Gifts of the Gods?

Are UFOs alien visitors or
psychic phenomena?

John Spencer

Virgin

First published in Great Britain in 1994 by
Virgin Books
an imprint of Virgin Publishing Ltd
332 Ladbroke Grove
London W10 5AH

ISBN 0 86369 821 2

A catalogue record for this title is available from the British Library

Typeset by TW Typesetting, Plymouth, Devon
Printed and bound in Great Britain by
Cox & Wyman Ltd, Reading, Berks

This book is dedicated to witnesses worldwide, in acknowledgement of the fact that they *are* the subject

Contents

Acknowledgements

This book has taken five years to write, counting the many months of experimentation, interviews and globe-trotting necessary to meet and work with people who have assisted me.

Very special thanks are due to Bertil Kuhlemann, a UFO researcher in Sweden who has for many years been a good friend and a source of valuable information. If his involvement in some areas of this book had been any deeper he would have deserved to be listed as a co-author, though that might not have been fair on his opinions. When I am not in Sweden, Bertil is the main reason why the paper in my fax machine runs out regularly.

Thanks are also due to Tony Wells. Tony is a former computer consultant for the London Stock Exchange who turned his hand to an impressive collection of sophisticated equipment for ghost and other paranormal research. He and I have worked together for some time now, and Tony has helped in depth with many of my UFO-related experiments. Indeed, he was a test subject for a series of hypnotic regression experiments.

Thanks also to Ken Phillips. He has a difficult task as facilitator of the only Witness Support Group of its kind in the country, a group whose witnesses have generously invited me to many of their gatherings. Ken works very hard to tread a straight line down the stony path between witness belief systems; I respect his dedication to UFO research and to BUFORA.

Thanks to Lucien Morgan for contributions in respect of regression theory.

Thanks to James and Lorraine Parry. Although Lorraine is listed in the book as a witness, and her story recounted, James and Lorraine are more than that. They have become friends as they joined me in the search for the deeper meanings to UFOs than are generally accepted. James is a TV producer who has searched thoroughly to design the 'treatment' that will present UFOs as they deserve to be presented.

Of course more than mere thanks is due to the witnesses who have allowed me to use their stories in this book. They are what UFO research exists for; they are the UFO phenomenon. They knew that I did not always share their interpretations of events, but they also knew that I never doubted their honesty in relating real and extraordinary events that they were experiencing. For many it took a lot to 'go public' and I am honoured that many chose me and this book as their first vehicle to do so. I would like to point out that I never pressed or persuaded any to do so; indeed I still have far more cases that witnesses have not yet felt ready to expose publicly, and I have always respected that position without question.

A point about the witnesses' stories in this book: I have done my very best to keep my opinions out of their recall. Except for grammatical correction, and editing for readability, the stories in this book are in the witnesses' own words, denoted by quotation marks. Where I have had to interject phrases for reader comprehension I have shown this with brackets. Each of those interjections comes from informal discussions with the person concerned. The principal witnesses have seen drafts of this book and have made what corrections they believed necessary.

A great many other people cannot be named simply

because of limitations of space, and because to name a few might be unfair to others. To all those who have supported me and worked with me inside and outside the field of UFO research, my sincere thanks.

As always, and in a book like this particularly, I want to make it clear that the opinions expressed are mine alone. None of the people mentioned above, or others, are responsible for the views stated, other than where they are clearly expressed as quoted views of others.

Illustrations

Introduction

'You can only find truth with logic if you have already
found truth without it.' G. K. Chesterton.

Over twenty years of study of UFOs, including some
very recent cases never before presented to the public
which are discussed later in this book, have convinced
me that the UFO phenomenon is a basically positive,
beneficial experience for many people. I have few doubts
that the UFO phenomenon is a very genuine one, with
people experiencing extraordinary events. I do not believe that most witnesses fantasise the events they
report, though I accept that that must happen in some
cases – as must fraud and simple misperception. Import-
antly, I do believe that there is a component of UFO
experiences which is external to the witness. In other
words, there is an element of every UFO experience
which is not generated by the witness's mind but which
comes from an external source.

That said, I do not believe that we will understand
the UFO phenomenon, nor will we understand or derive
the benefits available from the experience it offers, while
we are hidebound by a probably negative belief that
UFOs represent some kind of alien invasion.

If I thought the evidence pointed to that conclusion,
then I would say so. Many UFO researchers *do* believe
that that is the case, and they have said so in well-
written and well-researched articles and books. But
there are always two elements to UFO study, as with
any paranormal research and research dependent on

anecdotal accounts. One is the collection of data, and the other is its interpretation. The collection of data has been done, in many cases, very thoroughly by researchers such as myself in many parts of the world. But the interpretation is always personal. The interpretation in this book is my personal belief based on the data; others will have their own interpretation.

My one reason for wanting to outline an alternative to the so-called extraterrestrial hypothesis (that UFOs represent flying saucers full of invading aliens) is that, apart from the fact that I don't think it is correct, I also don't think it is helpful; indeed I think it is harmful. Worse, I think that the UFO phenomenon offers the potential for great development in people, and that this potential is being stunted, or missed, because of fears generated by one dubious interpretation which has come to dominate the subject. Close encounters, rather than being the frightening, negative experiences so often portrayed by the popular media, often have in fact the capability to improve our lives immensely, in all manner of ways. They can be life-enhancing and positive; a gift to the witness, whether it comes from their own consciousness, a living earth, alien beings or the gods themselves.

There are many cases outlined in this book which have never been presented to the public before and they offer the perceptions of witnesses whose thinking is much broader and much more open than that of many of the researchers working on their cases. But I have included several witnesses who very firmly believe in the ETH; had I been trying to impose a belief in the reader I would have left them out. I have included them because they are genuine beliefs, whatever I think lies behind them. Sten Lingren's, in Sweden, is an example of such a case.

I have a principle for UFO study, bearing in mind that we are dealing with difficult concepts, belief systems and the like. It is a principle taught in business training for good decision-making, team-building and change programmes. When two people disagree there is an unfortunate tendency to ask the question *'Why can that person not see things the way I do?'* This is the question that has been asked in UFO research for far too long, and it can be traced to an over-dependence on 'traditional' scientific beliefs.

The question that I ask, and that I believe we must all learn to ask, is *'What is it that this person sees that I do not?'*

Such a viewpoint allows for better understanding of witnesses' thinking, and it leaves open the possibility of accepting new sciences.

Of course the answers do not suddenly fall into place when you apply this new question, but they will become apparent one day. The first question, however, virtually makes certain that no answers will ever be found.

But before we can examine the good news, we have to look at the bad news. The first part of this book is a detailed reasoning of why I believe that the extraterrestrial hypothesis is wrong, has been falsely created and why it has become so predominant. There is no question that the majority of people who have looked at UFOs even from a moderately interested spectator's point of view see the extraterrestrial hypothesis as the predominant, or only, explanation. This viewpoint must be changed before people can see the alternatives.

My personal belief is that it is in the alternatives that the truth will be found. It is time that you as the reader were given a more honest appraisal of the UFO phenomenon from inside the UFO 'industry'.

The second part of the book contains the variety of

expressions people use to come to terms with their encounters: artistic, communicative, and so on. It shows how witnesses, and UFO experiences generally, are more closely related to what is termed 'the paranormal' than is usually admitted. These areas have for too long been ignored by researchers and authors.

Throughout the book I tried to allow the witnesses to speak to you, the reader, in their own words. In all cases I have personally interviewed witnesses in various countries face to face, and I have edited the transcripts of those interviews only to make their sentences more readable. I have long believed that it is for witnesses to give their own accounts.

Some of the cases will stretch credibility; no doubt some are the result of wrong-headedness. A lot of the book will one day probably turn out to be incorrect at some level, though we cannot yet say what will be valid and what will not. More work needs to be done, and I hope that this book represents a new and useful direction.

Throughout the book, then, please bear in mind the question that I want you, the reader, to ask yourself while reading:

'*What is it that this person sees that I do not?*'

Section 1
The Myths and the Mythmakers

1 How We Got Where We Are Today . . .

24 June 1947.

In the Cascade Mountains of the Pacific coastal state of Washington the pilot of a light airplane – Kenneth Arnold – was informally engaged in a search for a lost transport plane when he was distracted by a distant and unclear sighting.

It was an event that may well have changed the social perceptions of the human race forever.

Near Mount Rainier he saw what appeared to be a formation of objects in flight. He assumed at first that they were jet planes, but noticed that they moved in a curious way, flipping up and down. He described them later as moving 'like a saucer would if you skipped it across the water'. He could hardly have foreseen the consequences of his phrase.

A reporter picked up Arnold's term, giving to a long-existing phenomenon a name that the public found it could identify with: 'flying saucer'. The name caught the mood of the moment and attracted unparalleled attention in the media. The claim that readily came to the fore was that these flying saucers were extraterrestrial alien spacecraft bringing beings from other worlds to Earth. At this time no one had yet claimed to have met or talked to any of the crafts' occupants. But it was inevitable that, given the widespread hype, someone

3

would eventually come forward to say that they had met aliens. And so they did . . .

In 1953, after six years of 'flying saucer' sightings, George Adamski published a book revealing that he had made frequent contact with beings from another world. He described them as graceful, beautiful beings, Nordic in appearance, tall, slim and blond. Adamski's claims were not hesitant or modest: he claimed that he had journeyed throughout the solar system to several planets, and had had many types of contact with the beings.

Other contactees (as such people became known) followed on Adamski's heels, upstaging him and each other: they met Jesus, they saved the Earth, they saved the Universe . . .

Sceptics will argue that these were all fantasy-prone people or greedy people telling stories for money. That some were frauds was inevitable, and those that argue *none* were frauds are denying basic and proven human nature; when claims are made in any new or challenging field, fraudulent copycatting follows as inevitably as night follows day. But some of the witnesses may have been trying in a curious way to explain experiences they undoubtedly had had, by associating them with 'flying saucers', the mythology of the time. We will come to this later.

Over the next couple of years contactee encounters developed in their complexity, and, perhaps inevitably, romance entered the subject. Contactee Truman Bethurum met a beautiful female spaceship captain, Aura Rhanes, and whiled away the night with her. In 1956 Elizabeth Klarer met an alien, Akon, fell in love with him and had his child. Their offspring now lives with his father on his planet. Reading the account of her romance with Akon in her book *Beyond the Light Barrier* is like reading the mushiest of Mills and Boon romantic literature. Yet Cynthia Hind, an African-based researcher for whom I have great respect, has spoken to Klarer and, although unable to support her claims, told me that she could not doubt Klarer's obvious sincerity.

In the early 1960s abduction claims took the UFO phenomenon into a new phase. They started with the account of 'two lost hours aboard a flying saucer' in John G. Fuller's book *The Interrupted Journey*, which examined the claims of an American couple, Betty and Barney Hill.

In September 1961 Betty and Barney Hill were travelling towards their New Hampshire home after a short break in Canada when they saw a bright light in the sky (later they believed that the light was pacing their car). Eventually they stopped to look at it more clearly and were able to make out a structured object. Barney left the car and walked into a dark field towards it, where he was able to make out rows of windows and several occupants watching him. He became very scared and ran, screaming, back to the car and his anxiously waiting wife. They drove off, and saw nothing significant until they reached home that morning. Some time later researchers discussing the case with Barney pointed out to him that he might have lost two hours during that night; this was the birth of the 'missing time' phenomenon.

Immediately after the encounter Betty became an avid reader of UFO books and literature, and wrote to Major Donald Keyhoe, a prominent author on the subject, after finishing one of his books in a single sitting.

During the next two years Betty became increasingly concerned about a series of dreams she had had shortly after reading Keyhoe's writings, and therefore also shortly after the encounter. She had dreamt that their car had been stopped by a group of humanoid aliens, that she and her husband had been removed from the car and taken aboard the landed saucer, where they were led to separate compartments. There, each had been stripped and forced to lie on a medical 'table'. Betty recalled that the aliens shone bright lights on her and closely examined her hair, removing some samples; they looked closely at ears and eyes and removed pieces of ear wax. They cut off a piece of her fingernails, and scraped off particles of skin. They explained to her that they wanted to check her nervous system, and they wired her up for the purpose. They gave her a 'pregnancy test' by inserting a needle in her navel. Betty became convinced that the dreams were not just dreams, but memories of what had really happened that night. She consulted Boston psychiatrist Dr Benjamin Simon and underwent a series of hypnotic regressions designed to take her, and her husband, back to the events of the night of their sighting. Sure enough, the regressions drew out memories that matched the dreams exactly, seeming to suggest that the dreams were in fact memories and that the couple had indeed been abducted by aliens that night.

There have been many such reports since that time, and most alarming of all is the fact that they are all very similar. In many of the cases the aliens are of the same type: short squat beings with oversized heads, huge black, featureless eyes that wrap halfway around the head, a pasty complexion and reduced other facial features. In many of the cases the descriptions of what happened are similar: the medical examinations are often identical and the interiors of the spacecraft often have much the same features. In one case, that of Betty Andreasson, the witness underwent exactly the same examination of her abdomen as did Betty Hill. English contactee Rohan Hinton describes a classic abduction with a medical involvement concentrating on her ovaries; it will be discussed later in the book.

There is, however, an interesting bridge between the contactee and abductee phenomena, one that with hindsight probably shows the abduction claims to have been inevitable. In 1957 Brazilian Antonio Villas Boas claimed that he had encountered an object late at night while driving a tractor on a farm. He was captured by strange entities and taken aboard the object where he met an attractive female alien. 'Her body was much more beautiful than any I have ever seen before,' described Villas Boas. 'It was slim, and her breasts stood up high and well separated. Her waistline was thin, her belly flat, her hips well developed, and her thighs were large.' He went on to describe the naked alien as having blonde hair, pale skin, large blue slanted eyes, reduced lips, nose and ears, and high flat cheekbones that gave the impression of a pointed chin. Villas Boas said that he had been covered in a substance that he later reasoned was designed to stimulate him to mate with the woman. Whatever the cause, he did have sexual intercourse with her, twice. It was apparently a perfectly normal act which he found exciting and pleasurable, despite the woman's habit of barking like a dog occasionally. Villas Boas, many years later, also admitted that she extracted sperm from him (in a less pleasurable way), which he assumed was preserved for later use.

What a perfect bridge between contactee and abductee this case seems to be – or, alternatively, what a natural sequel the abduction phenomenon as we now know it came to be. The 'Adamski-like' aliens were quite human in appearance and frequently went about on Earth unnoticed by people 'not in the know'. They cared for people, and warned us of dangers to the Earth.

The aliens who dealt with the abductees, however, have been shown to be dwarf-like creatures with reduced facial features, slanted oval-shaped eyes and pointed chins. They abuse people and seem to show only as much concern for their 'victims' as is necessary to control them. And they would have some trouble passing themselves off as human in a crowded street! The woman Villas Boas met was human enough to be almost the female of the Adamski aliens, yet shortish, with slanted eyes, reduced facial features and a pointed chin. And while treating Villas Boas as a sexual subject, she appears to have used him for a purpose and then discarded him. The progression appears to be from human-like compassionate people, to nearly human and not very compassionate people, to non-human, non-compassionate aliens.

More recent abduction reports have veered away from the 'lonely road at night' pattern; so-called bedroom visitations are becoming more frequently reported. You wake in the night, and the aliens are standing around you; they take you out of your bed, out of your house, and into their saucer. In all other respects the reports are similar to the early accounts. The most recent version of this suggests that a flying saucer abducted a woman from the window of a New York apartment block in full view of witnesses.

Do we see, in these most modern abductions, the emergence of the real UFO phenomenon? Many prominent American researchers believe so, and their view, that aliens are visiting astronauts conducting experiments of the life forms of Earth as we might do if we went to other planets, is spreading.

I do not believe that. I believe that there is no UFO case that has ever arisen which *demands* an extraterrestrial explanation. The evidence suggests a more extraordinary truth behind abductions and the UFO mystery, and that truth almost certainly has nothing to do with extraterrestrial beings. Even if it involves aliens, I doubt that it is as simplistic as the 'alien doctors' theory would suppose.

How that theory arose, and why I believe it misses so much of the truth, is what this book sets out to explain.

2 ... And Just Where Are We Anyway?

After more than four and a half decades of research all over the world we do not have a solution to the mystery of the UFO phenomenon. The reason, quite simply, is because we have failed to define the problem correctly.

Let us look at that statement with a broad list of what is currently thrown into the UFO 'pot':

Sightings of distant objects and lights

Close proximity sightings, often by aircraft crew

Traces of landings

Varied effects on witnesses (physical and psychological)

Crash retrievals of saucers and aliens

Contactees claiming kinship and communication with aliens

Abductions by 'alien doctors'.

A look at this evidence suggests to me that we have basically two phenomena: **sightings** and **experiences**. I believe that it is highly unlikely that there is any connection whatsoever between the two.

When we look at **sighting** reports over time and location we find that they are seen by an average of around 2.5 witnesses. A similar examination of abductions shows an average of not much more than 1. In other words, abductions are largely the experience of a single individual whereas sightings are shared phenomena. In some cases these statistics do seem to merge – in the

Travis Walton case several people witnessed a UFO but only one had an abduction experience, and in one case in the north of England several police officers saw a UFO which was later assumed to be connected to an abduction report that same night – but in fact no such connection is demanded by the evidence.

Most sightings seem to take place while the witnesses are in a 'normal' frame of mind, the sort of frame of mind we are in when we are at work for example. However, abductions seem to have a quality about them – even to most witnesses – that suggests an altered state of consciousness (ASC). In other words, people are perceiving abductions while they are in a state of mind that is not normal. This is something I have noticed in other areas of paranormal research. I have a very business-oriented career which takes up most of my working day. If I go directly from work to a ghost vigil or a paranormal experiment, I rarely see anything. Yet on the three occasions in my life when I have submerged myself more fully into my paranormal work, and divorced myself from more routine business, I have observed such things as poltergeist activity and other 'paranormal' phenomena. It leads me to conclude that a certain frame of mind is needed to perceive 'paranormal' energies, and this is something that has been confirmed to me over and over again by witnesses. Whether the ASC is caused by the event, or whether it actually *causes* the event, is something we will consider later.

So why do UFO researchers link the two categories of UFO phenomena? They do so because it fits the Extraterrestrial Hypothesis (ETH) that many people are *seeking*. And the reason that the ETH fits so well is not that it answers the evidence, but rather that researchers, out of the mass of data available to them, have selected only the evidence which supports the theory.

The researcher who studies distant lights and objects is eventually forced to answer the question 'But what are all these apparently piloted flying saucers in the skies actually doing? Why don't they land? What do the occupants look like?' and so on.

Those researchers studying abductions have to answer the question 'If all these landed spaceships are lurking about by the sides of roads waiting to grab passing motorists, why doesn't anyone ever see them flying about?'

Linking sightings and abductions gives both sets of researchers their answer.

However – and it's a big however – no reliable witness has ever reported a sighting develop into a landing resulting in an abduction witnessed by a third party. We do not have even one reliable case where a witness says something like 'I was walking across the hills and I saw this UFO fly past, and then when I got to the top of the hill I looked down into the valley and saw this flying saucer parked by the side of the road, and this car rolled to a stop and a host of little grey people grabbed the occupants and took them into the flying saucer ...' There is, it should fairly be stated, a case that has been brewing in America since 1989 which might fit this criterion; however, it is so fraught with problems that even many Americans devoted to the ETH seem to believe that it is 'a bridge too far' and the case will only raise massive controversy.

Crash retrievals form one potential bridge between sightings and abductions. These are the (largely American) claims that flying saucers have crashed and been recovered by special military teams; on examination, they contain dead aliens of the type so often reported in abductions. However, crash retrievals may well be an urban legend in the making – they are a fairly new construct which began in the post-Watergate era, and they reflect the distrust of governments which that scandal so highlighted. It is, however, important not to be dismissive of this bridge without examination. It will be examined later in the book.

The two phenomena of sightings and abductions *must* be examined separately. The fact that people have taken photographs of distant 'blobs' in the sky is no confirmation of the reality of the abduction experience.

It is only once we have divorced those artificially connected ideas from each other that we are free to see the wider possibilities.

3 The Mythmakers: The Media

THE PRESS

You very rarely see a bowler hat in the City of London nowadays and despite over four years living in Barnet, one of the northern extremes of the London urban sprawl and the terminus of the London Underground Northern Line, I never saw a bowler hat in the streets of that area. This may be surprising news to readers of the *North American Sun* newspaper who read in the late 1980s of a dramatic UFO invasion.

The report was accompanied by a photograph showing literally dozens of businessmen, mostly in bowler hats, lying all over the street, apparently knocked out by green gas from a landed UFO. The newspaper carried the article under the headline 'Thousands are knocked out by UFO gas!' and began: 'Hordes of curious gawkers were flattened when a UFO suddenly landed on a crowded city street and emitted greenish clouds of potent knockout gas that put thousands of them to sleep!' The newspaper went on to describe the bodies of gassed bowler-hatted businessmen all over the pavements of 'the city of Barnet, England, a suburb of London'. Apparently, a command centre was set up in an abandoned warehouse and interrogations of witnesses were undertaken there. One witness, businessman Reginald Upjohn, saw the green mist emanating from portholes around the 50-foot spaceship and then said: 'Me and the boys were on our way to lunch when suddenly there was this high-pitched whine and this large ship just plopped right down in the intersection. My pipe fell to the sidewalk – I was flabbergasted.' (I can only assume that 'Mr Upjohn' trained for his report at the Al Capone School of Linguistics!) Barnet Council, when asked to comment, said, 'If a UFO has landed, nobody told us about it. If anyone asked us to take them to our leader we will introduce them to Councillor Leslie Pym or Chief Executive Max Caller.'

It is difficult to believe that even the most gullible of Americans would have been taken in by this story. On the other hand it is certainly not unique, and the English newspaper the *Sunday Sport* has certainly carried equally bizarre claims such as 'World War II bomber on the moon' and 'London bus trapped in ice at the South Pole'.

Early Press Coverage

For all practical purposes the modern UFO phenomenon started on Tuesday, 24 June 1947, when Kenneth Arnold, flying alone in the mountains of Washington State, USA, reported seeing unknown objects, coined the phrase 'flying saucer' and sparked off the widespread media interest that has not abated to the present day.

The Kenneth Arnold sighting does not represent the first 'UFO' report: some researchers claim that prehistoric artists were trying to report their own close encounters in some of the more thought-provoking diagrams found on cave walls around the world. What's more, Arnold's use of the term 'saucer' was not itself the first; the *Denison (Texas) Daily News* in 1878 reported that Texan farmer John Martin had seen an object over his farm 'about the size of a large saucer'. However, UFOs first became of public interest after the Arnold sighting and the media interest generated by it; it is by any practical definition the start of the UFO era.

It is important to note that at the time of the sighting Arnold did not claim the UFOs were extraterrestrial or that he had direct or telepathic or other contact with aliens, and he reported the sightings out of concern for national security interest. Arnold himself reported seeing the objects because 'I thought it was my duty to report these things . . . I kind of felt I ought to tell the FBI because I knew that during the war we were flying aircraft over the Pole to Russia, and I thought these things could possibly be from Russia,' he said.

However, the very next day after the Arnold sighting newspapers were speculating on the possible explanations, and listed as the top possibility – you guessed it – spacecraft from another world. Since then, the extraterrestrial hypothesis has been the only explanation for UFOs ever offered by the popular media.

However, it must be said that it is probably the introduction of that theory which made the phenomenon one of interest to the public, which kept the subject in the public's attention and which probably attracted most people to the subject in the first place. I was certainly first attracted to the subject at the age of eleven, reading of sightings in the English town of Warminster, reports that clearly leaned towards the extraterrestrial hypothesis, and entered BUFORA believing that there I would find that that was the most probable explanation for UFOs.

UFO research has therefore probably been influenced by a combination of:

(a) the press inventing the extraterrestrial hypothesis; then;

(b) the ETH attracting to the subject people who are

interested in that part of the spectrum of possibilities;

and then;

(c) biased and slanted investigation influenced by the
existence of the ETH.

The extent to which the tabloid media have empha-
sised the extraterrestrial hypothesis in their coverage of
UFO stories cannot be understated. This is true even
when the newspapers are working alongside UFO researchers, though it must be said that they have a
tendency to seek out and work with UFO researchers
who are committed to the extraterrestrial hypothesis in
preference to those who are not.

In May 1987 the *Sun* newspaper in England prepared
its readers for a forthcoming final episode of *The Colbys*
soap drama in which one of that programme's leading
characters, Fallon, was to be seen abducted aboard an
alien spacecraft (it was a desperate – and failed – attempt to lift the ratings of the show). The *Sun* devoted
a page to what they called 'Crazy close encounters of a
real kind'. Their headline was 'I met a thing from outer
space!', and in their introduction it was stated that: 'According to hundreds of *Sun* readers . . . they, too, have
had close encounters with real ETs and seen alien spacecraft'. Four cases were reviewed and these are the
introductory paragraphs from each of the cases:

THE CASE OF EDWIN WILSON KEMBERY
Edwin Wilson Kembery was visited regularly for three
months by two aliens who took biscuits and cheese
from his fridge in return for galactic 'diamonds'.

THE CASE OF JIMMY BROWN
Irishman Jimmy Brown had a close encounter with
three spacemen walking up the middle of the A23.

THE CASE OF PAUL DEVINE
Six months ago a space surgeon beamed Paul Devine aboard his ship and stuck needles in him.

THE CASE OF LINDA TAYLOR
Businesswoman Linda Taylor thinks a blond male alien used her for a medical experiment.

There is very little here to suggest that there are alternative, non-extraterrestrial explanations for UFO sightings.

On Tuesday, 26 January 1988, the *Star* reported the case of policeman Alan Godfrey under the headline 'Cop: I was kidnapped by aliens'. The article contains very slanted language such as: 'A policeman told last night of a close encounter with creatures from outer space'; 'Tiny robot buzzed around peering at the shocked earthling'; '[At] the start of his inter-galactic experience Alan ... added that when he saw the low flying *starship* [my emphasis] he tried to call for help'.

The *Daily Mirror* of Tuesday, 10 October 1989 broke the news of UFO activity in Russia. The headline was 'Look out comrade, the aliens have landed ...' and strap line 'Flying saucer drops into a Russian park!' The first paragraph opened with 'It's official, comrades! Aliens have landed their spaceship in a Russian park.' The article goes on to announce that 'The visitors from outer space were up to 12 ft tall and had little heads. They went for a short walk but didn't stay long. And the three strangers had a small robot-like creature with them.' They are referred to as 'extraterrestrial tourists'.

All the above stories came from national tabloid papers. Coverage in the quality Press is rare; one example was from *The Times* of 16 August 1991 following Press releases announcing the 6th International UFO Congress organised by the British UFO Research

Association in conjunction with a local Yorkshire group. The *Times* leader of that day covered the reports of aliens and others but offered alternative explanations to its readers (they may or may not be valid but at least they were alternatives). For example: 'Sociologists say that the current craze for the supernatural in a decommunizing world is part of a quest for some new faith'. Mention is made of geological and meteorological explanations and the attribution the phenomena to meteorites, earth satellites and weather balloons. It is true to say that the leader was somewhat tongue-incheek, referring to 'The only convincing explanation of the Kennedy assassination: he was about to spill the beans on UFOs' and so on, but at least the general tenor of the leader was not one to positively reinforce a belief in extraterrestrials as the source of unidentified flying objects.

The cumulative effect of the slanted coverage given by the tabloids is not, of course, that people believe the stories, but that they don't know which stories they should believe. They protect their own credibility by rejecting too much.

But why should newspapers seek to report stories that are blatantly untrue? In the spring of 1989, Media Studies student Julia Burton chose for her dissertation a study of 'Press coverage of the subject of UFOs'. She interviewed a wide range of people in the Press, in UFO research groups (several in BUFORA, including myself) and people in other areas offering a useful perspective.

'Press Coverage on the Subject of Unidentified Flying Objects' by Julia Burton (extracts)

Of one case involving witness Paul Kafno, Julia Burton made the following observations:

'Although Mr Kafno did not feel that he had been badly treated by the Press it is significant that he said he would not report another similar event to them. He felt that the media "had a low level of enquiry. They are just interested in filling space and they approach a problem with their minds already made up. I wanted to speak to someone who would help me make sense of what I had seen." He felt that Ken Phillips [BUFORA investigator] was genuinely interested in what he saw and would have no hesitation in reporting a similar event to him.

'We can see that the approaches of the media and of BUFORA are very different. The Press carried no technical details of all. Only the *Hampstead and Highgate Express* actually interviewed a witness and left a margin of doubt as to the origin of the object. Obviously the aims of an organisation will reflect the methods of research and the perception of a certain event. Thus BUFORA which cites research as a main aim will place more emphasis on research, and the Press which must sell its produce to a public and has limited space will concentrate on publishing a short interesting story. It should come as no surprise, then, that these organisations treat the subject differently.'

Of the second case in her study, relating to Zena Sfeir, Julia observed:

'Zena said that if she saw something again, she would not report it to the Press but she would report it to Ken Phillips. Zena did not give the impression that she felt her privacy had been invaded in any way. Although she felt that the Press and the *Breakfast Time* TV programme showed a lack of depth she was well aware that her experience was no more than a story to the media and did not feel personally affronted . . .

'I spoke to Peter Dunn of the *Independent*, who wrote this story, and to Christine Aubrey, a member of the Aetherius Society. Peter Dunn contacted the Aetherius Society because he had written articles about them in the past and knew that they were interested in the subject. "I knew that they would produce a relevant quote." He went on to say: "If there was an accident on the M4 I would contact the fire brigade and because they [the Aetherius Society] believe in flying saucers I contacted them." I asked Mr Dunn why, if he thought the founder was "dodgy", did he approach them for a quote and not BUFORA, which undertakes a more scientific approach to the subject, and he replied that he had never heard of BUFORA. I asked Mr Dunn if he thought this area was particularly open to Press interpretation in that a reporter could go to any "expert" source which fitted his/her interpretation of a story, i.e. if a UFO story was to be given an extraterrestrial slant the Aetherius Society could be guaranteed to supply it. If a more objective opinion were required, BUFORA could be contacted. He replied: "This is true of any area and is not just applicable to UFOs. I like to keep an open mind on these things." '

Julia spoke to Sylvia Jones, a journalist closely involved with the story:

'I asked her why the story had been presented in such a light-hearted way. [Her reply:] "There has never been any physical evidence of UFOs and photographs usually raise more questions than they answer. UFOs have all the ingredients for humorous stories. A tabloid, like the *Daily Mirror*, is interested in a cross-section of stories, both humorous and serious. In the case of UFOs we have well-meaning people who have seen something, but they are relying on their memories alone. There is no proof. Of course UFO stories will still have to be investigated like any other story."

'I asked her why, in the light of other explanations for UFOs, the Press concentrated on the extraterrestrial theory.

' "Tabloids are not the medium for serious, scientific exploration. I think that the Press keeps the subject going and the public are very interested." '

This section of the dissertation concluded:

'Zena Sfeir [and] Paul Kafno . . . agreed that they received the kind of Press coverage that they expected. Neither Paul Kafno nor Zena Sfeir said that they would report another sighting to the media, despite being content with the media coverage. In both cases it was felt that the media could not help them resolve the mystery that they had experienced. This is curious as the Press did in both cases put forward a resolution to the sighting, which closely matched BUFORA explanations of the time, and both witnesses said that they would not hesitate in contacting Ken Phillips in the future should such an event occur again.

'We can conclude that the reason why the witnesses would approach Ken Phillips again is because, whatever his ideas on explanations may have been, he took time to treat the witnesses seriously and to explore and question the technical details which surrounded the sighting.

'Zena thought that Ken Phillips "spoke my language". Both witnesses felt that Press was not the place for a serious investigation of what they had seen.'

Of the ETH, Julia comments:

'Although the Press do not accept that there is any

proof of extra-terrestrial life, they are quite happy to put forward this theory in their coverage of the subject. The lack of proof does not stop the Press putting this theory forward; it merely leaves the subject open to be interpreted in a humorous way.

Of the 'conflict' between the Press and UFO research, she observed:

'I have attempted to draw attention to the complexities of this subject as perceived by those who have spent many years researching it. There is a clash however between the way that researchers see the subject and how the Press portray it. Witnesses prefer the approach of the researchers in respect of BUFORA investigators. The clash between the Press and the researchers is a basic one and springs from the fundamentally different roles of the two parties.

'The Press have to sell their products, they have a market to satisfy. They manufacture a commercial product. They function in the sphere of business where deadlines have to be met in a pressurised environment. This is pointed out by the Royal Commission on the Press as a consideration when assessing Press performance: "Moreover, the pressures which the nature of the market imposes upon journalists are important too. Fairness also requires that judgements about the performance of the Press are made in the knowledge of the physical restraints under which newspapers are produced. Journalists have little time for enquiry or deliberation and ought not to be judged by the standards which apply to workers in research centres."

'Historically, in the case of UFOs, this interpretation has centred around the extraterrestrial theory. These stories are seen, for the most part, not as an area of serious study, but one which lends itself to humorous and superficial coverage by the tabloid Press. Although articles do appear in the quality Press, the subject is not given as regular coverage as in the tabloids. This is because the qualities do not view the topic seriously and thus do not think it is a suitable topic for their serious readers.

'Researchers in general and BUFORA in particular do not operate under commercial restrictions. They exist primarily for research and can take a long-term view of the subject and investigate its complexities. However, some researchers are also authors. It is important to note that they also have commercial pressures to sell their books. The extraterrestrial theory sells books so it is profitable to discover proof for this theory.'

The dissertation concluded:

'The function of the tabloid is to put news in an entertaining way and social theories do not fall into this category. As Tom Baistow points out: "The traditional broadsheet popular, even when make-up became bolder, was essentially a text newspaper . . . In the down-market tabloid the packaging has become at least as important as the content: the massive monosyllabic headlines in WAR DECLARED! sanserif type and huge pictures can take up to two-thirds or more of a page, leaving space for barely 700–800 words."

'He goes on to write that the qualities seek to inform the public on a variety of topics which include the "political, industrial, business, economic, social, home and foreign, sport and leisure", whereas the "formula" of the popular tabloids leads journalists to "look primarily for stories with a sensational theme, preferably involving sexual scandal or crime, popular 'celebrities' or public figures."

'The quality Press is more appropriate to this but the lack of seriousness attached to the subject hinders it.'

There is therefore a clear division of attitude between the UFO 'industry' and the Press, as Julia Burton so well demonstrates. Generally speaking UFO investigators, researchers and witnesses regard the subject as worthy of serious investigation, whereas the media clearly regard it as a form of entertainment.

As we will see with other sections in this book, the difficulty for those involved in UFO research is that almost everybody else regards it as entertainment as well; though that is because they are being led by the nose by, mainly, the media.

If we assume that the media are principally concerned with entertainment then we need only look at what the media are likely to regard as entertaining to see where the principal UFO theories arise from.

In the United States the belief in an extraterrestrial interpretation of UFOs is very strong; but outside that country many people find that the longer they are exposed to the serious, genuine material of UFO reports, the less they are likely to accept that UFOs are extraterrestrial. I have already stated my belief that, while some cases are thought-provoking enough to make the 'alien visitors' explanation a possible one, however vague, no UFO case that has ever arisen **demands** an extraterrestrial explanation. There is a spectrum of possibilities that ought to be reflected by a serious Press. However, as we have seen, in its 45-year history tabloid or 'popular' Press coverage of UFOs has never failed to speculate on extraterrestrials as an origin for the subject, has reinforced that possibility either implicitly or directly and has paid very little attention to alternative, more mundane possibilities. Serious (non-tabloid) Press coverage has allowed a more reasonable range of possibilities but because of the image created by the tabloid Press, coverage by the serious Press is rare.

In short then, the Press chooses to cover the UFO phenomenon because it is an entertainment and a 'seller'; and the theory which sells newspapers is that UFOs are extraterrestrial.

The vast majority of people in the world (other than those with a more than passing interest in UFOs who perhaps subscribe to magazines or join organisations and so on) get their information by reading the Press. Therefore the Press's misguided (though perfectly logical seen from their perspective) attitude towards the subject has reinforced beyond all proportion one highly unlikely and unsubstantiated theory.

Nevertheless the Press attitude towards the subject has never changed because, quite simply, the Press wants entertainment and they have never found a more entertaining explanation for the UFO phenomenon.

TELEVISION

Any UFO researcher or author will tell you that they feel they don't get proper media coverage. That is nothing unusual – many politicians, scientists and sportsmen will tell you the same. Most UFO personalities have stories to tell of annoying or irritating occurrences in TV studios. I have had them happen to me. But I write business books as well, which is an area about as far removed from the paranormal as you can get, and that offers me a useful and unusual perspective because I know what it feels like to be treated fairly and sensibly. Radio and TV appearances related to UFOs, while dogged with the usual problems of dealing with the media, also have special problems. Occasionally you get an incident which throws the problem into such sharp relief that you realise what is wrong. Such an event happened to me.

Timothy Good, an author and UFO researcher of many years' standing, had recently published the book *Alien Liaison*; a television company decided to do a late-night debate on aliens. You can probably guess the sort of thing: 'Do aliens exist or are UFO authors all loonies?' Researchers for the TV station asked me to take part; when I asked who else would be there they listed science correspondents, scientists, the Aetherius Society (a UFO-based religion/cult), some who claimed they had been abducted, a science-fiction author and others – all for a 25-minute discussion! I asked what the focus of the discussion would be. The researcher's ensuing silence seemed to me to be just a fraction of a second too long. 'We-are-going-to-debate-the-existence-of-aliens,' it was patiently explained to me.

I was at the time in the middle of a heavy schedule of radio and TV appearances as I had had three books published that previous month, and I had to ask if my involvement was really of value; after all, there are plenty of well-qualified people who could have appeared. If I was not needed I promised I would certainly see to it that someone local went to the studio. But they assured me that my involvement was crucial, they had a major role planned. Even as I heard this I heard the hollow clang of the not-quite-truth. However, Timothy Good is a valued colleague and I wanted to support him, so I agreed to go to the studio.

We had to arrive at 9.30 p.m. – we were due to go on live at 11.30. The interim time gives the presenter a period in which to get to know his guests, form his last-minute ground plan and so on. I have been on over a hundred TV and radio shows and after a while you can 'feel' what the show's ambience will be like.

I arrived punctually and was taken to the hospitality suite where I was greeted by the researcher for the programme. I introduced myself. Smiles all round: OK so far. 'We will be discussing alien life, whether it exists,' she said. 'You will be telling the viewers that aliens visit Earth in flying saucers, won't you?' (It was a question, I think.)

'No,' I said. 'I've never been persuaded that UFOs are flying saucers. I don't think UFOs are likely to be anything to do with aliens, or probably not anyway.'

Stunned silence. But the researcher's professional smile stayed in place. I could imagine what was going on in her head: *a flying saucer nut who doesn't believe in flying saucers!* We invited him here to be the person who says UFOs are full of aliens visiting the Earth in flying saucers! She waited for me to come up with something to save the situation.

I confess I deliberately remained stoic; I wanted to see what was going to happen next. I could see her problem. What would her bosses say when they discovered she had invited not only the wrong UFO nut, but one who didn't seem to know 'his proper place'?

She broke the silence by going over the 'domestics' – where I would be sitting, how the presenter would come to me during the show. And she told me he would look me out over the course of the next hour or so.

If I thought that I had been wrongly invited I had, I suspect, missed part of the point. During the hospitality time I discovered that the programme would be linked by telephone to Bob Oeschler, our researcher in America. Now I began to get the full picture. Live TV shows have a number of risks and what happens if they go wrong? Easy – you invite a number of guests as 'spare parts'. They may not be needed but they are there just in case. I don't know now if I was only invited for that role or if I acquired it when they realised I might say something a little too 'out of line' but at this point I certainly got put on the back burner. My allotted place in the audience was moved to a 'secondary' sitting, out of the way of the aisle where the presenter walked. And the presenter never even bothered to seek me out to discover who I was (he still probably doesn't even know I was there, I certainly never found out his name).

As it happened I had been with that American researcher in Gulf Breeze, in Florida, not long before and had discussed with him the work which he was now going to be talking about. We had swapped some current research data. I was probably the only other person there in the studio who could have broadened the conversation with him. All of this was of course lost because no one even questioned me about my views or told me that he would be joining the programme by satellite link.

At one point I asked what the direction of the talk would be, given both Timothy's and Bob's concentration on the technological side of UFOs, and the non-technical views of the Aetherius Society. The TV researchers clearly didn't even understand the question. Not only was the idiot not going to say the right thing, they were obviously thinking, he was going to alienate the guests (sorry about the pun)!

We trooped down to the studio, the programme went on and I was ignored throughout. The show was a ragbag of diverse opinion with no direction whatsoever. Timothy described dead alien bodies which the government would put on display; the American researcher talked about government cover-up. The Aetherius Society said they were in touch with an alien on Venus.

One man said he had been abducted by aliens. David Whitehouse, the BBC science correspondent, said he found the suggestions improbable, Professor Archie Roy of Glasgow said he believed aliens existed but he couldn't regard UFOs as evidence, and Heinz Wolf said the whole book was bollocks. (Oh yes, he did!) As a debate on the probability of extraterrestrial life it was a shambles.

The abduction witness never had a chance to speak properly. His is a valid story, rich in detail. Before we went into the studio I asked him, 'Were you abducted by aliens?' He said that he thought he probably had not been and it was something a little different to that. When asked the same question by the researcher with a microphone pushed into his face he said, 'Yes.' He was railroaded.

The Aetherius representative got to show his model of a flying saucer just as he had shown it on a previous television debate of similar quality many years before. He admitted afterwards, 'They just invite us for the loony side, we are used to that.' He was railroaded.

Since I couldn't be railroaded I was shunted into a siding. Basically the same effect.

So what did the whole thing bring into focus? Well, these types of shows have been produced for decades; the format virtually never changes and they never get anywhere.

Let's look at why that should be.

Firstly, we have to go back between 20 and 40 years, when UFOs were certainly the domain of train-spotter fanatics and the loony fringe. No one else would touch the stuff. TV shows covered it – rightly, probably – from that point of view. But times have changed. The loony tunes are still there, of course, but now a massive army of professionals from business, science and the medical professions and other fields has taken the subject by the scruff of its neck and is trying to transform it. However, the media have chosen not to bother with such people.

Secondly, TV companies have been blinded by the loony fringe so long that they can't see the direction they should give to any other programme. They see the subject of UFOs as a single issue and try to cover it all in half an hour. In fact, it subdivides into many quite diverse areas: crash retrievals, abductions, flying saucers, mythology, sociology, technology, psychology, folklore, global cultural variation, cultural tracking, cult and cult power, and others. You can't adequately cover any of these in half an hour but you can have a discussion along a direction – you are wasting time to try to deal with all aspects. Short programmes have impact if they have a topic. TV researchers for UFO programmes simply don't know how to subdivide the boundaries. Would the producers of *The Sky at Night* insist that every time Patrick Moore made a point the Flat Earth Society or the Creationists should chip in their opinion? Obviously not.

That brings us to the third point: a bridge of the previous two points. UFO researchers are never called in to consult in the weeks running up to a show; they are only ever called in at the last minute. That stems from the fact that UFO 'people' are thought to be all nuts, and that it's all one subject anyway and that the TV company knows best. If programmes used researchers to help them select and direct their programmes, the results could become very meaningful.

Fourthly, there is the element of risk. TV companies know that they can get good laughs if they present UFOs the way they do. What more could they want? Would the soap-opera audience take to highbrow stuff? But this is a wrong assumption. The genuine UFO researcher is looking at a subject that is serious, funny, vivid and rich in detail. Almost certainly we are looking at the borders of a new science yet to be discovered: a natural science but a very exciting one.

In Sweden, when a UFO programme was directed with the help of UFO researchers, it worked well, getting a massive response from the public to the opened telephone lines. Such an experiment has yet to be conducted by British television companies.

To be fair to the other side of the coin, television producers are themselves under a great deal of pressure. Recently the message that I have set out above, and which I have been table-thumping around TV studios for years, is beginning to get home. Several producers are actively working with me and other researchers to set up programmes planned in collaboration with UFO researchers. John MacNish, the producer of a BBC programme that I appeared on who had demonstrated common sense in pre-planning – and who went on to produce an excellent crop circle video *Crop Circle Communiqué* – is a good example. But the progress is slow. Many of them are, in turn, finding that the TV companies are slow to take the risk of a new type of programme. The public's perception of UFOs will change for the better when TV companies take this vital initiative.

4 Mythmakers from Other Worlds: The Influence of Science Fiction

The influence of science fiction and the cinema on the progress of the UFO phenomenon cannot be overstated. Researchers and witnesses strongly committed to the extraterrestrial hypothesis will reject this claim out of hand, yet there can be no doubt of an interaction and one which I believe is very influential indeed. There have been a number of analyses of this interaction, including one in my previous book *Perspectives*, and I do not propose to go over the whole 'decade by decade' build-up here.

The purpose of this chapter is to examine, in detail, the few very influential films which have formed a great deal of the imagery that has become incorporated into our interpretation of the UFO experience.

Barbarella, like *2001 – A Space Odyssey*, is the story of an astronaut's voyage in space, but the two films hardly belong in the same category: whereas *2001 – A Space Odyssey* is a futuristic construction attempting to be as factual as it can be in its use of hardware and human attitude, *Barbarella* is clearly fantasy with no obvious extension of existing technologies or attitudes. The latter film was an embodiment of the 1960s New Age attitudes that 'love conquered all'; at its most basic level it was a film that sought to show as many ways as possible to get its star, Jane Fonda, out of her clothes. We do not expect images from *Barbarella* to be incorporated into our library of UFO images because they cannot be seen as potentially real. Images from *2001*, a more factually based and 'realistic' film, are more likely to be 'trusted', and, in fact, the Lee Parrish abduction in 1977 did include 'entities' not unlike the famous monolith from that film.

Contactee Rohan Hinton, whose case is discussed later in the book, made the point to me that the latest wave of science-fiction films, such as *ET* and *Cocoon*, presents aliens as friendly, beneficial creatures. It is a portrayal reflected in many recent UFO reports. Kenneth Arnold's sighting in 1947 marked the beginning of the UFO phenomenon, and as early as 1951 the first really significant film based on the UFO reports of the time, *The Day the Earth Stood Still*, was released. That same year brought *The Thing from Another World* and *The Man from Planet X*. 1953 brought *Invaders from Mars*, *War of the Worlds* and *Killers from Space*. 1955 brought *This Island Earth*. 1956 brought *Invasion of the Body Snatchers*; the absurd *Plan 9 from Outer Space*; the brilliant remake of Shakespeare's *The Tempest*, *The Forbidden Planet*; and, significantly, *Earth Versus the Flying Saucers*, adapted from the first book acknowledged to be inspired by UFO literature, in this case the writings of Donald Keyhoe. 1957 brought *Invasion of the Saucer Men*, *Enemy from Space* and *Not of this Earth*, and 1958 *I Married a Monster from Outer Space* and *It!*, *The Terror from Beyond Space*.

1947 brought the first disc sightings and these continued until 1952, when George Adamski offered us the first contact with aliens from another world. These contacts continued through the 1950s and it is not until the very late 1950s and early 1960s that we begin to see the emergence of the abduction phenomenon. The images, imagery and some underlying meanings of the UFO phenomenon are easy to find in these science-fiction forerunners that were so popular across America, and, to a lesser degree, England, at that time.

THE THING FROM ANOTHER WORLD (1951)

Workers at an Arctic establishment discover a flying saucer frozen under the Arctic ice. Presumably the expense of building a flying saucer was too great, and the film provides only the fin sticking up through the ice; the saucer shape is made visual by the men from the outpost forming a circle as they stand over the edge of the object they can see through the ice.

At this time no UFO reports had involved aliens. Film makers had only the flying saucer as the 'real' basis of their film; the rest was pure fiction and in this instance they created a highly watchable horror movie in which the alien (who had conveniently been thrown out of the saucer when it crashed, to be separately frozen in another part of the ice) turns out to be a carnivorous vegetable in the shape of a man. That there have been no reliable UFO claims involving man-shaped carnivorous vegetables is actually very important to our study. As I state elsewhere in the book, reports of UFOs 'coloured' by interpretations from science-fiction films need to be *credible*, both to the reporter and the world at large; a report of such an entity would *not* be credible. Also, the alien displayed no particular intelligence, and the substance of UFO claims is that there is scope for human–alien interaction. The UFO phenomenon would not have developed very far if all those reporting it had been describing bloodsucking, rampaging vegetables. Furthermore, there would be an obvious need for, and lack of, physical evidence in such claims.

The Thing from Another World, therefore, is merely a horror story based on the reports of flying saucers at the time, and has no particular alien interaction.

We might at this point ask ourselves why we do not get claims of events based on films such as *The Incredible Shrinking Man*, the 1957 movie which depicted a person affected by an anomalous cloud who eventually shrank to atomic size? It is because UFO contactee claims provide answers to mankind's big questions ('Is there other life?' 'Is there a God?' et cetera). *The Incredible Shrinking Man* offers no answers to people's needs and, while a highly watchable film, is little more than that.

THE DAY THE EARTH STOOD STILL (1951)

Well ahead of its time and one of the most influential films in UFO imagery, *The Day the Earth Stood Still* offers leads into abductions, contactees, crash retrievals, and 'ordinary' sightings. The film starts with a military radar discovery of a UFO, reinforcing immediately the belief that the military 'know' about flying saucers. 'This is not another flying-saucer scare,' the film tells us. 'Whatever it is, it is something real.'

The first appearance of the spaceship does the whole UFO range in seconds; it goes from being a light in the sky to a cigar-shaped light to a classic flying saucer as we see it landing.

First on the scene are the military and the first thing that happens to the visiting, peaceful alien (Klaatu) is that he gets shot, putting paid to any questions like 'But why don't they just land on the White House lawn?'

Interestingly, Klaatu's first appearance shows him with a bald, dome-shaped head, virtually no facial features except the slightest impression of a nose, and dark slit-like 'eyes' almost suggestive of the 'grey' aliens. Actually this is just a helmet and when he takes it off he bears an uncanny resemblance to the actor Michael Rennie, but it's a thought-provoking start.

The reason for Klaatu's coming to Earth is hinted at but not stated early on in the film. We soon discover the beginnings of 'contactee' imagery; like Adamski's later aliens, Klaatu is here to warn us to mend our wicked warlike ways. He comes from a world without war, a world that has made great advances in medicine and healthcare. His knowledge of mathematics and technology is highly advanced. **His coverall clothing is also uncannily similar to the outfit George Adamski's alien wore.**

By the end of the film Bobby (a boy befriended by Klaatu), Bobby's mother, a friendly professor and a whole host of others become 'special' contactees, in that they are given a message to help develop mankind or the Earth will be in danger.

The ship (and a companion robot called Gort) are resistant to blowtorches, oxyacetylene and a diamond drill. 'Toughest material I ever saw,' says one man engaged to break into the saucer. **In crash-retrieval stories we get much the same claim: *Crash at Corona*, by Stanton T. Friedman and Don Berliner, reports Jesse Marcel's description of the recovered material from a saucer crash as 'could not be broken, could not be burned ... I tried to bend that stuff and it won't bend. I even tried it with a sledge hammer. You can't make a dent on it.'**

There is also a crash-retrieval hint in the way the saucer is treated by the military; unable to move it, they build a wall around it and post guards to keep everybody out. **There have been hints for many years that some crashed saucers were buried in the desert where they fell rather than risk moving them.**

Klaatu wants to get out and live with people to understand them better. **This desire to understand is a recurring theme in both abductions (working with aliens to gain insight into their technology, as suggested by Timothy Good in *Alien Liaison*) and contactees (where the aliens frequently live and work amongst us – see Sten's story in this book.)** The religious overtones of the film won't have escaped those comparing it to contactee claims. Klaatu adopts the name 'Doctor Carpenter': a suggestion of Jesus, I think, and one reinforced towards the end of the film when he is killed and resurrected.

Klaatu says that he has travelled 250,000,000 miles to Earth. That would have to put his starting point in the inner planets of the solar system, with Mars and Venus as frontrunners. (I suspect, however, that no particular location was intended; the filmmakers probably thought that this distance was about as far as the audience would stand without laughing. It might have given a sense of direction to contactees, though.)

Several images seem vaguely indicative of 'Men in Black' imagery. Klaatu makes his first appearance in a human home in shadow, in a rather sinister way, and the military all run around in shiny black cars. There are, however, none of the rather bizarre MIB descriptions that were to arise in UFO reports.

Klaatu decides to stage a demonstration of his abilities. He causes a selective blackout of all electricity across the world, though to avoid causing harm, he is able to keep aircraft in flight and hospital power running. **UFO reports have, since the outset, been connected to electrical effects and UFOs were associated with the Great North–East Blackout around New York in November 1965. In that event, as in the film, many people were trapped in traffic jams ('car stops' in the film, failed traffic lights in the Blackout), and in elevators.**

When Bobby follows Klaatu back to his saucer and then tells his mother she insists it was all a dream. Wet clothing from the wet grass he was running about on makes his mother wonder if he was telling the truth. **Many abduction reports follow that pattern of 'discovery'.**

Inside of the ship itself is a circular corridor around the perimeter of the inside of the saucer. Within that there is a room containing a platform bed (used in the film for medical treatment of Klaatu). There is no obvious point of lighting shown though there is bright lighting in the room. At one point Bobby's mother is 'abducted' by Gort and taken into the room with the platform bed against her will. **The interior images emerge again and again in UFO reports.**

INVADERS FROM MARS AND IT CAME FROM OUTER SPACE (1953)

Aliens are bad guys in *Invaders from Mars* – normal for the time. It's interesting, though that the bad guys come from Mars (also see *War of the Worlds*), the planet named after the God of War; George Adamski's kind, gentle and beautiful aliens came from Venus – named after the Goddess of Love.

Standard flying saucer lands at night in lonely place (as does the crippled craft in *It Came from Outer Space*). One boy sees it land and throughout the film fights to convince a disbelieving world of the truth – a forerunner of David Vincent's role in the TV series *The Invaders*. And, of course, this is the frustrating plight of John Putnam in *It Came from Outer Space*. (Are UFO researchers seeing themselves in this role?) The aliens are capable of taking on human form – something which is occasionally a feature of UFO reports, and might be held by some to explain the 'Adamski' aliens' similarity to humans: what started as a movie-maker's cost-cutting exercise has become part of the fabric of UFO reporting. In *It Came from Outer Space* the aliens tell Putnam that 'It is within our power to transform ourselves to look like you.' **Much the same thing was said to abductees Peter and Frances by 'their' aliens on the road to Beitbridge while heading for South Africa. Peter said, under hypnosis, 'They can make themselves appear in any form in our minds. They can say to you, "I look like a duck," and they would look like a duck in your eyes.'**

The police in *Invaders from Mars* are no help at all since their key people have been 'taken over'. Do conspiracy theorists believe something like this with their firm belief that governments will never tell the truth? They use ridicule – a clear forerunner of disinformation theory – to discredit the boy. **Incidentally, belief that aliens are working in the Pentagon and other military areas in league with humans has been an undercurrent belief in UFO research for some decades; it is only just surfacing again in a new and revised version, linking UFOs with cattle mutilations, abductions and super-technologies.**

Although unable to perfectly re-create humans – due to their lack of emotion – the aliens blend in fairly well with the social environment. Could a 'real' alien do that? Consider the problems a man would have fooling an ape that he was another ape for any period of time. This is a device for the film, it keeps the cost of props and make-up down, but it seems to have been imported into UFO stories. **The early contactees all reported aliens that were almost perfectly human – they met them in normal Earth surroundings such as burger bars and on Greyhound buses.**

It is interesting to note that in this film the scientists

decide to believe the boy because his claims 'can't be disproved'. Only a fiction film could be so generous to science! *It Came from Outer Space* got it right: the scientists won't believe because they are 'much less inclined to witchcraft' and the news media spend the whole film acting the goat and ridiculing the main characters.

The aliens 'control' their humans by inserting implants into the head. One scientist immediately theorises that the aliens control humans by some form of 'transmission'. **It took a few years for implants to surface in UFO reports; but now abduction reports are full of them. In one of the saddest twists of the UFO phenomenon, advertisements in America offer to 'remove your implant' for a large fee.**

The aliens are not very 'grey' or foetus-like, and could hardly be said to be a forerunner of the 'greys'. They are tall humanoids, have three long fingers and huge reflective eyes. Their only resemblance to a foetus is that they run as if they are wearing oversize nappies. The result of this cost-cutting for the filmmakers is an alien lacking in the credibility needed for it to be imported into UFO claims. (In fact, the 'real' form of the alien in *It Came from Outer Space* is a walking trifle with one eye and a sparkling slime trail behind it.)

The boy blasts the aliens in *Invaders* with one of their own guns. A nice touch, that, and one I expect to see in a mutated form in UFO researchers' claims in the next few years – perhaps abductees will use the alien implants 'against' the aliens.

The ending of the film is curious; the whole thing turns out to be a dream, and then there is the implication that it is all going to happen again. Bedroom visitation and dream-state experiences – throw six to start here!

EARTH VERSUS THE FLYING SAUCERS (1956)

This film was, according to the titles, 'suggested by *Flying Saucers from Outer Space* by Donald Keyhoe'. This was the author whose book Betty Hill read avidly following her own sighting, which was soon to become the archetypical abduction. One week after her sighting, Betty Hill wrote to Keyhoe, and this film came out five years before her experiences.

The flying saucers are very 'classical' right from the opening, scene-setting shots, confirming a solid, structured craft. The 'scene-setters' state that 'Air Intelligence Command in Dayton, Ohio collects UFO data from all over the globe'. The narrator confirms there is 'increasing' investigation. The film picks up on a few standard UFO images before the film 'proper' starts. Consider the events related by Betty and Barney Hill when reading these opening film scenes.

We see a car containing a married couple driving down an isolated road. Prior to the 'encounter' there are other cars moving in both directions; by the time the flying saucer approaches the car there are no other vehicles to be seen. **Betty Hill and her husband Barney were driving through the night on lonely roads**.

The UFO makes a close approach, frightening the couple. They pull over and stop the car, and see the UFO leave. During the encounter they have heard a strange buzzing sound. **Betty and Barney first saw a light in the sky that quickly came closer and was perceived as a large, structured object. Barney in particular became alarmed. They pulled the car over to verify if what they were seeing was really moving. At one point Barney confronted the UFO at close range; it was hovering at treetop height close enough for Barney to identify figures**

on board. As they left the scene of this encounter they heard a curious 'beeping' sound that has never been explained.

The first words spoken after the encounter are 'It was a saucer – a flying saucer?' spoken as a question seeking confirmation. **The first words spoken by Betty after the encounter were to ask her husband: 'Now do you believe in flying saucers?'**

The buzzing sound they hear is recorded on a tape in the car. It turns out later that this is actually a voice message for the occupants but transmitted from the flying saucer at an incredibly fast rate. In other words, the occupants of the car receive more information than they know at the time, though they discover this only later. **Hypnotic regression on the Hills indicated the possibility of an abduction where they underwent medical examination. This was 'blocked' from their conscious recall and came out later during investigation**.

The aliens eventually abduct a human who is then subjected to a 'weird' interrogation by a crystal 'eye'. He acts like a zombie with his mind blacked out. **Obvious parallels with the abduction claims: Betty and Barney have recall under hypnosis of a rather 'drugged-like' state, allegedly brought on by the aliens, when being moved to and from their car**.

The aliens speak to their captives in English (through a translation device). **The Hills' aliens spoke English.** (It would be difficult to see how the film, or the UFO phenomenon in this guise, could develop if they did not!)

Eventually the film leads to the landing of a saucer. Watches suffer electro-magnetic effects as a result of exposure to the flying saucer's drive energies. **Both Betty and Barney Hill found that their watches had stopped when they got home that night**.

The aliens that emerge are anything but the 'classic'

type – though they later turn out to be! When we first see them they are ungainly, robot-like creatures that owe some kinship to Gort, the giant robot from *The Day the Earth Stood Still*. However, by the time one of them gets shot and has his helmet removed, we see a fairly familiar face looking up at us: bald, flat-nosed, large eyes. (He does look rather more aged than the average 'grey', and his mouth is much more prominent.) **Betty and Barney encountered aliens similar to the 'greys' but more human-looking than is normally reported nowadays. Their eyes were much more human-like, with a pupil, and the heads were not ludicrously over-big. (Over the years aliens have been getting increasingly more alien.)**

Incidentally, the still shots advertising the film were enhanced before being turned into posters: they show the main characters of the film walking under a flying saucer and being hit by an angled beam of light from the saucer – very 'Gulf Breeze'!

The other imagery in the film is clearly designed to 'make a movie' and owes little anyway to Keyhoe's writing. There is much fighting and military-versus-alien confrontation but this is mainly designed to give us a cracking good story and an exciting and uplifting ending.

The subliminal imagery (and the alien description) has all come through in UFO reports in the years since. None of it arose in UFO reports prior to that time and therefore was not described in Keyhoe's book.

(Humorous note: one reviewer compared this film with *UFO*, a 1956 documentary about the phenomenon, and concluded that *Earth Versus the Flying Saucers* made more sense!)

Many people will point out that in this chapter I have selected those aspects of films which have come through to UFO reports and ignored those that have not. But that is the point. If we assume, as I do, that people are creating the 'flying saucers and alien' interpretation of their otherwise real experiences from an image-bank of science fiction, then there will also be a selection process, by the reporter, of those things that to him or her seem credible and those that do not. The most bizarre aspects of the films should not, and do not, come through to UFO reports; the more likely possibilities should, and do, surface. The reporter is not just seeking to convince others, and I am certainly not dismissing these claims as hoaxes. The problem for the UFO recipient is that first he or she must convince themselves of the credibility of what they have seen.

Incidentally, the degree to which some people can accept as real what they hear on TV, even in fiction, is astonishing. I was told by one individual that the makers of the TV series *Outer Limits* could actually control your TV set in your living room (which was what the programme spookily claimed in its opening titles). He firmly believed that the broadcasters could, for half an hour, control the volume and focus knobs of his TV set. To this day he is convinced that someone else could do that 'if they could do it all those years ago'. No amount of explaining from me would convince him otherwise.

What the future holds is uncertain. In the days of the films described above UFOs – flying saucers for the most part – were just entering the collective consciousness, particularly in the West. Like it or not, and from whatever basis of reality it comes, awareness of UFOs is now a fact. People 'know' about UFOs whatever they believe about them. Films now are being made directly from the claims of UFO witnesses. In this book there are many references by witnesses to images they recall from movies such as *Close Encounters of the Third Kind* and *Communion*. There are no longer any UFO virgins. The interaction between science fiction and UFO reporting has changed forever; it will be many years before we see quite what the effects of that have been.

5 The Mythmakers: The UFO Researchers

D r Ivan Grattan-Guinness, who has had a long-time involvement in the paranormal, once said, 'If ever a subject needed rescuing from its advocates, then ufology is the one.'

No study of the public face of UFO research would be complete without a look behind the 'closed doors' within 'the industry'.

As Julia Burton has pointed out in her dissertation, reproduced in Chapter 3, one of the problems that any diligent newspaper reporter has is finding a spokesperson for ufology – there isn't one. There are no shortage of spokespersons, of course, but no consistency. Some speak for organisations with particular viewpoints. Many of the highest profile ufologists within those organisations are only spokespeople for themselves. 'Independent' ufologists – belonging to no groups or bodies – at least have no conflict of interest in this way but their viewpoints are no more representative of the subject.

BELIEF SYSTEMS

Many people dismiss UFO reports because they don't fit into their accepted frame of thinking. UFO researchers are no exception – and they show up their worst side when they do so.

For example, in the 1950s it was quite acceptable to talk about objects in the skies, but regarded as very 'suspect' to take seriously the claims of those who said they had seen aliens. It was once unacceptable to consider the claims of 'repeater' witnesses; now it is recognised that most close-encounter witnesses have a life history of paranormal self-reporting. It was once quite acceptable to believe that flying saucers could do manoeuvres in the skies that our planes could not do, but not acceptable to believe that they could – for example – move through solid objects. In fact this kind of conditioning is largely the result of science fiction; what could be done by the special effects of film studios and therefore 'seen' by everyone was acceptable; what could not was ludicrous.

More recently it has become acceptable to believe that aliens are ugly little grey 'doctors' performing genetic manipulation on humans, but quite unacceptable to believe that they are tall, Nordic benign creatures who have selected certain people to bring a salvation message to the world. Why is one better than the other? Both versions have their claimants – in fact there are probably more claimants to the latter than the former. The reason, rather simplistically stated for the moment, is that the abductions present a level of challenge to our everyday thinking that we can tolerate – alien hardware and attitude is an extrapolation of our own abilities, or even what we might suspect we would do if we had a flying saucer and could go to the planets around a nearby star. Contactees represent claims that the majority of people simply cannot allow to be true: the idea of a vastly superior race that feeds us tit-bits of help along the way is just too ghastly for human pride.

If we argue that aliens are formed in our self-image, then it is a sad reflection on us that we more easily accept malign, manipulative aliens than we do benign, caring aliens.

PUBLIC PROFILE

Ufology as a subject is largely being written about – and at least to some extent created – by the researchers. Abductions turn the witnesses into victims and the researcher becomes Special Top Dog, riding in on his white charger to Save The Day. Contactee claims, on the other hand, make the witness special, reducing the researcher to the level of journalist. The more manipulative of UFO researchers are creating a niche for themselves which is challenged by contactee claims. Bias here is not all one-sided; some contactees have sought to take control of these experiences for themselves – a good thing by any standard in my view – but that does leave the door open for contactees to become Special Top Dog in cult followings and pseudo-religions. We have seen it happen since the 1950s.

There is no question in my mind that the majority of researchers and investigators belong here, in the Mythmakers section. A subject started by the media picking up a few claims during 'the silly season' of the summer was manipulated by those media to produce dramatic copy-selling stories of alien invasion. It was attractive for a number of reasons explored elsewhere in this book: the post-war need for a new enemy to keep nations united, a need to search outwards rather than inwards, and so on. But presented as it was, it obviously attracted those people to it – to become the researchers – who were attracted to that line of thinking. This is natural and honest, and was modified over time as the evidence was shown to be more complex. People dissuaded of that belief 'dropped out'. Some were not dissuaded of course, and the subject opened up to accommodate those with different viewpoints. A much wider discussion of the origins of UFOs is to be had on the subject today than, say, twenty years ago. Certainly more than was there 40 years ago.

However, the media attention has never really deflected from the ETH – the 'alien invasion' theory. And that has sadly meant that some researchers have been forced to be less than honest, particularly those who seem to have a desire to see themselves on TV and in print.

I am not saying, of course, that adherence to the ETH is dishonest. Researchers such as Timothy Good, for example, have never wavered in their belief that extra-terrestrials are involved in UFO events, and I have every admiration for him and others who stick to their guns. Rather, I am considering the sort of situation that arose a couple of years back when one prominent British UFO researcher kept announcing to English audiences that they did not feel aliens were involved. Transcripts of addresses to foreign audiences however, promoting books clearly steered towards the ETH, were less certain. Then that person was offered a US tour (where the biggest bucks are to be had talking about aliens) and suddenly started trying to persuade others that 'Well, maybe there is something in this ETH after all.'

MAGAZINES

Books and public lectures are not the only outlet for material. Ufology is a subject littered with as many 'industry' magazines as there are viewpoints – and then some. Of course some of those magazines are highly valuable, but many are frighteningly manipulative. This is always a subjective opinion and I will not be so unfair as to list my opinions of good or bad magazines. However, readers might consider dividing magazines into three types:

'In house' mags that are the outlets for organisations.

It is sensible that these organisations should have a voice: their job is to collate the work of their researchers and members and make it more widely known. Such magazines are also a valuable arena for articles and discussion.

'**Fanzines**' which promote (usually) extreme viewpoints and can be edited by individuals or on behalf of organisations. They are valuable but have the drawback of being highly selective in what they print in terms of content and present material not supportive of their viewpoint in a deliberately jaundiced way.

'**Cult leader' mags**. Avoid like the Black Death. These magazines reflect the viewpoint of just one person. They are never balanced, never add anything to the subject, and almost always the person responsible has never seen a witness or gone 'into the field'.

ORGANISATIONS

Eduardo Russo, a prominent Italian UFO researcher, said once that research is never conducted by organisations but by individuals. That is a fact; all work in this field is done by individuals.

However, there is a genuine reason for the existence of organisations beyond just a 'train-spotters club' for fans. The best of the organisations – including BUFORA – are there to collate that work, present it to a wider public and be a channel for information exchange across the world to share as widely as possible the work of others. However, all UFO organisations have problems.

Organisations can be slow and plodding to respond to needs; they are usually run by a committee of volunteers who just do what they can in their spare time. There are of course no full-time or professional (i.e.

paid) ufologists in the UK, despite publicity-seeking claims to the contrary by one or two individuals.

Organisations can be manipulated for a time by individuals seeking to use them as publicity machinery for themselves. A well-disciplined committee can fight off these attempts that arise from time to time though the public – and the members – rarely understand what is happening.

Organisations can become cults if an open policy towards belief systems is not encouraged.

Organisations, being largely amateur, seem afraid to adopt 'business-like' attitudes, fearing the worst of the business world might affect them. In fact, they would benefit from such areas as team-building, goal-orientation and so on. Many organisations have aims, but few short-term achievable goals.

There is also a natural conflict between being serious and scientific, and being 'popular'. Organisations need money to fund research but there is a fine line between 'selling what people want' and offering the truth, however unpalatable. Some people will pay a lot of money to be fed popular stories. An organisation, such as BUFORA, which shuns 'sell-outs' also finds itself rejected by a great many people whose interest is marginal, and belief-system-oriented.

BUFORA and other organisations are essential, though, and should be encouraged without at the same time being allowed to dominate a subject where domination is always detrimental.

UFO RESEARCH IN CONTEXT

Aware that my own viewpoint was in danger of reflecting only the problems of BUFORA rather than a wider scope, I sought the views of others. They have helped me in the points raised in this chapter and elsewhere in this book. One colleague who appears frequently in this book, Bertil Kuhlemann from Sweden, is not a member of any UFO organisations but has had experience of the problems of UFO-group conflicts in his own country. He offered the following observations:

'When we come to the question of UFO research organisations we can see that different organisations are formed for quite different aims. There come into play very subtle energies within the individual, for instance fear and also in many cases courage, and it is important to understand this in order to understand the research done by these people.'

I pointed out that UFO research organisations now have very cynical, sceptical people involved; people who are usually trying to 'wish away' the subject with the same fervour – and lack of scientific principles – for which some scientists are renowned. He agreed:

'We could benefit by trying to retrieve from the sceptics the basis they have for their scepticism. What is the background they are coming from? For instance the difficulties you may have in the BUFORA Council and in the British ufological scene are to some extent caused by people not defining what the basic stand from which they are coming is. You may think that you can analytically come to an understanding of what's implied behind the words but when you question people, ask them directly about what kind of basic framework of reference they are coming from, they become very vague because very few people have thought deeply enough.'

LEGAL MANIPULATION OF UFOS

This section would be a good deal longer and more specific if it weren't for the strict libel laws in England and, to a lesser extent, America.

The UFO phenomenon is driven in large part by the United States, a country which itself is driven almost entirely by lawyers. Lawyers, particularly in the United States, are in turn driven by money and little else. While the UFO phenomenon was a 'game played for fun' it was left alone by lawyers; there was no money in it. There have always been legal threats of course, mostly caused by individual egos being bruised, but by and large they were settled by the parties calming down and coming to their senses rather than actually resorting to law. And it was obvious from the outset that the threats themselves were designed to rebuke critics rather than actually seek legal redress.

However, of late we have been seeing and hearing of the most deliberately manipulative use of the legal system. To explain the broad position: anyone can take anyone else to court. The plaintiff (accuser) makes a claim and the defendant is then forced to defend the allegation. The most lucrative ploy for a 'plaintiff' to try is to allege libel (false statements which damage the credibility, standing and financial earning-ability of another). Defendants in libel cases are not able to claim 'legal aid' (a government-backed defence fund); faced with a bill of several thousands of pounds of legal costs, the defendant will often 'back off' even when he or she knows they are in the right. Many people in UFO research simply cannot afford the fight and have to 'cave in'.

The problem, from my point of view, is that the person 'caving in' unfortunately has to concede that the plaintiff was 'right' and they were 'wrong'. They cannot then come forward to me and say 'Ah, but I only said that to get out of the case'. If they did that then they could be sued again and this time they would almost certainly lose in court because they had 'admitted' the offence previously.

I have heard, in the 'backstage' and informal chatter at UFO meetings and lectures, prominent UFO researchers advising others to threaten legal action simply because it will suppress good research contrary to that person's own beliefs. The whole of UFO research and history is gradually being rewritten using legal manipulation. And the motive is very simple: the more ludicrous the view the more the media will pay for the story. Use the legal system to get the critics out of the way and then 'take the money and run'.

I must be fair and say that this does not mean that recourse to the law is always to be rejected. There are vicious and unfair attacks on UFO researchers and it is right and proper than these people should have redress to the law to defend themselves from those attacks. I have seen cases of perfectly legitimate complaints; it is the misuse that is of concern. What started as an American disease is now spreading to the UK, and UFO research bodies in the UK are powerless to stop money taking over from research as a driving force.

This is a very serious point. These events must – when witnesses wish – be placed in the public domain. It is important that people are given every opportunity to understand these experiences witnesses are going through. And any attempt to control it, beyond the witnesses' own control of their story, is censorship of the most devious kind.

If these events are real then they belong in the public domain. In my view those researchers who 'tie' witnesses to them for financial gain, selling their stories and so on, are making the subconscious confession that they do not think these stories do belong in the public domain; in short, they do not really believe the stories to be anything other than constructed fiction.

It would be nice to end this chapter on a practical note; unfortunately any practical recommendation is beyond the scope of this book. The fault lies not with UFO research but with the legal system. Faulty legal systems, in all areas of life, have their devious manipulators and UFO research is no exception. I can only hope that changes in the law can one day make it easier to speak openly and without threat of suppression.

6 The Mythmakers:
The Conspiracists

On 17 June 1972 five burglars were arrested breaking into the Democratic National Headquarters in the Watergate office apartment and hotel complex in Washington DC, USA. The burglary was one manifestation of a conspiracy and corruption which reached to the highest levels of the American administration. To have covered up Watergate should, by the logic of most UFO researchers, have been easy. The highest authorities in the country had reason and power to contain the conspiracy; only a limited number of people in any case had the information necessary to break the conspiracy; and all could be made subject to threat and/or bribery.

Furthermore, the conspiracy had to be contained only for a reasonably short time. Richard Nixon had been elected President on 5 November 1968 and had nearly finished his first term in office. The next election was to be held on 7 November 1972; Nixon, therefore, had to contain the conspiracy for just a little over four years.

In fact, on 8 August 1974 Nixon announced his resignation and resigned the following day. The efforts of two determined investigative reporters, working for a little over two years and starting with a minor burglary, had forced the United States president out of office.

Compare even the basis of Watergate with the idea that just one flying saucer had crashed in America in the desert 45 years ago, presenting the military science and politicians with an alien spacecraft and dead (or, even, alive) alien beings. How many people would have, in practice, have been exposed to the alien material? There would of course have been some civilians who saw the crash or the damaged alien craft; there would have been the immediate military who recovered the craft; there would have been those needed to transport it; there would then be the scientists, law enforcement agencies, security agencies and various departments of the military needed to contain, study and examine the material. There would have been scientists, some probably employed by private industry (given the American privatised economy), working on developments learned from discoveries of the alien material. On the bases holding the alien material there would have been a whole range of janitors, cooks and other workers, all of whom would, over 45 years – in the course of the way the world works – have had some exposure to the material (albeit they would have been under military orders). There would have been politicians, who have a disarming way of forcing themselves into each and every aspect of projects, about. Four example, on 12 April 1985, Space Shuttle 51D took off for a week-long flight into space. One of the occupants was Senator E. J. (Jake) Garn, the chairman of the Senate Committee responsible for overseeing NASA's budget. Apparently he felt he could sanction the requests for money from NASA more easily if he better understood space travel first-hand. Such dedication to duty would surely have arisen in crash-retrieval research.

Furthermore this UFO conspiracy has apparently lasted 45 years – as compared to the brief life of the Watergate conspiracy – pursued by an incredible number of researchers across the United States and other countries.

We can look at Watergate because (a) we know it was

a conspiracy; (b) we have a documented way in which to analyse how it was defeated and unravelled; and (c) we can examine the consequences of the revelations.

The same might be said of the exposure of the Manhattan project or the revelation that for a time the British security service was virtually being run by Russian agents. Being contemporary and involved as it is with the American administration, Watergate provides us with the best parallel to UFO cover-up and conspiracy.

Let us first then look at the Watergate conspiracy.

The following timetable is a brief synopsis of the 'real time' work of the principal pair involved in the Watergate revelations: the *Washington Post*'s Carl Bernstein and Bob Woodward. It covers only a short period of the early days of the investigation, since Watergate is not the topic of this book, but illustrates the type of in-depth analysis that was the Watergate investigation of some two years.

17 June 1972. Burglars were arrested breaking into the Democratic National Headquarters in the Watergate complex in Washington. Bob Woodward was asked to report on the burglary. That afternoon Woodward went to court for the preliminary hearing. Seeing Caddy (unknown to him) who seemed to be in unfamiliar surroundings Woodward sat next to him and asked him if he was in court covering the Watergate burglar. The man replied, 'I am not the Attorney of Record, I am acting as an individual,' but introduced the man next to him as the Attorney of Record, Joseph Rafferty Jr. From Rafferty, Woodward got the names and addresses of the five burglars. Caddy did not want to talk about the burglary, but confirmed that the burglars were not his clients. Persistent questioning by Woodward revealed from Caddy: 'I met one of the defendants, Bernard Barker, at a social occasion.' Later Caddy admitted to Woodward that he had arrived in the court because Barker's wife had phoned him at three o'clock in the morning ('she said her husband had told her to call me if he hadn't called her by three, but it might mean he was in trouble'). During the hearing Woodward heard James McCord give his occupation as security consultant, recently retired from the CIA.

Called to the case Woodward had intuitively, and very quickly, found a source and despite that source's reluctance had already found out something of the burglar's pre-burglary motives.

The *Post*'s managing editor, Howard Simons, was worried about the story, thinking 'it could be crazy Cubans'. Since President Nixon was well ahead in the polls and the Democratic party was in a shambles, it was thought highly unlikely that the Republican party could be in any way behind the break-in.

So this 'conspiracy theory' did not even arise out of expectation.

18 June 1972. An item on the *Associated Press* news wire indicated that James McCord was security co-ordinator for the committee to re-elect the president. Neither Woodward nor Bernstein could immediately identify a particular meaning to that fact.

The same day, former US Attorney-General John Mitchell, the president's campaign manager, stated: 'We want to emphasise that this man and the other people involved were not operating on either our behalf or with our consent.' Bernstein assumed that the White House would not be involved in so tacky an activity as a burglary and asked for confirmation that that was not the case. His contact did not deny it, indicating only that he believed whoever had organised the break-in was politically naive.

*Woodward and Bernstein started by expecting an outcome different to the one they got. It was the **facts**, not their predisposition, which changed their minds.*

22 June 1972. President Nixon announced: 'The White House has had no involvement whatever in this particular incident.'

Bernstein and Woodward were attracted by the phrase 'this particular incident'. It was as if Nixon was not prepared to declare the White House was clear of all illegal activities but wanted only to take the heat off the immediate problem.

Woodward and Bernstein were subject to considerable scrutiny. Ben Bradley, a *Post* executive editor, challenged Woodward on the source for his claim that Howard Hunt was conducting an investigation into the Kennedy family. Because the source was not at a high enough level Bradley greatly diluted the claim and told him, 'Get some harder information next time.'

If Ben Bradley were adjudicating on UFO cover-up and conspiracy revelations this is a phrase he would likely use many times!

Bernstein found out early on in the investigation that Howard Hunt's lawyer had been paid $25,000 in cash in a brown envelope to defend Hunt and was told, 'At least $100,000 in CRP's [Campaign to Re-elect the President] budget was earmarked for "convention security". The money is the key to this thing.'

At this early point Bernstein and Woodward could not progress the Watergate story. Other newspapers had been delving in other areas; the Long Island newspaper *Newsday* reported that White House aide G. Gordon Liddy, a lawyer for the CRP, had been fired by Mitchell for refusing to answer FBI questions about Watergate. The *New York Times* ran a story indicating that there had been many phone calls from one of the burglar's telephones to the CRP and an office used by Liddy. Bernstein used contacts at the telephone company to follow up these claims. It was there that he discovered that one of the burglar's (Barker's) phone records had been subpoenaed by the Miami local district attorney, Richard Gerstein. Bernstein spoke to Gerstein, who claimed that he did not know what was in the records but that Martin Dardis, his chief investigator, would know. Gerstein said he would instruct Dardis to co-operate with the *Post*. Dardis phoned Bernstein later that evening. He invited Bernstein to fly to Miami to discuss the documents and admitted on the telephone that more than $100,000 was involved and that it had come from Mexico City. Little of this made sense to Bernstein at the time, but he diligently plugged on to verify and understand.

Bernstein was very persistent and eventually was able to extract a good deal of information from this district attorney's investigator. He was able to confirm that the money coming from Mexico had been 'laundered' (in an attempt to cover up the source of the money).

At one point Dardis was refusing to allow Bernstein to photocopy the bank statements and cheques but for no clear reason allowed Bernstein to hand-write and copy out all of the information.

Dardis did not want the source to be proven to have originated at his office and there was no particular reason why he ought to have shared it with a reporter. Yet it is a major factor in the unravelling of the Watergate and other conspiracies that people who have secrets show off by sharing them or feel compelled to talk when there are no obvious pressures on them to do so.

In examining the cheques a $25,000 cheque payable to Kenneth Dahlberg was discovered. Dahlberg turned out to be the Mid-West finance chairman for the Committee to Re-elect the President, linking the laundered money to the president's campaign funds.

Interestingly for our study, when Dahlberg was challenged by Woodward and asked whose the $25,000 was, he said, 'Contributions I collected in my role as Mid-West finance chairman.' Dahlberg went on to say, 'I know I shouldn't tell you this.' Dahlberg even went on to add, 'At a meeting in Washington of the committee I turned the cheque over either to the treasurer of the committee or to Maurice Stans himself.' (Maurice Stans was the finance chairman of the CRP.) As Woodward and Bernstein's book goes on to say, 'Woodward couldn't wait to get off the line', and as *Washington Post* city editor Barry Susman said, 'We've never had a story like this.'

*But why **did** Dahlberg talk? Because secrets burn holes in your pocket far quicker than money ever can . . .*

When Woodward telephoned Clark MacGregor, Mitchell's successor in the CRP, MacGregor did what most people do and blamed everything on his predecessors on the – quite reasonable – basis that he was in the clear. 'These events took place before I came aboard. Mitchell and Stans would presumably know about this.'

People with nothing to hide are a very useful source of information against those with plenty to hide, particularly if there is the slightest doubt that allegations not specific to a person can be made against the innocent party. The innocent party usually makes the effort to ensure that the allegations fall where they deserve to. Again a very valid source of information in unravelling conspiracies. Where are these people in the UFO cover-ups?

Further investigation resulted in the *Washington Post* running a story indicating that more than half a million dollars of campaign funds had been mishandled. The same day United States district court judge Charles Richey confirmed that sworn statements by Mitchell, Stans and others would not be made public before the American elections. Richey had apparently reversed his own decision with no pressure from CRP lawyers claiming to be acting for the constitutional rights of those under investigation. Richey personally telephoned Bernstein at the *Washington Post* and said, 'I just wanted you to understand the basis for my decision.' Richey went on to confirm, 'I wanted to be very clear that I haven't discussed this case outside the courtroom with anyone and that political consideration played no part whatsoever.' As Bernstein and Woodward's book indicates: 'Bernstein was dumb-struck. He had never met Judge Richey. The call came out of the blue.'

Investigative reporters who are 'on to something' do not have to dig and chase and extract all the information they need. Once something starts to unravel there is a lot of information thrown at the investigators who are themselves sought out by those wanting to tell stories which reflect well on them. As other events in the Watergate conspiracy show, good investigative reporters use those pieces of information to seek out and verify other information and to cross-check. In similar circumstances UFO investigators have accepted one anecdotal story as evidence without further investigation. Indeed both Woodward and Bernstein developed an unwritten rule: 'Unless two sources confirmed a charge involving activity likely to be considered criminal, the specific allegation was not used in the paper.'

Despite the fact that a small number of people and a short time scale were involved in Watergate, Woodward and Bernstein had several hundred names on their list of contacts and kept up their pressure by ensuring that everyone on the list was telephoned at least twice a week.

It takes pressure to get people unwilling to talk to feel that there is a compulsion to do so. There is no indication in any of the writings on UFO cover-up and conspiracy that anything like this degree of pressure has been applied to force the unwilling to come forward. Indeed a cynic looking at the cover-up and conspiracy work would conclude – as I do – that far from wanting people to talk, UFO investigators have all too often shown that they want people to keep silent because unconnected unverified information is thought-provoking and exciting, whereas detailed deeper information usually ends up confirming either that the person is a liar or mistaken, or that the UFO investigator is getting hold of the wrong end of the stick. These are comments that will be strongly refuted by cover-up and conspiracy investigators but I still come back to the basic fact that I think cannot be refuted: it takes pressure to get people to reveal what they wish to conceal, and UFO investigators do not apply pressure anything like Woodward and Bernstein's efforts.

There was no question of Woodward and Bernstein having a 'right' to the Watergate investigation. They had to earn their right to keep the investigation and they had to keep earning their right. 'They sensed that as long as the stories continued to come, there would be no problem.'

UFO investigators are not subject to 'quality control' and as such have an automatic 'right' to work on whatever they want to. The downside of Woodward and Bernstein's problem is, however, even greater for UFO investigators: if the UFO investigators are to have information worth sharing, i.e. in books and magazines, then 'the stories must continue to come' – the more exciting the better.

If there is any doubt that Woodward and Bernstein met opposition, then consider one person on whose door Bernstein knocked. 'Please leave me alone. I know you are only trying to do your job, but you don't realise the pressure we are under. I hope you understand I am not being rude, please go.' However, another said, 'I want to help. God, it's all so awful.'

There may have been pressure but there was also a need to relieve that pressure. If a person has a secret and is being threatened in one way or another that revealing the secret could result in their coming to harm, then it is very easy to conclude that the fastest way to become permanently safe is not to hope that the secret stays a secret but to assist in some undercover way in making this secret public, so that the pressure becomes irrelevant and the threats invalid. We hear all the time in UFO cover-up that people cannot tell the truth because of immense government threats; the fact is that the more pressure that is brought to bear the quicker people ensure the secret becomes a secret no longer. UFO cover-up and conspiracy theorists will argue that a great many people have come forward and tried to reveal the truth, but as the Watergate case reveals, people know that anecdotal stories do not reveal the truth and that someone somewhere usually produces the hard unambiguous evidence (as was the case with Watergate). Despite 45 years of investigation, the hard unambiguous evidence of government conspiracies to cover up a detailed knowledge of UFOs has yet to materialise.

It would not be possible here to outline all of the information gleaned by Woodward and Bernstein, but many, many small items added up to an unravelling story. One of the key factors in the unravelling of Watergate was that one person would often detract attention from themselves by giving Woodward and Bernstein the name of somebody else to go and pester. Gradually the somebody else got higher and higher up in the administration and nearer and nearer the authoritative sources of proof.

Many times people revealed to Woodward and Bernstein that those higher up in the White House administration were concerned about where and how often Woodward and Bernstein were getting their information. It was genuinely a mystery to people at the Campaign to Re-elect the President and in other areas of the administration.

There is little reliable evidence that UFO investigators have got government officials on the run yet.

Other people's opinions of the power of cover-up and conspiracy are interesting. Several quotes from Woodward and Bernstein's book as relayed to them by frightened witnesses are intriguing: 'You'll never get the truth. You can't get it by reporters talking to just the good people.'

'I'll tell you, but it won't do any good.'

'The whole thing is being very well covered up and nobody will ever know what happened.'

People often argue along the above lines against the contention that a 45-year-old conspiracy could not be concealed.

It is not practical to examine the whole two years of Watergate in such detail as this but the above points indicate the contradictions between Watergate and UFO cover-up and conspiracy. All that we have examined above took place in slow plodding steps between June and September, a three-month period. In that time a minor burglary had, through diligent examination, been shown to represent a slush fund of money laundered through Mexico, handled by the president's campaign-fund committee and apparently involved in clandestine operations. The Watergate burglary had ceased to be of any particular significance; Bernstein and Woodward were now examining the mechanisms of the White House administration under a microscope.

What we can examine with interest are one or two other facets of the Watergate revelations that perhaps throw some light on the UFO cover-up and conspiracy theory.

DEEP THROAT

Woodward had a source in the executive branch whose name was not revealed (such sources are referred to in newspaper jargon as 'deep background' but this one became known as Deep Throat after a famous pornographic movie of the time). Deep Throat would never be quoted even as an anonymous source. It was clear from the outcome of the investigation that he had considerable authority or position, and presumably a lot to lose by working with Woodward and Bernstein. He made elaborate arrangements for contact in order to protect himself. In their book Woodward and Bernstein make one reference to Deep Throat: 'His friend was displeased, even angry at him. What struck Woodward even more was how frightened Deep Throat seemed. The fear had been building, but Woodward had not recognised it until now. Only a part of it was personal. It had more to do with the situation, the fact, the implications of what he knew about. Woodward had never known him to be so guarded, so serious. At their last meeting, he had seemed *weighed down*. If Woodward was reading his friend right something was horribly amiss.' (My emphasis added.) Deep Throat seemed weighed down, according to Woodward; in other words he had a need or a desire to assist Woodward in his investigations, but was presumably threatening his own safety. Threats did not dissuade him; furthermore it was Deep Throat who kept Woodward and Bernstein on track and provided them with the authoritative evidence they needed.

There have been no shortages of potential Deep Throats in UFO cover-up and conspiracy, but none have turned out to be in any way valid. Either they or the information they allude to turns out to be false, ambiguous, dubious or, even if potentially true, unproven or unauthoritative.

THE PRESIDENT WHO BUGGED HIMSELF

In unravelling the Watergate conspiracy it is not always obviously recognised, though of course it is there for all to see, that one of the main confirmations of cover-up and conspiracy was provided by President Nixon himself. Nixon had Oval Office recollections and conversations taped and stored the tapes, presumably for posterity. He was literally the president who bugged himself. The knowledge of the existence of the tapes was confirmed to a few, but Woodward and Bernstein were able to identify their existence as they worked their way up the chain of the White House command bit by bit. They were able to reveal the existence of the tapes and force the judges dealing with the case to subpoena their presentation; despite the president's best efforts, they were able to force the transcripts into the open.

Many famous figures have indicated that (though they might not put it this way) their vanity has forced them to 'bug themselves'. British politician Tony Benn taped recollections of his political life each evening and these have recently been broadcast on Radio 4; and the memoirs of most political leaders indicate that they start out by keeping some kind of record in the knowledge that one day it will become either politically interesting or commercially viable as a published book, or some such other document for posterity.

Forty-five years of the concealing of crashed UFOs by a great many military people, including not a small number of generals (who often display a Patton-like vanity) cannot have failed to produce a charismatic general who has a complete day-by-day, blow-by-blow, account of his dealings with flying saucers and captured aliens. Forty-five years of covering up the existence of crashed saucers and aliens cannot have failed to produce at least one soldier with a desire to make money (and as we shall see this is the least of all the motivators) by photographing, stealing or in some unambiguous way proving to the likes of Woodward and Bernstein that the UFOs are really there in some underground United States Air Force base. Not that there have been any shortage of candidates coming forward to UFO researchers with an offer, but the offer is fool's gold, not the real stuff. The people who have come forward are generally people who either believe the government is covering something up and feel that it is wrong to do so (but can offer little more than anecdotal statements in support of their belief) or people who want to make money by selling stories to UFO researchers (but whose goods turn out to be from a back-street market stall rather than from Harrods or Macy's).

So does this chapter prove that governments are not covering up information relating to UFOs? Not at all. Those who seek to promote conspiracy theory deliberately mix up two aspects of the problem: (a) that governments cover things up; and (b) that they are covering up knowledge.

The evidence, when examined critically, indicates that there is no doubt that governments lie and cover up their involvement in UFO research. However, there is nothing that proves they are covering up knowledge; only that they are covering up their ignorance. I do not believe that governments know very much more than UFO researchers about the meaning behind UFOs. But they don't like to be seen to be in that position.

There will also be, must also be, good reason for some cover-ups. Some UFOs will have been military flights or secret manoeuvres, and some UFO reports will have been revealed through clandestine spy equipment. It is expected that governments would cover up those aspects of their own work. They will use disinformation, they might even use UFO mythology as a part of their cover-up.

But what of unrevealed conspiracies, you might ask? I will rely on the belief that you can keep a small secret for a long time and a big one for a very short period of time. The big conspiracies that seem to have got away suffer from the same problems as UFO conspiracy theory.

Consider it like finding faces in random wallpaper patterns; as soon as someone shows you where the 'face' is you can always see it. Unless shown you might not see it, or you might see something else. UFO conspiracy theory consists of first knitting together the story, then finding the evidence to 'make it work'. Most of the evidence for a conspiracy in the Kennedy assassination, the 'Elvis is alive' theories, the death of Robert Maxwell, and so on, seems to have been constructed that way. There is a need, the story is constructed, and the conspiracy to have covered up the evidence is worked out last. We might consider the conspiracy that got away: it was often said that when a man broke into Buckingham

Palace, climbed across the roofs and ended up sitting in the Queen's bedroom talking to her in the middle of the night, the story would have had no credibility had it not been for the fact that the Queen verified it herself. Indeed, if put into a fictional book it would have been derided. But even more likely, if the Queen had been found murdered the next morning there would be an endless run of conspiracy theories around the IRA, Middle East hit-men and so on. The idea that a lone, wandering man could have done it would have been dismissed out of hand. The newspapers would have had a need for the conspiracy theory, they would have taken the result and constructed the evidence of cover-up last of all.

The UFO conspiracy was knitted long before the 'evidence' ever surfaced to support it.

Real conspiracies work the other way round.

Section 2
Perceptions

7 How We Perceive the Outer World

There are 3,000,000,000 people in the world and no two of us see the world the same way. Given close cultural backgrounds, groups of us are able to perceive the world with enough agreement to make living together possible (consensus reality) but when examined in depth even such consensus reality breaks down.

UFO reports, whether of distant sightings or close encounters, deal as they do with an area where there can be no consensus reality. Effective perception and communication are impossible. Let us examine the stages of each to see the problems. To make life easier for ourselves, let's leave UFOs out of it for the time being and consider an apple.

HOW WE LEARN

Go and take an apple from the fruitbowl and put it down in front of you while you are reading this book.

How do you know it is an apple?

You might think that a silly question – anyone out of their pushchair ought to have learned by now what an apple is. True.

But how does the learning mechanism work? We learn by experience. In simplistic terms we are given our first apple and told it is an apple. Eventually we make a connection between the word 'apple' and the object we are holding.

But what happens when Mum isn't around to use the word 'apple' and we want one? How do we find one in the fruitbowl? What happens is we have a 'picture' of an apple in our minds, as if on one card in a card index, and we call up the pattern – the picture – in our mind. We carry the image to the fruitbowl and make a match between the objects there and the picture in our minds. When we can match an image and an object we know we have found an apple.

A number of questions, from the practical to the philosophical, arise here, and all have a bearing on UFO reports.

Firstly, suppose the only apple you have ever seen was red. You would carry the image of the red colour around in your 'card index' in your mind as part of the characteristics of an apple. Would you be able to recognise a green apple if there was one in the fruitbowl? You would match up certain other characteristics – general shape, the stalk and so on – and you might make a guess. But it would be only a guess. You would then eat the green apple and the taste would further confirm your suspicion that this was indeed an apple, albeit one of a colour you had never seen before.

If you checked with others that there were such things as green apples, and you ate enough over time, you would eventually incorporate this colour into your card index and you would be able to identify a green apple easily in future.

We can take this one stage further: supposing I used extraordinary artistic talents to paint (with tasteless paint) the skin of an apple not just orange, but with the apparent texture of the fruit we call an orange. Now you would see this object and your mind would be forced to call up two index cards: one of an apple and one of an orange. And what would you decide this fruit was? Shape would suggest an apple, but colour and apparent texture would suggest an orange. Your senses would be baffled and you would have to employ others to check out other characteristics on your index cards; you would use taste and that would again confirm that it was an apple.

We can get into a philosophical argument on this. Suppose that I was able to take an orange and shape it perfectly into the shape of an apple. What would it actually be: apple or orange? Based on shape it would be an apple. Based on taste and inner texture it would be an orange. I suspect that we would eventually come down in favour of acknowledging that it was an orange, but that would depend on knowing its history. After all, how do you know that I didn't take an apple and genetically mutate the structure to produce an orange-like taste and texture? Your decision would depend on knowing what I had started with in the first place and demanding that it therefore be 'labelled' according to the type of tree it originally came from. But without that knowledge, and given my ability to alter the fruit 'either way', you would be forced to make a guess, or simply to agree to a consensus reality for the sake of simplicity.

ATTITUDE AFFECTS UNDERSTANDING

Is the glass half full or half empty? The joke about the optimist and the pessimist is actually not a joke. Much of our perception of the world is dependent on our attitudes.

Returning to our apple: what does the fact that it's an apple mean? To one person – a scientist presumably – it would represent the fruit of an apple tree. To another – say, an artist – it might represent a basically globular object with particular patterns of light interplayed on its surface. To yet another it might mean a sweet, juicy fruit that he or she enjoys eating. But one person might enjoy eating it in bed last thing at night and just before sleeping. To that person the apple might impart a subliminal message of drowsiness or comfort, or whatever other sensation he or she associates with going to bed. To another person the apple might be part of breakfast, and make him or her think of a fresh and sharp vigorous start to an exciting day.

We could consider manipulation: what if every apple you had ever eaten in your life was – by extraordinary coincidence – dry and tasteless? A sweet and juicy apple might not taste like an apple at all to you.

If every apple you had ever eaten contained a maggot, you would expect to find one in apples you selected in the future. And so on.

We know that some people like apples and others do not. Why this should be so is too complex to go into in this book, but it is obvious that we do not all appreciate the world in the same way.

THE WORLD OF ILLUSIONS

Given the limited perceptions available to us, it does not take much accidentally or deliberately to create a false world. One of my friends built up a very funny 'act' with his dog based on this fact. He taught the dog to obey commands: 'roll over', 'sit', 'play dead' and so on. But he taught the dog the wrong association of words so that the dog would roll over to the command 'sit', sit to the command 'play dead' and so on. Of course the dog was being obedient and responding to the 'card index' in its mind very accurately. And it was a stunt guaranteed to break the ice at any dinner party!

As a teenager one of my Saturday jobs was working in a supermarket re-filling shelves overnight. It was a slick operation, and done at fairly high pressure. Chains would form along the aisles and heavy boxes of tins, jars of jam and so on would be thrown from person to person and placed along the aisles ready for stacking. One of the tricks we played on each other was to re-seal an empty box and then throw it to someone in the aisle, accompanying the action with all the groans and staggering that suggested great weight. The recipient, watching the efforts apparently made by the thrower and remembering having caught heavy boxes before, would catch the box poised for great weight and would feel no weight at all. The tensed muscles in the arms would not be able to adjust quickly enough. The box would fly up in the air, usually over an aisle or two, and the 'catcher' would fall backwards. Silly stuff, but a useful object lesson.

Our physical structure cannot help but play these tricks on us either. In the eyes are receptors for colour. But these receptors also produce false after-images. It's natural, and cannot be stopped. Draw a brightly coloured picture of the Union Jack in yellow and green, look at it for a minute or so, then cover it with a white sheet of paper. What you will see is the Union Jack in its proper red and blue colours; these are the 'after-images' of yellow and green. Although no red and blue light has been emitted, that is what the eye tells you you saw.

Consider now the following image:

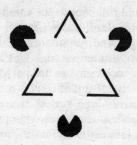

How many triangles do you see? There is the black triangle pointing to the top of the page. There is also the white triangle laid over the top of it, pointing to the foot of the page. In fact, of course, there are no triangles at all. Faced with an unclear image – and a leading question – you have been forced to create a consensus reality to fit the apparent image and the matching question. It is a complex process, too. We can actually see three dimensions in this (non-existent) image because the white triangle, being apparently 'unbroken', seems to be laid over the top of, and obscuring part of, the black-edged triangle. The 'breaks' in the lines create that illusion. What has happened is that you have gone to the card index of your mind, sought out the word 'triangle' and then overlaid the image on to the picture to find a 'nearest match'.

The reason why the brain works by searching for patterns is quite simple: it is programmed to survive. Patterns it can recognise can be dealt with from experience, patterns that cannot be recognised must be approached with caution. The brain is also, therefore, seeking to convert the unknown to the known – a crucial factor to understand when examining UFO reporting. The subconscious is the area of the brain that protects the rest; it can find it convenient to accept a constructed lie for a time while it searches for truths and while it is educating the conscious mind to deal with a situation it is gradually learning about.

We are more dependent on these illusions than we know. Take your newspaper and look at any photograph. What do you see? The Prime Minister smiling out at you? An attractive film star? No, you don't. Actually what you see is a collection of unconnected dots laid out on the page in such a way as to fool you into thinking you are looking at an image of the Prime Minister. Using colour tones and proximity, something that hits the eye as looking like the Prime Minister is created. Move in really close and look very closely at the photograph, take a magnifying glass to it if you can. You will see the dot matrix. The same principle is used in so-called dot-matrix computer printers. You don't actually see letters, you see patterns made to look like letters.

Physics has even provided us recently with an even more alarming thought: when you look at the actual Prime Minister or film star in fact even then you are only seeing a swirling mass of electrons arranged in such proximity as to look like what we call a human being.

Funny old world, as a former Prime Minister said. And it will get a lot funnier as we go through this book.

There are many such optical illusions as the diagram on page 60; get a book out of the library and play with your consensus reality. (How will you know it is a book?)

Let's go back to the apple, and get a little closer to UFO reports. For the moment we will stay with the relatively safe ground of distant sightings.

RECONSTRUCTION WITHOUT CLUES

Imagine pressing the apple into an ink pad and then pressing the inked apple on to a clean white page. (Or do it, if you feel so inclined.) What you have will look something like this:

This is the impression left by the apple after it has gone. Similarly, a UFO report is an impression left after the UFO itself has gone. At least the apple image is left on something simple like a piece of paper, and not something as complex as a human mind.

Imagine giving your UFO report – I'm sorry, I mean your inkstain of an apple – to someone who has never seen an apple before. Could they reconstruct the shape of the apple from the image? Probably not, but supposing somehow they could, then could they reconstruct the texture? Even less likely. Certainly they could not reproduce the internal texture, but let's for the sake of argument say they did. Could they reconstruct the taste and the smell? No. But even if they could, could they reconstruct an understanding of your enjoyment and appreciation when you eat the apple?

No. Yet in the early days of UFO research we deluded ourselves into thinking that we could construct the shape, propulsion systems and motives of 'alien visitors' based on distant sightings in the sky seen for fractions of a second. Of course we could build a logic around what we saw, the effects on the environment and so on – yes, we used the clues we had. But not only may we not have had all the clues, or interpreted them correctly; the problem was we had a preconceived notion of the end result.

If I give you the inkstain above and tell you that it was made by an orange then you will direct your thinking in that direction and perhaps never think of an apple.

Rubbish, I hear the call go up! 'I would see the textural differences straight away and switch my thinking from orange to apple – you couldn't fool me!'

Oh no?

Just take a look at the celebrated Gulf Breeze photographic case that arose in America in 1987 and still continues as a point of debate. One witness, basically, took over fifty photographs and video footage of UFOs over a small town in northern Florida. I have seen 'scientific' analysis of the photographs 'proving' that they are genuine for all manner of reasons. I have seen equally 'scientific' analysis 'proving' they are faked. I have heard conflicting 'proofs' of how they were faked. I don't know the truth behind Gulf Breeze though I have my opinions, but only one analysis can be right. Even if the photographs are faked, only one explanation of how each photograph was faked can be valid. But each of the analysts insist that they are right – because they know what they are looking for. One wanted an apple, and built an apple from the inkstain image. Another wanted an orange, and built an orange from the inkstain. Both were, in fact, looking at the 'triangles' image shown earlier in this chapter, and perceiving what the card index in their minds expected to see.

And just to show how complex it can get, bear in mind that the triangles image shown earlier could arise in two ways: it could be drawn two-dimensionally, in which case there would be no real triangles there; or it could be created by taking an aerial photograph of a white triangle overlaid on a black-edged triangle, in which case there really are triangles there (genuine UFOs?).

There is a further problem with our mental card index. It has all our patterns built up from experience in our lives stored there, ready for recall when needed. Supposing an apple passed by giving you just a few moments to identify it, and you had never seen one before. What then?

Firstly the mind seeks out a 'nearest best fit'. It would call up, for the sake of argument, the image of a pear, and say 'I assume the object must have been a pear because it looks pretty close to one.' If you were given time, resources and educational support you might learn that there was such a thing as an apple, but probably – at least for a time – you would go on thinking that the apple was just a type of pear.

WE SEE WHAT WE EXPECT TO SEE

The second thing that happens – very important in the case of UFO research – is that given a period of time after the 'sighting' of the apple and your connecting it to the image in your mind of a pear, you will begin to adjust your recollection of the apple, gradually making it more 'pear-like' as you keep comparing the sighting with your image bank of 'realities'. If you see a 'some-thing' in the sky called a UFO – which the newspapers tell you are spaceships from other worlds – and your image bank is full of science-fiction imagery (which is very prevalent in the Western world) then you will soon be calling up pictures of flying saucers and changing the apple into a pear; blurs of light become portholes, spinning motions, and so on.

It is said that the native American Indians were unable to see the 'iron horse' – the railway – when they were first exposed to it, simply because there was no pattern in the brain to receive the image. They looked at the physical structure and literally saw nothing they could comprehend. A similar claim is made of native islanders first seeing Captain Cook's ships.

So when we see a 'something', a strange light form perhaps, and we search for a 'nearest best fit', what do we come up with? Do we go through a process that starts with the word UFO, because we read about these things somewhere, then remember that we read in the tabloid newspapers that UFOs are alien spaceships? And do we then start to remember the structures that 'reveal' to us it was an alien spaceship – 'that blurred dark area was probably a porthole and that dark shading underneath, I think I could see some landing gear in there' and so on.

NINETY PER CENT OF SIGHTINGS ARE EXPLAINABLE

For decades the statistics on distant sighting claims are fairly consistent; something like 90 per cent, perhaps slightly more, are researched to a reasonable safe, satisfactory conclusion. A report of a single, bright light in the sky at a time when it is quite certain that, say, the planet Venus would be visible in that location, can be fairly certainly explained as the planet Venus if the witness did not see another bright light at the same time. Some sightings are clearly explainable as air traffic. Some have more exotic but nonetheless 'normal' explanations – birds in flight, sparking lights caused by electric trains crossing points, mistaken geography leading to people thinking car lights are actually high in the air, and so on.

However, if 90 per cent of sightings are comfortably explainable, and even if we assume that the other ten per cent deserve an 'extraordinary' explanation (and many of them probably do not), then even on that basis nine out of every ten reports are the product of misperception. Nine out of every ten reports arise because people see something ordinary, often something they have often seen before, and decide that it is so extraordinary that they must seek out someone to tell. We need to know why that should be. We do know that a certain amount of 'wishful thinking' comes into it; when a researcher asks a witness the question 'Well, what do you think it was?' the answer is very frequently a variation on the theme of 'I've no idea, but there must be life on other planets after all' – a very clear indication of the interpretation they have in the back of their minds even if they are consciously trying to remain neutral. For some people the need to reinforce that belief becomes slightly dishonest. The example I gave above of the planet Venus was a real case, though typical of many others. In the case I was dealing with I had established that the light was almost certainly Venus and I had asked if the witness had seen any other bright lights in the sky. The answer was an emphatic No. I pointed out that Venus was visible and would have been bright at that time. The witness was visibly very disappointed, obviously wanting a more exotic explanation, and came back with the statement: 'Oh I didn't know you meant that. I know Venus and of course I saw that as well.' But I was certain that she was now modifying their claims to keep something of the excitement I was unfortunately taking from her. If I had pressed her further I believe she might well have modified their own memories enough to really believe she could remember seeing Venus. I left my conclusion with her; there was nothing further on that case I could do.

The 90 per cent of solved sightings, and the way in which they are presented to researchers, suggests there are a lot of desires in people's sightings that are coloured by the mythology bound up within the subject.

SO HOW RELIABLE ARE WITNESSES?

When witnesses describe a sighting the assumption is made that since they were there, their account must be reliable. In fact if a researcher, having identified the stimulus – Venus, say – for the sighting, suggests that the witness is probably wrong about this or that detail, the response is often one of hostility. The last line of defence is often 'Well I was there and you weren't. I know what I saw.'

It is certainly true that the witness is the only real contact with the sighting, but experimental work indicates that people are very bad at recalling what they saw. This cannot be ignored when faced with the comment 'I know what I saw'.

BUFORA, and specifically its former Chairman Bob Digby, have conducted several tests with various sizes of audience to examine this reliability. I reproduced one such experiment on live TV (*Daytime Live* at the BBC studios at Pebble Mill). The audience were shown a faked picture of a fairly 'classical' flying saucer for fifteen seconds. The image was then turned off and everyone given pencil and paper and asked to draw what they had just seen. The results were extraordinary. Fifty totally different and almost entirely inaccurate images came back. One image was a circle with four huge wings radiating out from it, the product of such a creative descriptive ability that the artist in question must have been an estate agent!

Had I been researching a genuine sighting, I could have been in the position of receiving fifty reports, with drawings, from fifty witnesses to a single event. How would I ever have unravelled the real image? Yet this sighting was real – the audience all really saw the image which they were drawing. And the chances are that, if pressed, the majority of those people would have called themselves reliable witnesses.

In BUFORA we have expanded that experiment to include time-sense. The image we put up in our lectures (the test is done to random audiences without warning to simulate actual sighting conditions as closely as possible) is held in place for just ten seconds. In addition to asking people to draw what they saw we ask them to state how long they saw it for; estimates range from one second to around one minute. One estimate was three minutes!

We have all seen the classical optical illusion test:

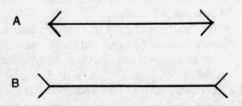

Before it became so well known 90 per cent of people believed line B to be longer than line A, when in fact of course they are the same length. When a great many witnesses tell the same story some researchers claim this proves the validity of the claim, that the simplest answer must be correct. This simple illusion shows that is not always the case.

If people are not terribly reliable within themselves about what they have witnessed, the problem is made worse when researchers begin questioning. Most researchers simply do not realise how easy, almost unavoidable, it is to 'lead' witnesses. Eye movements, body language, and vocal shifts are powerful influences on a person's recall.

But this leads us into the more difficult problems of perception in *close* encounters. All that I have described in this chapter relates, in fact, to both distant and close encounters though I have used examples only of distant encounters. But close encounters have a few other problems of their own. We will come to these next.

You can now eat the apple. Enjoy it!

8 How We Perceive from the Inner Self

We must never forget, as Dr Allen Hynek reminded us, that we do not study UFOs, we study UFO reports. And we must acknowledge that a UFO report is the result of an attempt at understanding by the witness to the event. But just what is behind the witness's own understanding? If we are to understand how close-encounter reporters perceive their experiences, we must first understand how people perceive anything.

WHO CREATED US

Analysts of personal development have long held the belief that people must make a planned and sustained effort to make changes in their lives. People who simply accept 'they are what they are' are not the choosers and leaders in life; some of the most successful business training is designed to tease out qualities people never realised they had.

The highest-level need, in self-motivation, is summed up by the phrase that 'everyone must become the person they know they have the ability to become'. This is the essence of self-fulfilment and of happiness. Vandals, muggers, drug addicts and other people society regard as 'failures' all display characteristics of being frustrated in their attempts to 'become the person they know they have the ability to become'; their criminal acts become protests at a world they see as hostile.

The problem for most people with all of the above is that the starting point is muddled, so muddled that many people live a dissatisfied and unhappy life intuitively knowing that there is more, but not knowing how to get it.

The reason for this, for the most part, is that the 'you' now sitting here reading this book was not designed and created by you, but by a variety of people throughout your life. Most people are a Creature stitched together by a number of Baron Frankensteins. From childhood, your beliefs, attitudes, opinions and values were developed by the influence of parents, grandparents, siblings, other relatives, teachers, clergy, friends, neighbours and people in authority. You have been influenced by law, society, the arts, the media, advertising and a host of subliminal messages received through day-to-day dealing with people even in brief encounters: on the trains and buses for example.

Influence has been direct or subtle: repeated suggestion, reward and punishment, related experiences, censored views, guilt and fear.

You have, like it or not, accepted other people's beliefs about the 'way the world works'. Even if you have rejected their beliefs, that is still a response to them.

HOW WE RE-CREATE OURSELVES

The essence of self-development is to take control of your own life. If I had the ability to fulfil every one of your goals you would soon become unhappy and dissatisfied because you would have no sense of achievement; the 'you' I would create would be a gift, not a victory. Intuitively everyone knows they must find their own path. Gurus, whether 'religious' figures dealing with enlightenment or business trainers dealing with personal development, are guides whose job it is to show the roads ahead, not to drive the bus. Mostly, these tease out of people what is in them already; they do not put things in.

To begin to take control of our own lives we all have to start by finding something which belongs to us, and us alone. That is the anchor-point for us to 'become the person we know we have the ability to become'.

Fortunately the world offers us a variety of possibilities. As Johannes Kepler said, 'The diversity of the phenomenon of Nature is so great, and the treasures hidden in the heavens so rich, precisely in order that the human mind shall never be lacking in fresh nourishment.' For some people the 'thing' (event, experience, revelation, et cetera) that becomes their anchor-point is, at face value, benign. For others it is, at face value, bad. A simple example might be winning a million pounds in a lottery. People who have spent their lives struggling financially tends to set their own restrictions according to the money they have; once they 'come into a fortune' they can destroy those restrictions and become free to develop themselves (a limited and often unsuccessful development in that particular case, it must be said). On the other hand, war is a terrible thing, but some people personally come through battle hugely enriched. When you have seen horrific death you gain insight into the value of quality of life. For some people their life-changing experience has related to disability; they become enriched by the way they deal with the onset of physical impairment. Forced to take control of their lives they find their quality of 'inner self' improved. Their biggest hurdles are then the ones society sets up by its lack of consideration. Of course, for some it is the reverse which causes the change; one woman spontaneously recovered her sight after a lifetime of blindness and was able to pursue avenues of self-development she had probably never dreamed possible. The story of Janice Georgou, related in Chapter 18, is an excellent example of an encounter leading to greater personal development by the witness.

For some people the experience that belongs to them and them alone is an exposure to what we call the paranormal, and in this book we will primarily consider UFO experiences. While several people have 'used' distant sightings to enhance their own development we are talking here, for the most part, of *close-encounter* cases.

During a close encounter a person experiences something they have never before seen or felt. It may be an abduction, a 'contactee' message, channelling, visions or other variations on this theme. Because these things are not yet socially acceptable the individual has to deal with the experience in isolation, at least at first.

But there are many problems – problems which I think are partially solved by what I have termed witness-driven investigation.

THE PHASES OF PERCEPTION

As we must have a scenario, I will describe one I think highly possible as an explanation for some UFO experiences. I believe that there are energies in and around the world, the mechanisms for which we do not yet understand. For the most part I suspect these energies are natural and 'non-intelligent'. Liken them to wind and thunder, natural forces that exist around the world. When we did not understand them we personified them and assumed they were created by gods.

Gifts of the Gods?

As we developed we learnt how they happened; we didn't need to attribute them to human-like beings but instead learnt the physics involved. Indeed, we went on to harness these forces as a source of cheap and clear energy. In ancient times to have suggested harnessing the 'powers of the gods' might have been blasphemy, but we know better now. I believe there are still energies that are yet to be understood, and perhaps yet to be harnessed, and that these may be in part responsible for paranormal experiences. When we have understood them we shall no longer need to personify them as the creations of non-human beings – i.e. alien visitors.

But now we are like primitive cave-dwellers surprised by the onset of a lashing thunderstorm. Some of us fear the unleashed power, particularly if we believe it to be intelligently directed; some enjoy the sensations of the rain and the wind. All of us are ignorant of the cause. And we are all seeking a greater understanding.

The researchers and the scientists are studying the reports for clues, the witnesses are using their intuition to find the answers. Who will succeed, or how the answers will be revealed, is anybody's guess. One thing is certain. If 'research' in those cave-dwelling days had focused on the motives of the gods, the mechanisms of the gods and the interaction of gods and man, then we would still not understand meteorology. It took a radical, and probably intuitive, change of focus away from the gods and on to other areas before rainfall could be understood. And I suspect that the person who got the answers got wet on his way: no room for armchair research here.

So therefore we can speculate that a natural energy is being perceived by people as UFOs. Presumably this energy can become visible, has electrical properties, interacts with the environment and can perhaps affect the mind. Michael Persinger in Canada has long theorised that such a force is released naturally by geo-physical strain.

The interaction with this force becomes, first and foremost, a personal experience instantly 'owned' by the recipient. From that point on it is theirs to do with what they will. This is not exclusive to the close encounter; it is true of any and every experience.

These are the phases we go through:

Phase One

Firstly, we have a natural tendency to personify, or attribute intelligent direction to, any unknown event, until proven otherwise. If the energy had luminosity, or some kind of visible form, we might be tempted to think of, say, ghosts or aliens. If we are walking on a moor late at night, particularly one known to have its share of 'white lady' reports, we might think of a ghost. If we have a love of science fiction, and a mental image bank full of such images, we might think of an alien.

Perhaps the experience is not visible; it might be the apparent reception of a message directly into the brain. Again, depending on our background, we might think of a voice from 'the other side of the grave'; if we have seen enough *Star Trek* episodes we might think of an alien contact.

Adherents of the extra-terrestrial hypothesis raise many questions: but *why* do so many people think of aliens and alien contact? If close-encounter experiences are so personal, why is there so little variety? The answer to the first question is that we, in UFO research, are a self-selected sample: they come to us because, broadly, they believe their experiences can be explained by UFOs. Get out and do parallel research as I do and the other interpretations are there: some people believe they have experienced a oneness with God, some that they have made contact with their own higher consciousness; some believe they have had an inner revelation, and of course some have bad interpretations, demonology and so on. These people are having similar, perhaps identical experiences to those of close-encounter witnesses, but they interpret them differently.

The answer to the second question lies in the next phases, and in just how much of the experience ends up being 'our own'.

Phase Two

After an experience we seek out further clues to confirm that 'we weren't just imagining it'.

Part of that is a selective process, what Canadian therapist Dr David Gotlib refers to as 'the ratchet effect': turns of a ratchet screwdriver in one direction have effect, turns in the other direction do nothing. So in UFO research: evidence *for* is added to the pile, evidence *against* is ignored as irrelevant; the initial impressions, based on personal views, are thus strengthened.

UFO ground traces are usually found 'after the event': first, the witness experiences or sees something and then looks for clues. Marks on trees and on the ground (as in the Rendlesham Forest case of 1980) perhaps take on more significance than they should. Marks that would be ignored in any other circumstance suddenly look like just the sort of mark a flying saucer landing leg would make. And so the ratchet effect tightens . . .

Phase Three

There is, then, a checking of the event itself against expectations, with the unfortunate effect of creating false memories, in line with expectations of what really happened. Again, this is not merely a property of the encounter but a normal way we deal with the world; it would therefore be *abnormal* for it not to be part of the encounter experience. I remember once seeing a woman walking along the road I live in, towards my house, dressed in strikingly bright colours that just happened to be exactly the same leggings, sweatshirt and jacket that my wife wears. She even looked a little like my wife. I looked at the child running along next to her and could easily identify one of my two daughters; in fact I was wondering where my other daughter was. When I got closer I could see that the woman was not my wife, although she did look quite like her, but the child with her turned out to be not even a girl. The boy had short, blond hair and glasses. My daughters don't wear glasses, both have long hair and neither is blonde. I recognised that I had 'created' the vision of my daughter because it was 'logical' that she would be walking with my wife. Presumably the daughter I thought I had seen was the nearest 'best fit' to the real vision in front of me.

There is evidence from some multiple-sighting reports that the differences in description of objects depend a lot on what each person thought they would be seeing, once they had 'decided' what they were seeing.

TAKING CONTROL

The real problems for close-encounter witnesses start here. It is at this point that we either use the experience to 'take control of our lives', or we surrender the experience to others. Those who do the latter seem, for the most part, to spend the rest of their lives regretting it.

In most ordinary experiences, the person is forced to

take control of the event for themselves. Imagine a situation where a person becoming disabled was prevented from helping themselves. It would be perceived as wrong; indeed the best care of such individuals is to train them to help themselves. The language we use allows them to keep their own self-respect.

But do we do that with UFO witnesses? The truth is that people who have had close-encounter experiences have to fight UFO researchers, the 'fanzine' editors, the media and the sceptics to keep control of what has happened to them. Everyone wants to claim a close encounter for their own. And we have no guidelines for 'allowing' close-encounter experiencers to retain their self-respect.

Of course there is nothing wrong with using other people's experiences for your own development; we don't have to fight on the battlefield to be aware of the horror of death. But we must let our development be ours, and the witnesses' development be theirs.

The 'classic', or at least front-runner, work on abductions in the United States, based on regression hypnosis and using the Hill-generated abduction as the model, takes away control of the experience from the witness and leaves it with the researcher. This is to the detriment of the witness. In fairness, that is not the specific fault of UFOs, UFO researchers or UFO witnesses. I believe it is the fault of American society, which encourages the surrendering of personal responsibility to others: the dependence on an analyst is often no more than a request to 'take away my problems' in the manner of 'sin-eating'; liposuction is saying 'please make me slim but take away my responsibility to diet'; plastic surgery is 'I don't like myself, take away my responsibility to become something I do like'; and so on.

If you believe your experience was essentially a bad

thing, and this belief is reinforced by your convictions about aliens and UFOs as highlighted by prominent UFO researchers and the media, then your UFO researcher can only reinforce that belief, because the chances are that you will have sought out a researcher whose name you read while reading about bad experiences (ratchet effect). If you think the experience was a good thing, your opinion will be reinforced by those aspects of your reading you think are most like yours, and you will probably seek out a researcher with a 'nicer' viewpoint.

Philip Mantle, a BUFORA director, told me the story of an abductee who had spent time analysing his own 'case' and come to terms with it, though he still wanted to know more. He went to America and was 'researched' by a prominent researcher there, and came back a much unhappier person. As Philip said, 'What good did it do him? Now he spends every night sitting in the pub, crying.' And I would also ask whether the research took that person any nearer the objective truth, or only nearer the truth as seen by that researcher.

Of course some witnesses are traumatised by their experiences and seek help. That is quite fair. To maintain the analogy, disabled people seek help and it is right that structures exist to offer that help. But the question is still one of the quality of help offered. It should not be a smothering help that takes away personal control of the person's life, but a form of support that guides and is there when needed, while offering the maximum possibility for personal development.

9 Perceptions through Communication

In England we call a flat a puncture; in America they call it an apartment.

Well, perhaps Americans and English can communicate fairly easily, but in fact even a commonly understood language is not an effective medium of communication, even if it is the best on offer.

The phrase used by many in training for effective communication is: 'I know you believe you understand what you think I said, but I'm not sure if you realise that what you heard is not what I meant.' In the two previous chapters I have explained the problems of how the mind and memory work. This chapter examines the flaws of communication.

Communication models can be very complex; a simple one looks like this:

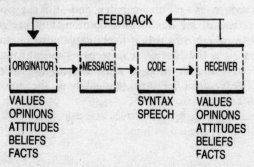

In dealing with an extraordinary event for which neither the witnesses nor the researchers have a solid factual basis, communication can often be highly subjective.

Let's look at the problems.

If we have had an experience (seen a UFO, eaten an apple, and so on) how do we communicate that experience to someone else?

Standard UFO investigation (investigator-driven) arguably takes the view that the witness has stored in his or her mind an objective 'photograph' of the event. In other words, the witness has seen, heard and perhaps experienced something that happened *outside of him*, and any witness standing where he had stood would have seen, heard and felt the same thing.

In order to re-build that snapshot the investigator then has to ask the right questions or perhaps use hypnotic regression to take that witness 'back in time' to remember the incident more clearly. The event can then be related factually and accurately.

That is the theory. *But that is simply not the way the mind works, not the way the memory works, and not the way communication works.*

The witness has perceived an event for which he has no 'card index' in his memory and is struggling to understand it. He has formed opinions and prejudices which lead him towards a likely explanation – that is normal, it is the process that keeps us safe throughout our lives – and, in the case of close encounters particularly, he is deciding how to deal with the emotions aroused by the event.

Then the investigator arrives and asks for the 'photograph' to be related to him.

STAGE ONE

The witness has to work out what the experience meant. This means drawing on a lifetime of beliefs, attitudes, experiences, comments of friends and relatives, TV programmes and films, religious teachings, having been told what is right and what is wrong, fears of being laughed at or disbelieved, prejudices and cravings, likes and dislikes and so on, and so on. The list of impressions that you receive every second of the day and that go to build up the character and attitude of the person you call you – the person reading this book right now – is literally endless. And at some point a UFO experience happens; the you that experiences it is the 'now' you; if you had experienced it yesterday or tomorrow the you that would have experienced it would have been the 'then' you – a different you with a different list of impressions, and perhaps a different priority of what impressions were most important. Sometimes it can be more obvious than at other times: if tomorrow you are told that your first-born child has contracted a fatal disease and will live no longer than three months, then clearly the 'you' that will exist for the rest of your life will be very different from the 'now' you.

STAGE TWO

You have to decide what the message is that you want to explain to the investigator. It is not just a question of 'the facts'; life is just not like that. Firstly, long before you open your mouth you will be deciding if you believe the experience to have been basically good or bad. That decision – and it is a decision, not just a fact or an opinion – will determine a lot about how you view the details of the experience.

Then you will have to decide what are the most important attributes of the experience that you want to explain. If you think you have been abducted by aliens from another planet then you will automatically seek out and bring to the fore those details of your 'memory' that confirm and strengthen that belief. Those areas which, if not contradictory are at least unsupportive, will be downgraded. Again I must stress that this is not a factor unique to UFO experiences; it is a normal re-action and the way we operate in our lives every minute of the day: it is the basis of a simple decision to cross the road here or 100 yards further down the road, to eat an apple or an orange, to save or to spend. In any de-cision the facts are outweighed by subjective aspects nine to one. If you have another belief system (you don't like science fiction but you do think God and Satan are the only forces in the universe) then you go through a similar process, but come forward with a different pri-ority of what 'facts' are important to 'get across' to the investigator.

STAGE THREE

You have to say something, or write it down. This means that you must translate already muddled thoughts, maybe angry and frightened, maybe enriched and enlightened, into spoken words or written senten-ces. But there is a huge gulf between our ability to comprehend and our ability to convey that comprehen-sion. There are many things – love, for example – for which we have no really effective vocabulary at all, a point I will come back to in Stage Four. But even if we examine our various vocabularies there is a shock in store. The average person has something over 50,000 words in what is called the Recognition Vocabulary. This is the 'pool' of words that we would recognise if we saw or heard them in an appropriate context; they are not words we would normally use or even understand without a contextual setting.

A more immediate pool of words exists in our reading vocabulary; something between 20,000 and 50,000 words. These are the words we recognise when we read or hear them, even if not in context.

Then consider our written vocabulary of around 15,000 words, these are the words we use when we write. Even if our UFO witness writes an account of her experience she is probably limited to this number of words to express all those muddled feelings.

Lastly we have the spoken vocabulary. For most people this is around 8,000 words, and can be as low as 4,000, even in fairly well-educated people. The witness is limited to these few words if he is verbally to express all those feelings.

STAGE FOUR

This last stage is the most damaging of all. The receiver of the information receives a report which has been filtered by the beliefs and attitudes of the witness, translated according to a subjective set of criteria and expressed in a limited fashion through the witness's vocabulary. Then the receiver of the information has to understand it.

We must never forget that the receiver – the UFO investigator – has also had a series of lifetime experiences, also has a set of subjective criteria, and also has a limited vocabulary. The investigator who hears a UFO abduction account today is not the same person as the investigator who hears the same account tomorrow. Perhaps in the intervening night he has seen *Close Encounters of the Third Kind*, read Budd Hopkins's *Intruders* or even perhaps this book. That is not to say that the investigator is some sort of programmable robot – he or she will not believe everything or react to everything in any film or book – but he will be influenced, however slightly. Even rejecting a theory causes the person doing the rejecting to encompass and consider some aspect of that theory – even if it is negative.

In order to overcome the difficulties of expressing these emotions and feelings the investigator cannot but help, offering words from his or her own vocabulary. This is how we live in the everyday world. But it does mean that with no consensus reality it is easy for an investigator to steer a description towards his own preconception without even the witness knowing that the image the investigator is building up is not the image in his or her own mind. In Stage Five we can see the problems of 'shared world' knowledge.

STAGE FIVE

If we give an obviously incorrect or deficient description of a UFO (say, we leave out its size), then that information can be asked for by the researcher. Problems arise when the researcher unconsciously uses preconceived images from their own mental data bank to fill in the details. The result is a false image. Two people sharing a world knowledge is useful; it makes for better comprehension: the danger lies in not realising that the world we think we have in common is not in fact shared at all.

For example, consider the following passage:

> John went to live in London. He courted a young
> lady named Penelope but she came to prefer a
> friend of his.

It seems to be a simple communication and you as the
reader should have some image of the situation in your
mind. Now try an experiment: think of one other fact
about this situation that you would like to add, perhaps
that John works for London Transport driving buses
from King's Cross station, perhaps that the name of the
friend Penelope came to prefer is Martin, the date of
John's move to London is 1994, and so on.

But what if I suggested to you that the London mentioned is not the capital of England, but a town in
America? What if I suggested that this happened in
1594? When did Penelope come to prefer the friend?
Had John and Penelope been married and lived together
happily for forty years before that happened? And what
if the friend's name was not Martin, but Sarah – what
would that tell us about the dynamics of the situation?
And so on. When you read the passage you might have
thought that you and I, as the author, shared a world.
But the world you thought we shared was one largely
created by your image bank, not mine; I had not provided you with enough data from my image bank so you
filled in the rest yourself.

Incidentally, language can also carry strong subliminal meanings which are often not appreciated. A
version of the above phrase has been used over the years
by several management trainers working with me. Several hundred people have been exposed to it and their
analysis studied. Two interesting points came out.
Firstly, the word 'courted' suggested to most people a
gentle and 'olde-world' feel to the whole situation.
When I suggested that perhaps John was sleeping rough

under Waterloo Bridge in London, England, and that Penelope was a drug pusher, over 80 per cent of people found that impossible to reconcile with the word 'courted'. Secondly, over 70 per cent of men aged between 30 and 45 thought Penelope was blonde. We wanted to know why this should be, and when this was examined further we discovered that for that age group the most powerful 'image' of a person named Penelope they were carrying in their image bank was the blonde puppet character Lady Penelope in the TV series *Thunderbirds*. Furthermore, we realised that we had accidentally reinforced that image by linking the words 'lady' and 'Penelope' in the passage.

This suggestibility has serious implications for hypnotic regression, because the input of data from the researcher to the witness is not just misleading, but can lead to reinforcement of the false image.

What researchers also seem to fail to take account of is that in an interactive situation, only a relatively small proportion of communication takes place through words. In a normal conversation only about twenty per cent of the meaning is expressed through words; 80 per cent is expressed through eye contact, vocal shifts, body language and so on. Even researchers who are diligent about avoiding leading questions often fail to avoid leading the witness in these other ways.

I was once sent a tape by a researcher as a defence against my suggestion that the witness had been led. In my view, however, the tape proved me correct. The witness, under hypnosis, said he could see small people around him. The researcher requested further information, but instead of saying 'How tall were these people?', asked: 'Do you mean people about three or four foot tall?' The witness agreed he did. Did the implied command under hypnosis re-direct the thinking of the witness? Bryan, whose case is described elsewhere in this book, described entities two inches high – small people indeed. Just who created the three- or four-foot-tall entities in the witness's videotaped recall?

Consensus reality is enough for us to 'get by' in our everyday world. Take the simple example of seeing a particular car – say a Ford Escort – drive past. The witness sees the car, identifies it, and describes the sighting to another. That person knows of the Ford Escort type of car and creates a pattern in his or her mind that is probably close to the truth. As I've outlined in earlier chapters, even this consensus reality can break down, but it suffices for our everyday life.

But go a stage further: how do we express concepts like, say, love?

To tell someone that you love them you use certain body language to generate a 'warmth' between you, you moderate your voice to a soft, gentle pitch. And you say 'I love you'. Because both people involved in the conversation have, we suppose, a common background, the 'receiver' can understand enough consensus reality to comprehend and respond sensibly. But the 'receiver' does not 'feel' the love the way the 'originator' does. There is no way – even using descriptive words – that one person can truly explain the pain in the chest and the sense of excitement and trepidation that comes from emotion. But the receiver will have had experiences of her own, and will feel *her version* of the pain, the excitement and the trepidation. She will respond not according to the concept which triggered the communication in the first place, but to *her own* concept of love. Their 'understanding' is based on her own lifetime of experiences, not the experiences of the person speaking to her.

But what happens when there is no consensus reality?

Like it or not, there is no worldwide consensus as to what a UFO experience is or what it means. We do not really know what a UFO abduction is – and don't be fooled by those who tell you otherwise. What those people – investigators *and* witnesses – are doing is trying to impose their interpretation on others. As the previous chapters have demonstrated, witnesses are as flawed a set of humans as any other, and just as prone to misperception and misunderstanding due to preconceptions as anyone else.

Between all the stages from initial sighting or experience, through to coming to terms with it and seeking out an investigator to trying to explain an experience, there are many, many filters and barriers to true comprehension. Without a consensus as to what we are all involved with any understanding is fatally flawed.

So do we give up? No.

What we do is recognise that we need clues to those areas of the experience that can be reduced to objective study. Where we can we can try to use 'neutral' recording equipment to 'catch' experiences on film or tape. Skywatches were an early attempt to take the witness out of the loop and allow investigators to see the reality for themselves. They didn't work.

They didn't work because close-encounter experiences are about *people*. The UFOs spotted in the distance and caught on radar might be investigated by this method to some degree; one day they will be mostly understood. But close encounters are not about 'things'. We can't take people out of the loop any more than we can study human love or hate without studying people.

But we can reduce the filters. Witness-driven investigation recognises that the closer we get to the witness's own thoughts and feelings – without imposing our own on to his statement – the closer we get to the clues we shall eventually need.

And witness-driven investigation serves the needs of witnesses very well. One witness whose case is outlined in this book, 'Mark', suffered anguish because of his encounter. James Parry greatly helped him to come to terms with the experience, and introduced him to me. He said after our initial meeting: 'What helped me so much was just that you let me talk.'

An investigator who is part of our research team, Chris Walton, commented that there was something different about my previous book *Perspectives* that he at first couldn't put his finger on; he later realised it was that I was allowing stories to develop slowly, at the witnesses' own pace, rather than forcing them along.

Of course many of the flaws of investigation will still be there. But witness-driven investigation will make one huge difference: there are thousands – perhaps in the end millions – of witnesses but there are only a few investigators – perhaps a few hundred really active people all over the Earth. The standardisation of reports of close encounters arises because investigators subconsciously lead witnesses into their own belief systems and their own framework of possibilities. That is why one investigator gets one type of encounter, say alien 'nice guys', while another gets the 'bad guys' and so on. By removing the filtering of investigators from the loop and keeping them more passive, we will not see the standardisation of accounts we are currently seeing, but millions of stories, rich in their variety.

We will still not see the objective truth, but we will be one major stage closer. There is a component of these otherwise external, and quite real, experiences that belongs in the mind of the witness. We need to understand what that is; at the moment we are mostly looking at the component of the experiences that belongs in the mind of the investigators.

10 Perceptions through Memory

In preceding chapters the problems of perception have been examined. Clearly, any recall based on these misperceptions is itself going to be faulty. This will be the case even using hypnotic regression. However, there are also special difficulties in recall where there is suppressed memory.

THE RELEASE OF SUPPRESSED MEMORIES

One of the effects of close encounters would seem to be that memories of certain incidents are suppressed. There are various theories to account for this: trauma, the deliberate action of aliens, the lack of a language of expression, and so on.

To examine this phenomenon I decided to add to the long list of abductees with 'missing time' a few stories of strange, but perhaps not paranormal, memory perceptions, including one of my own. Two were offered to me by Bertil Kuhlemann. The second of his stories, relating to a near truck crash, is particularly interesting as it relates to the exact opposite of suppressed memory: enhanced recall.

The first story Bertil offered concerned a five-year-old child who had been standing at the top of a staircase. After a second or two she found herself at the bottom of the staircase having received no injuries, but with no memory of her path down the staircase. The young child said afterwards that it must have been her guardian angel who took care of her so that she was not injured.

This is very similar to a claim made by Lorraine Parry, though Lorraine attributed the 'flying' part of her experience to an out-of-body experience:

'When I was five we lived upstairs in a flat. I often was on my own, my brothers were in the garden.

'And I was at the top of the stairs and I looked down the stairs and I wanted to fly down the stairs, I really wanted to fly. And so my experience was that I did. I jumped off the top of the stairs and I flew down and landed very gently just below the last stair.

'I told my parents, "I flew down the stairs, I have flown down the stairs." They said, "Oh, very good, yes." That was nice. They didn't want to say, "No, you didn't." They didn't want me to think I hadn't because I was so excited, I was so elated. And what actually happened, at the time I probably couldn't actually put this into words but it's a memory that is most definitely there. And while I was actually flying down the stairs I was very close to the ceiling which was like our landing. And as I was going down I sort of went a little bit along before I went down. And the ceiling was there and that was fine, this was all part of flying, and it was all very commonplace to me, I was fine and I looked down and there was me, slowly holding on to the banister and very slowly going down the stairs. [It didn't seem] unusual to me, that's just . . . flying.

'And when I actually landed just below the bottom of the stairs I in fact entered into my body from the top and went in [with] a kind of a slight jolt.

'Then I dashed up the stairs – inside my physical body

– to tell my parents I had just flown down the stairs. [This] gave me a great deal of bustling and blowing and exertion, which was quite different to the flying down the stairs. And I always remember that I did fly down the stairs.'

The second case concerned a friend of Bertil's who had been employed as a truck driver. At this time he was driving a very heavy load of roof tiles to two locations in northern Sweden, and having delivered the first, and biggest, part of the load, was now on his way to the second stop.

He was driving over a fairly steep hill in the middle of the winter and so the road was very, very slippery. At the hilltop he changed down the gears in order to save excessive use of the brakes. Suddenly he saw a car turned over in the road; another car was approaching and he needed to use the brakes in a hurry. It was wintertime and the road signs were covered with snow to a couple of metres high so he couldn't find anywhere to go off the road. The brakes wouldn't work correctly; the driver suddenly realised that he was not going to make it, he could not prevent a collision. But at a crossing he saw a chance to drive to the side of the road and out into a field. Throughout the experience he was not only conscious of every move, but experienced them as if in slow motion. Had he not been able to appreciate the manoeuvres in that way he could never have performed them. The whole thing could only have taken seconds, yet it seemed like a long time to the driver.

Debbie Tomey ('Kathie Davis' from Budd Hopkins's book *Intruders*) mentioned something similar. She had seen an alien entity in her house, an incident mentioned in the book, and at first thought that it was her son, Casey. She was beginning to tell him to get back to bed, and went on: 'I got about half of the words out when it hit me that that wasn't my son. It seemed like time stopped, it was like I moved in slow motion, I thought in slow motion, and it was like this moment lasted for ever.'

MY OWN 'SUPPRESSED MEMORY'

During my teenage years I was a passionate, if somewhat reckless, cyclist. I travelled all over the United Kingdom alone or with friends. Like most teenagers I had little regard for personal safety and no thought of danger. I was once stopped by the police near Marnhull in Salisbury after speeding down a one-in-three hill; they assured me they had 'clocked' me at 60 miles an hour and threatened to arrest me. When I was sixteen I, inevitably, came unstuck. I was cycling from my home in Kenton in Middlesex to Willesden to visit my grandmother. Cycling through Kingsbury, in north London, I was – according to a witness – going far too fast down Church Lane when suddenly I seemed to be distracted by a multi-note car horn (probably directed at me!). I turned at just the wrong split second. Apparently at full speed I hit the back of a parked car, flew over the handlebars, cleared two cars and finally landed face first on the pavement, unconscious. I was taken to Edgware General Hospital where I spent three days under observation for concussion. I had been lucky. I had suffered a few physical injuries, several deep cuts around the eyes and on one ear. The skin on half my face was scraped off and I suffered damage to the nerves around my mouth which, even today, means that when I talk there is less mobility to the left side of my mouth.

When I woke up in hospital I had little memory of

anything. In fact I didn't recognise my parents in the first few hours after the crash, and it was several days before I could remember any of the journey that had led to the accident.

In the years since, mostly in the months immediately after the accident, I remembered details of the journey that day; they came back in stages. Firstly I could remember leaving the house, but not much more. Then I could remember some of the early part of the journey, but not the last roads. Finally I could remember turning into the road where I had the crash. But I cannot remember further. The last minute or so before the crash is a memory I cannot access. However I have been told what happened by a witness and I have a fairly vivid picture of it.

The problem is that if I were regressed through hypnosis and recalled the crash I would be uncertain whether I was remembering (a) the reality, (b) the description given to me by the witness or (c) some image of the whole thing that suits me. Regression experiments have been performed on me but so far have failed to retrieve any memory. Bertil Kuhlemann offered an interesting reason why I might have suffered a suppressed memory of it. He took the view that I am a person who likes to remain in control of myself – which I accept is largely true – and suggested that when I totally lost control I 'decided' not to acknowledge that fact to my conscious memory.

I feel it is at least probable that I would remember the basic incident as described to me but coloured by my own images of what I must have looked like that day. The reality is that there is probably no way that I could ever be certain now what actually happened. That is the problem for close-encounter witnesses. How do they 'check up on' their own memories?

A VEHICLE FOR DEVELOPMENT?

One reason for suppressed memory was suggested in a close-encounter witness support-group meeting. The witness, who does not want to be named, pointed out that he had acquired an almost obsessive thirst for learning since the experience. In particular he had increased his reading manyfold, and was aware that his vocabulary was growing.

'It isn't that the memory is blocked,' he said. 'It's that I don't know the words to describe what I feel. By reading I shall be able to tell people what happened.'

It is easy to see what he meant. Try describing the colour red to a person who has been blind all their life. We just don't have the words or the means of expression.

Those who have undergone what would seem to be a cousin of abductions – the near-death experience – have also described the occurrence as a learning process. Indeed, part of the 'classic' model of that experience is a vision of the highlights of the person's life, with a presumed view towards learning from the various key events.

Lucien Morgan, a clinical psychologist who has been working in paranormal research for some time, pointed out that routine actions can cause memory blocks and 'missing time'.

'Everybody has missing time every single day. Could be minutes, could be a few seconds. There are times when we disconnect ourselves from our surroundings. Familiar road journeys, train journeys and so on. Go into a trance in a lift, watching TV. It's totally natural. Can be a little fantasy – fantasy produces endorphines which release stresses. Missing time is probably very healthy, it is a stress release, a governor on the steam engine.'

We know then that close encounters usually happen in some sort of altered state. Such altered states are not so rare; they can occur during routine events, during trauma and in 'normal' life.

Highway hypnosis, states of hypnopompic and hypnogogic imagery at the threshold of sleep are all times when such altered states can occur, and close encounters are reported as occurring during such times. And all situations provide for the possibility of 'missing time' which, as Lucien states, may be both normal and necessary for us to stay mentally healthy.

But what happens during that altered state? Is the imagination taking over? Or is the mind only then capable of perceiving what it otherwise cannot?

11 Perceptions from Culture, Society and Religion

The UFO phenomenon is global; sightings and close encounters take place all over the world. The only limitations to UFO reports seem to be that there need to be channels of reporting for witnesses to use. (And of course that there have to be witnesses there in the first place.)

Areas of the world with fewer reports of UFOs usually just have fewer reporting channels. When a UFO researcher or journalist takes an interest in a country or an area of the world, UFO reports immediately come forward. The breakdown of the large communist blocks in the East of Europe and Asia, and the collapse of the Soviet Union, have led to access to UFO reporting channels and a surge of UFO reports where few existed before.

However, while the UFO phenomenon may well be global, it has national or cultural characteristics.

'Little men' reports are common in Europe and Scandinavia, which has a tradition of 'little' entities: leprechauns, fairies, elves and the like. When the first entity reports came out of Russia it was perhaps revealing that they were of giants; the folklore tradition of that country includes mostly giant entities. Aliens are presumably not creating specific entities for specific countries and cultures; the presumption must be that perception of aliens is coloured by expectation from folklore and stories heard in childhood. (Again I stress, as I do throughout this book, that I am not suggesting these experiences are from the imagination, just that the imagination plays a part in how we perceive them.) For some reason South America seems to have the widest variety of entity forms: hairy beasts, troglodyte-type cave-creatures, even a stone-walled spaceship. There is even a report of a red-skinned alien with one eye. Sexual-encounter claims are frequent on that continent, perhaps reflecting the 'macho' image Latin American men are traditionally driven by.

The case that seems to me to best display the African culture variation is that of Clifford Muchena. The case was investigated very thoroughly and expertly by the leading investigator on that continent, Cynthia Hind. Clifford saw silver-suited figures and a ball of red light. When asked what the figures might have been, he said that he thought they might be the spirits of his ancestors. A similar claim in the West, influenced by science-fiction imagery, might have led to a claim of alien entities. But are we really in a position to demand that one explanation is correct? Perhaps neither interpretation is correct; both are being coloured by cultural conditioning.

These cultural differences suggest that although the UFO experience may be universal, some component of it is always personal to the witness. We will not understand the nature of these experiences until we can separate the external elements from the internal components, and we can only do that by paying more attention to the accounts of witnesses.

One case that I found interesting in this way was related to me by Maureen Cresswell. As she comes from a specifically West Indian culture, her reasoning for some interpretations of the entities that she saw was fascinating.

MAUREEN

Maureen Cresswell is a Grenadian, now living in London. At the time of interview (February 1993) she was 38 years old. What follows is her own description of her experiences:

'Many things are a mystery when you are a child. As you get older eventually you come to understand them, what you heard or saw becomes clear and fits into a framework in your life.

'What singles out these "encounters" is that you never really get to understand them – and you spend your life searching for an understanding or at least you hold the event in the back of your mind hoping an answer will present itself some day.

'You can explain the world [about you] eventually. You can explain everything you might have heard someone say that you didn't understand, eventually. The one encounter, the one "thing" in my life that happened – and I know that it happened – was never explained and I know I am the type of person to try to explain it. I always thought it would have to be very rational and there must be an explanation for it somewhere.

'I have read a lot and sort of wandered all over the world and done things but I've never had [that experience] totally explained.

'Gradually over the years there have been things that have caught my eye and I've seen certain things. The first thing that made me remember the experience was a black and white children's science-fiction puppet show – I think it was called *Lost in Space*. [Maureen pointed out that that might not be the right title.] I remember watching this and they had these "people" and it was the shape [that caught my attention]. It sort of hit me – pow! It was that intense and I went straight into

120

remembering this time I had seen these "people" and I thought – wow – they [the film makers] saw them too! That was my instant reaction.'

I asked the obvious question – did she think her 'memory' was a false memory created by seeing the programme? She was adamant it was not.

'No. No. No. It was a completely real thing. It was something that had been in the back of my mind and I was trying to put into place, and I hadn't put it into place as yet. There had been lots of different types of fantastic being-type things in programmes you see but all of that I could dismiss. It was just this one particular thing.

'[It] happened in Grenada before I left at the age of four or five. My mother and father had come to England ahead of me and I was staying with my grandmother, and my grandmother looked after me. I remember this day of "wandering". We lived at the height of a clifftop in an area of subsistence farming, in Gouyave [west coast] in Grenada. I was walking behind this house where we were, high on the clifftop. It was all shrubland and bush, all jungly. I was going exploring, or whatever, and I wandered off. We lived at the point where it begins to get hilly. Lots of cliffs. The cliffs [were over joined bays]. We [all the children] played on one side and you couldn't really go into the other bay. It was too steep, no way down. Through landslide and torrential rains there were [scree slopes] of rocks into the sea. Fishermen could get to the bay by sea, but you couldn't walk to it. I was used to being in that area and playing as a child.

'I remember wandering on this brilliantly hot day, feeling very free because [it was like] you had "escaped"! I remember looking out to sea and then there was a glint from [below left]. The glint caught my eye and I looked down and right at the base [of the cliffs] there was a flat table – like a rock. It was there that "they" were; these "people"! I can't exactly remember how many there were. There were several and they were deep in discussion.

'They were completely bald – that intrigued me – and they were white, very creamy sort of white. That intrigued me too because everyone I knew was black.'

We discussed this and Maureen thought that she had probably not – at that age – ever seen a white person. She acknowledged shades of black/brown in different friends, but probably knew of no white people. The colour of the entities she saw was a clear 'outside' element of her experience.

'It was what they were wearing [that was also strange]. It was like a conical shape [a circular 'pyramid' tapering up to the head. Maureen drew the outline for me.] The shape was like a coat, but not billowing, it looked fairly sort of static. It was very white which also caught my eye because it shone, it gave off a shimmer. They were deep in discussion. The impression I got was it was some kind of meeting. When they moved from one place to the next it was a "float", a "glide", definitely a glide from one area to the next. I was fascinated. I stood there looking at them and then for some reason – I don't know why – I became very afraid.'

We discussed this fear; Maureen was sure it came just from the strange appearance of the entities.

'Perhaps it was because they were "people" from out of my experience. [A type of] people I had never seen before. I thought "they mustn't know that I've seen them" – that was the thought that went through my mind. I just ran away back to my grandma's. I never went back to that site. There was so much fright. I can still remember the fear. The first time I went back to

Grenada was after "O" Levels, [the trip] was a kind of present. I went back [to the cliff] but there was no way to get down into the bay so I just sort of roamed around and looked. I saw nothing; and the table-like rock was still there.

'I have a feeling that I'm going to know – that I'm going to find out who they are. I think it's extremely important [the wider subject, rather than just the experience] because of religion, because of the impact [it would have].

'I don't think at that time I specifically connected them with another world, I just thought they were people from "somewhere else", because I hadn't been everywhere else. I thought it was likely I would understand them one day. You see people like Buddhist monks and you think one day you'll find them [these 'people'] and you'll find they came from some island somewhere but of course I *haven't* found that.'

I asked why she thought they came from outer space since we had established that she saw no 'craft' of any sort.

'Because of reading about encounters that people have had and things they've said, from watching films very closely – the TV thing made me do that. I look to see if there's something I remember.'

I asked whether this conclusion could have been 'triggered' by a science-fiction programme and whether, with a different stimulus, she might have described them as 'ghosts'.

'That's interesting but I've seen ghosts and they [these beings] were "flesh and blood". [Maureen and I later established that she meant she had seen them in films, so she imagined ghosts that way and not 'shimmery' – she confirmed specifically she had not seen 'real' ghosts.] [These beings] were real.

'I just saw the "people" and I know they were intelligent people because they were in this deep discussion.'

We talked about how she 'knew' they were in discussion. By her hand movements and body language I understood how the 'people' had been interacting with each other – gliding to and fro across the table-like rock, et cetera. It was an impression she had, but a clear and definite one.

What Maureen was describing might well not belong in UFO reporting at all; certainly no 'UFO' in the conventional sense was seen. However, the case has entities that could be taken as alien, and her own interpretation is one of extraterrestrials. For that reason it deserves study. It also shows how the barriers we have set up around what we are prepared to call a 'UFO experience' may be artificial and even meaningless. She might have been inspired to report ghosts rather than aliens if her 'trigger' had been different and if she had a different view of what constitutes a ghost.

PERCEPTIONS OF RELIGION

'Religion has made an honest woman of the supernatural.' (Christopher Fry)

Imagine that I suggest to you that you should go to a designated place where you would join a group of like-minded others. You're told that when there you will be able to communicate with an extra-terrestrial and might receive guidance in the way you should run your life. Contact with the extraterrestrial will be enhanced if you adopt a meditative position, and indeed meditate. Furthermore, you will stand a better chance of making contact if you believe in the existence of the extraterrestrial in the first place.

An invitation to a skywatch? The stuff UFO cults are made of?

Perhaps. But isn't this also a description of something 'normal' everyday people do frequently? Isn't this a description of going to church to pray to God?

We have an ambivalent attitude towards God and prayer. As the old saying goes, 'It's okay to speak to God, but start worrying if you hear Him speaking back to you.'

The conventional religions, it is suggested, are just cults with political power. To put it another way, cults are religions that have yet to become socially acceptable. American writer Ralph Waldo Emerson once said: 'The religions we call false were once true.' Even recent controversy over the Dead Sea Scrolls suggests that the basis of the Christian religion may be a somewhat constructed and censored version of the whole truth. One analyst of the scrolls, Professor Robert Eisenman, said: 'Whatever Jesus was like, he's not like the picture we have in the Scriptures . . .'

For many people alien contact and UFOs are a religion. In some cases UFOs join sex, religion and politics as taboo subjects for discussion because of the intransigent belief systems of adherents. I have met very few people who have ever been persuaded in an argument that UFOs were or were not alien against their former beliefs. The majority of people who are persuaded by evidence to change their minds move from a position of instinctively thinking UFOs must be alien to one of thinking they might not be. Far fewer people 'turn' the other way and become convinced by evidence that UFOs might be alien. While most adherents to the extraterrestrial hypothesis will deny it, I would argue that for many their belief is based more on faith than on the balanced weight of evidence.

In fact much that has been said of religion has been applied to alien contact: consider Freud's comment that 'Religion is an illusion and it derives its strength from the fact that it falls in with our instinctual desires.' Indeed, I have seen that many witnesses view many experiences involving coincidences as having an extraterrestrial origin, causing many people to scoff. But when I asked a committed Christian how they knew God and Christ were in her life, she told me that 'It's just the many coincidences that happen to you.'

We instinctively need to believe in something 'bigger' than ourselves. Many find that need later in life, some only in desperation. It is said that there are no atheists on a sinking ship. But it is also clear that the conventional religions are progressively failing either to produce a convincing God or to bring people nearer to a real God. People's needs are still largely unfulfilled. Throughout Britain church pews are empty; even the normally complacent Christian religions are beginning to use covert threats such as 'fail to attend church and we won't baptise your children or marry you'.

The problem is widespread; I took the opportunity while in Sweden fairly recently to get some opinions from that country. I was told: 'In Sweden approximately five to seven per cent of the population is church-going. Hopefully some higher percentage believes in the Christian religion but still 57 per cent are private spiritual seekers. They are not necessarily within the realms of the Christian, or any other, religion but depend solely on some very fundamental basics, for instance that there is a creator. But there is no dogma. Many believe that each individual can get in touch with a creator without any intermediaries, and that in the past all spiritual groups of people in different parts of the world have degenerated into religious movements and gurus and so forth. They become driven by political pressure.'

It seems that the priesthood starts by becoming a channel to bring God to the people, and ends up becoming a block between people and God. The people then turn away to search for spiritualism which doesn't involve the church.

Perhaps there are people who are genuinely 'channelling' or are in touch with energies and pass them on. But when they become a formalised body like a priesthood they end up becoming a political compromise, probably bringing into that group people who are not actually channelling energies but only want power for themselves.

Certainly that is what is happening in areas of ufology.

12 Higher-Level Perceptions and Sexual Energy

There is an area of UFO research that is missed by most researchers and ignored by the few who have become aware of it. It may be that in a somewhat diverted way the American research methods using hypnosis on close-encounter witnesses are addressing this issue, though that is debatable.

The issue is that of sexual expression.

Over a decade of closely working with UFO witnesses it has become very apparent that there is some correlation between experiences, and particularly close encounters, and a rise in their inner, sexual, feelings. There are several possibilities that might account for this phenomenon:

- feeling special
- kundalini
- generally getting in touch with energies which we in the West naively tend to call sexual
- a deliberate ploy by the aliens designed to produce the sperm for genetic study (in my view not a very likely possibility).

FEELING SPECIAL

What is it that makes a person feel sexually 'switched on'?

The factors are manifold, but since we know that it does not take a UFO encounter to make people sexually attractive to others, or to turn themselves on to their inner sexual feelings, we can assume that any sexual feeling is probably a by-product of the UFO experience rather than the reason for the experience itself. That the person may manufacture (I don't mean lying or faking, but creating something within the 'psyche') the experience in order to turn themselves on is possible, but not, in my view, very likely. Sexual energy, after all, is just one form of expression.

Sexual attractiveness is something that comes from within a person, not from the surface. People in a lasting, loving, sexual relationship find sexuality in such areas as a sense of humour, inner assertiveness and inner strength, playfulness, mischief, experimentation (not just with sex, either!) the desire to give to their partner more than they take from them, and so on. All of these things require a level of confidence.

I suspect that the UFO encounter is a step towards building a certain kind of confidence. The result of UFO encounters is that the person becomes special – mainly to themselves, often to their immediate friends and family, sometimes to the world at large.

Many close-encounter witnesses have relationship problems with their spouses or partners after their experiences. Even long-standing marriages often come under strain. This would seem to be a result of the same 'feeling special'. A healthy, loving couple try to share their lives and experiences. Some do everything together, acquiring the same hobbies and interests; most allow each other their own hobbies but share them by talking and encouraging. But in stable relationships the 'level' of each other's non-shared interests is fairly even; 'he has his golf, she has her bingo' might be a bit outdated, but generally there is equal give-and-take. When someone has a UFO encounter it often becomes, for them, the most important aspect of their life – indeed it can become the whole meaning of their life. And yet their partner is excluded. Worse still, the experience cannot be shared vicariously by talking about it, because in most cases witnesses simply cannot express feelings about their encounters they don't understand themselves. Most witnesses take years to come to terms with their feelings; some never do.

Many close-encounter witnesses are divorced or otherwise alone. The tension and often breakdown of relationship between couples would seem to be a result of this imbalance in their relationship. One partner may become 'famous' as a result of a life-changing experience, and literally change character and outlook; the other party cannot 'break into' their feelings (because the witness doesn't know how to let them in) and their relationship suffers

The breakdown seems more likely when it is the woman who is the witness; in older couples particularly, women tend to live in the shadow of their husbands. When the man becomes 'special' the woman is used to him being the centre of their world; when the woman becomes special, the man feels left out or rejected. One couple I spoke to admitted that after the wife's encounter and local 'fame' their sexual life stopped for some time, and indeed the man indicated that he might have actually become impotent for a time. A pity; the woman said she had never felt so sexy!

This 'sexiness' seems to come about as a result of enhanced self-awareness. The person has the experience. If they can share it even at a local level then they are forced to deal with situations they have never had to deal with before: almost hostile criticism from some, glory-

worship from others. To deal with both constructively
helps the person to become more assertive, more confident. Some witnesses have to deal with appearances on
TV and radio; all these things develop their self-esteem.

They also recognise that they have had an experience
that is fairly rare and that singles them out as special.
Some believe the experience has spiritual or cosmic
meaning; those who do not convert themselves and their
experiences into something 'religious' channel the
'special' feeling into themselves. As a result they become
more confident, more assertive, more sharing with
others ... they become sexually attractive people.

Frequently the witness not only becomes that much
more attractive to others, but acts in that manner, seeking to express themselves sexually. Let me be clear: that
does not mean that they seek sex. It only means that
they emit the signals we often associate with sex. In essence they announce to the world 'Look at me, I'm
special, I'm re-born, I'm confident,' and so on. The observer can easily mistake that for a sexual message, and
the witness may find that quite agreeable. So we have a
mixture of increased overt sexuality and – more commonly – inner sexuality.

YOGA, CHAKRAS AND KUNDALINI

Close-encounter witnesses seem to be experiencing the
release of energies that they are not previously aware of.
Many of them, naively, associate the feelings with sexuality. This is the 'teaching' of the Western world; but
for Eastern people – or at least those raised in more
spiritual cultures – these energies are almost certainly
those that are released through yoga, meditation and
the following of a different way of life. It is interesting

131

to consider that the 'world' into which abductees are taken may be the same world that yoga and meditation can reach, and into which shamans go in order to learn and develop themselves.

To explain this, and to remove some misapprehensions, requires a little background information relating to yoga – information that may prove directly useful to UFO researchers in the future.

Yoga is not just a funny way of sitting and exercising, as it is often presented in the West. For more than 6,000 years it has been a philosophy of life in some of the most densely populated areas of the world. It teaches that the person is composed of mind, body and spirit, all needing to be in harmony and balance. Full development of the individual requires the development of all three components together; indeed yoga makes it clear that the three cannot be separated. It is not a philosophy that demands that the individual submerge himself for life in order to achieve anything; even a moderate 'paddle' in its waters will help relieve tensions, fight disease, create an ordered and tranquil mind, provide for relaxation and develop the intellect.

There are eight fundamentals on the path of yoga: physical posture (*asana*), breathing (*pranayama*), concentration (*dharana*), meditation (*dhyana*), avoidance of evil (*yama*), observances (*niyama*), withdrawal of senses (*pratyahara*) and self-realisation (*samadhi*). It is worth noting that most of these are forced on witnesses to UFO encounters in one way or another; in particular the withdrawal of senses would seem to match the sensory isolation that people report – a sudden lack of wind, animal or other sounds, a quiet that comes over the scene, and a feeling of being cut off as if under a bell-jar.

It is strongly believed that yoga enhances extra-sensory perception and awareness of the paranormal.

Certainly yoga is part of the explanation for those who can lie on beds of nails, suspend breathing and so on (though such practices are regarded as 'circus tricks' by true yogins and not a worthy use of the art). Clearly the techniques of concentration, meditation and self-awareness demand years of study before they can be mastered. Once mastered they release potential previously unused by the individual. Equally clearly yoga is not something that can happen by accident. However, it may be possible that forced circumstances (i.e. a UFO encounter) can bring about yoga conditions for a short time accidentally, and release immediately the energies that take a long time to release under control.

CHAKRAS

The spiritual component of the body, often referred to as the astral body, has seven energy centres known as chakras. Yoga helps people to connect with their own energy centres. Several revolutionary training programmes used for large companies now use meditation with colour in order to help corporate executives with stress control and decision-making.

The chakras are positioned along the *sushumna*, the astral equivalent of the spinal chord. At the base is the Muladhara chakra, with four energy channels (*nadis*) leading from it. Its location corresponds to the base of the spine. It is here that kundalini energy rests dormant – we will come to that later. The next chakra, moving upwards, is the Swadhishthana chakra, with six energy channels (located near the prostate); next is Manipura chakra (ten *nadis*; located at the solar plexus); Anahata chakra (twelve *nadis*; located at the heart); Vishuddha chakra (sixteen *nadis*; at the throat); Ajna chakra (two *nadis*; at the temple). The highest chakra – the Shasrara chakra – 1,000 *nadis* – is positioned at the crown where the pineal gland is in the physical body.

Yoga is designed to clear the *nadis* and allow the energies of the astral body to flow freely. If the effects of yoga can be momentarily caused by an encounter with paranormal energies, then these energies may flow and the person may experience sensations never before felt.

KUNDALINI

Kundalini is a dormant bio-energy depicted in yoga as lying at the lowest chakra, at the base of the spine. It is visualised as a sleeping snake, coiled three and a half times around the lingam – the sacred phallus. There are strong warnings about waking it! It is awakened with yoga practice (or, arguably, by accident when in contact with external energies we call 'paranormal') and moves upward through the chakras. It is strongly suggested that kundalini should not be awoken without the guidance of a teacher; its effects can be alarming. (Several people have even made a link between kundalini and the somewhat questionable phenomenon of spontaneous human combustion.)

Kundalini is linked to sexuality, but is not sexuality. Kundalini fully awoken in a fierce way is thought to have a shocking and life-transforming effect on the individual. However, yoga under guidance allows for a gradual and gentle awakening of kundalini. UFO encounters, however, may provide for a spontaneous awakening, not usually total, which may be translated in Western minds as an awakening sexual energy.

Typical accounts of the awakening of kundalini include tingling and irritating sensations in the physical body, spontaneous sensations of orgasm, feelings of 'hot and cold' alternations and headache. In the non-physical body the individual can encounter feelings of ecstasy and wonderment. To a mind expecting nothing of the sort the release of kundalini can be a revelation, leaving the individual feeling he or she is 'in touch' with the whole universe.

Kundalini is believed to be the energy that, when aroused, creates the awareness of close encounters, near-death experiences and electro-magnetic interferences (often associated with contactees and abductees). It could be argued that it creates a 'fantasy' image of 'cosmic contact'; in my view it more probably allows for a *genuine* contact with real and external energies – a contact which the mind interprets as fantasy.

The summation of the argument is, therefore, that close encounters (with a natural but not well-known 'paranormal' energy) begin a transformation of the spiritual self and – since they are inseparably linked – of the mind, body and spirit of the individual. I shall later describe the personal experience in 1990 that led me to study this link between yoga and close encounters; however, for the moment, let me mention that when I spoke to one contactee about my own experiences he told me I could either 'embrace it and develop the contact, or let go of it and it would go away'. I believe he meant that I could develop 'contact' with extraterrestrials – not my strongest personal interpretation of close encounters, by far, but nonetheless if the yoga theory of the release of these energies is true then his advice was almost certainly completely correct.

Many writers on the subject of kundalini have described it as a powerful transformation tool of the whole body, the 'mechanism' through which individuals – and therefore ultimately the whole of society – will evolve into New People. I believe that the UFO experience is part of that transformation.

MY PATHWAY TO THIS RESEARCH

All too often UFO researchers are studying academically what other people are experiencing for real. But it seems that more and more researchers are beginning to find themselves 'wrapped up' in their own witnesses' claims. In 1990 I was involved in the research of the claims of one witness when I underwent what for want of a better word can be called a paranormal experience.

This experience led me to study the practice of yoga as part of the whole UFO experience, for two reasons. The witness herself was involved with yoga (though herself never made the connection I made years later, set out in this section); and I had been through circumstances that had led me 'accidentally' to adopt yoga practices for a time prior to the event.

Not wanting to make a complete fool of myself I kept the experience more or less to myself for years, discussing it only with trusted colleagues and friends, and in one public speech which I was fairly (and rightly) certain would not make news in England. When I first tried to think through the experience, I assumed that one of two things had happened: (a) I had had a close encounter (in the 'alien' sense of the expression). I more or less immediately dismissed this on the totally unscientific basis that I don't think they are happening – in that way – to anyone. The witness was also certain I had had no such experience; (b) I had become affected by the 'experiment'. It is a belief of psychiatry that the experimenter changes the experiment and can become part of it him- or herself.

I discussed the experience with Hilary Evans, a colleague in the UK for whom I have great respect. He could offer no help other than to say 'I don't know what to say except that when someone like you tells me that all I can say is "wow!"' '

I knew what he meant; I'm the analytical type and not given to fantasy, yet now I was telling him I might have had an experience that neither of us believed in, at least on that level. It was the frustration of needing to understand that led me to study what had been happening to my physical and spiritual body that might have created the experience.

OF THE EXPERIENCE ITSELF

I had worked with the witness for some years and was due to meet her in Florida in 1990. We stayed at the same hotel in Orlando for three days, which provided me with a reasonably intensive period of time to interview and discuss with her the finer details of her case. We were not together throughout all the time, however.

During one of the days when I was working alone in the hotel, I had feelings of being ill at ease consisting of a strong feeling of 'being watched', or at least of being aware that I did not feel alone in the room. We are talking about a brightly lit hotel room in the middle of the day. I was someone who had never experienced 'spooky feelings' and this seemed a strange place to start getting them.

I perceived moving shadows of human shapes in the room, all slightly out of my direct line of vision. I also heard sounds that could best be described as a slight electronic speech-noise – certainly incomprehensible.

If presented to me by a witness my first conclusion

would have been 'cabin-fever' (single-man-alone-in-strange-country, et cetera). However, I was fairly certain that did not apply here, simply because my lifestyle is one that puts me in that position frequently. In 'real life' I am a trainer for the business world and as such can spend many tens of nights a year alone in various hotels in England and several countries abroad. This was my first trip to the States, but at least they speak English there (or very nearly!) and I have suffered no ill effects being alone in countries all over Europe where even simple communication is a struggle.

There were factors that did seem important, however.

(1) I had just had an overwhelmingly 'gushing' response to my address to the MUFON conference. (Not a factor of me or the talk, I imagine, but simply the over-the-top way Americans treat anyone who has been up on stage in front of them, especially a foreign guest with an English accent.) I had therefore been on an emotional 'high'.

(2) I was now on something of an emotional pendulum. The 'high' of the reception I got in Gulf Breeze was now leading to an adrenalin crash as I 'came down' from the hype there. Yet I had built up adrenalin again on meeting the witness for the first time.

(3) I had recently changed my diet and become vegetarian.

(4) I had not eaten, except once, for around three days for the rather stupid reason that I had simply not found the time.

(5) I had probably suffered salt deprivation as a result of not eating and I was in Florida, often in the open air, in temperatures around 100 degrees Farhenheit. I was sweating freely and therefore losing even more salt.

(6) During the day I had realised that for the first time

in several very busy months of work I was alone where no clients, friends or anyone else could get hold of me. I spent several hours 'meditating' (or at the very least quietly relaxing) in the knowledge that I could get some real peace.

Yoga has five cornerstone practices: relaxation; exercise; proper breathing; healthy diet; positive thinking; and meditation. My lifestyle is usually that of the average middle-aged businessman – the exact opposite of all the above most of the time. Now, for around five days I was totally absorbed, often by accident, in all five practices. I think I probably awoke some of the natural energies that are dormant in all of us, whether kundalini energy or not; but the same or similar energies that can be awoken by UFO experiences.

I wanted another perspective on these views and I discussed this chapter with my colleague Bertil Kuhlemann in Sweden, who has not only given much thought to these general areas, but who also introduced me to chakras when we were using 'New Age' techniques to study the abduction of a Swede some years previously. He is also the man who introduced me to this witness, and has given training in Sweden using chakras and colour-codings – a training programme currently being adapted for businessmen in several countries.

'I have been asking myself why a specific individual has chosen, or been chosen, to become a contactee or an abductee,' said Bertil. 'My general feeling is that these are extremely sensitive people. And I am not talking about sensitivity in the sense of 'the paranormal' necessarily. But there is a sensitivity that is a potential opening towards paranormal phenomena.

'These people are perhaps not exercising their sensitive energies but those energies are there – dormant

– and in many, many cases I think we would find secret sides of their lives where they are expressed. Creativity is a part of that spectrum.

'It's not so much that UFO-type energies are sexual energies; more that we have badly labelled sexual energy as such. It just represents a combination of other energies.'

ALIEN INTERVENTION

I do not find it very probable that the American view of abductions is correct. The somewhat reductionist and simplistic view that alien astronauts are capturing literally thousands of people all over the world, over long periods of time, and performing genetic and sexual acts on them, as part of a programme of genetic engineering, seems to be the product of the science-fiction culture that gave us flying saucers in the first place.

It is my view, as this book explains, that this scenario is created by the mostly accidental misuse of hypnosis to lead witnesses towards a stereotype of abduction carried in all UFO researchers' heads.

However, while a few people might find themselves 'afflicted' by such techniques and acquiring an experience they never had, for the most part I think that the witnesses themselves are genuine in their claims that they have experienced a strange 'something', though they may only later come to 'recognise' it as an abduction. What is interesting is that within those reports there are medical 'anomalies' pointed out by the researchers themselves. For example, Budd Hopkins, a prominent researcher who uses hypnosis and firmly believes in the scenario above, has tried to get non-witnesses to fake abduction claims and their 'alien' medical examinations in order to see what they would produce from imagination. He said, 'What we got was ninety per cent *Star Trek* and ten per cent their last medical examination.' In particular Hopkins noted that 'fake' medical examination claims centred around the heart, which is often the cause of most concern for those worrying about their health. There was little emphasis on the genitals, although virtually all 'genuine' UFO medical abductions focus on the sexual organs or on aspects of reproduction. Hopkins's interpretation is that 'the shortest route from A to B is a straight line' and that therefore UFO aliens are focused on their victims' reproductive abilities.

However, it does seem at least possible that if, as I believe, these people are having experiences with natural but as yet unexplored energies around us, and that those experiences are releasing kundalini energy – an energy we associate with sexuality in the West – from the region of the sexual organs then that might be the cause of the focus when under hypnosis. Frankly I have to admit that I think this is a long shot even by the standards of UFO-research guesswork, and I also have to admit that I have had no opportunity to do any structured research that would confirm or refute the possibility. It seems to be a legitimate area of study, however, and a possibility not to be missed. Anyone looking for a study project might like to take this one up, preferably starting in America.

13 Perceptions into the Paranormal

There is a tendency for many people to think of UFOs as a discrete set of events that have little or no connection to other areas of the world around us. (Particularly as they are popularly seen as not coming from the world around us!)

However, after many years of working closely with close-encounter witnesses I have realised that there are many overlaps between the UFO phenomenon and what is generally called the paranormal. Even those in paranormal research have shunned UFO research; the reputation it has earned for itself is not flattering. However, apart from the possible direct paranormal links in UFO claims, many witnesses to close encounters often also have other claims to make. This, and the nature of their claims, suggest that this link is crucial.

RAUNI-LEENA

Finnish doctor Rauni-Leena Luukanen-Kilde is used to a degree of publicity and attention that some contactees shun. She is a diplomat's wife, and was for years a leading light in the medical world. As a Chief Medical Officer in Rovaniemi she had responsibility for all medical and dental care in her province, Finnish Lapland. She has worked as a medical adviser in Indonesia, has been Acting Director at the Finnish Department of Health and Social Security and has represented the government of Finland in tropical medicine at the World Health Organisation. As a result of working as a Red Cross doctor assisting Vietnamese refugees in Malaysia she made the Finnish government increase their contribution for refugees tenfold.

She is charismatic, charming and confident, yet Rauni-Leena's claims are not moderate, even by contactee standards. She claims to have met and talked with extraterrestrials, and even flown with them in their spaceships. She believes they have protected and guided her; indeed she thanks them for twice saving her life.

Her first book, *There Is no Death*, covered her beliefs and personal experiences with such phenomena as healing, out-of-body experiences, telepathy, and more. Her belief in extraterrestrials is combined with a belief in the wider paranormal. One belief does not suppress others; rather it seems to make the percipient more open to other experiences. The last chapter of the book was, she claims, written by her dead grandmother, channelled through automatic writing.

Like many who claim out-of-body experiences, Rauni-Leena was undergoing surgery at the time.

'I saw the whole operation "from above" and knew in advance what the surgeon was about to do. Just as he was about to cut an artery in the abdomen by mistake I tried in vain to warn him!' She was lucky to survive.

She was hospitalised again when she nearly died in a car accident. When she woke up a small entity, a metre tall, stood beside her and gave her healing with his hands on the liver area, which the hospital later discovered had been damaged. Much later she became convinced that the entity was extraterrestrial.

These extraterrestrial guardians apparently dictated her latest book, *The Messenger from the Stars*: 'I was meditating when the pen started moving by itself,' she says. 'After thirty-seven hours in all the book was finished. The handwriting did not look like anything I had seen before. It was slanting in all directions. The message was unmistakable. The theme was universal love.

'I invited them,' Rauni-Leena explained. 'I said that I wanted to have a ride.' Rauni-Leena is certain that contact with extraterrestrials will change people's view of the world. 'We will understand that we are not the centre of the universe but are surrounded by entities at a higher level, both technically, intellectually and morally.'

One day Rauni-Leena looked outside her house in Finland. Astonished, she saw a spaceship hovering a hundred yards away. 'I have never in my life been so frightened! My whole picture of the world fell to pieces!' The encounter lasted around fifteen minutes, then the ship took off. A local newspaper reported that around a hundred people in the area had seen the object, though the official explanation was that it was a Russian rocket. As Rauni-Leena put it, if so it was a Russian rocket 'which stopped for fifteen minutes to say hello to me'.

Regression hypnosis revealed to Rauni-Leena that the following night she had had a much closer encounter:

'Under hypnosis I experienced what had happened inside the spaceship. Among other things the entities gave me a thorough medical examination and took tissue samples from different parts of my body. I still have the scars on my stomach and legs.'

She also has a simple, but uncommon, explanation for the memory suppression aliens impose on their 'guests'. 'It would be much too frustrating to live in two dimensions at the same time,' Rauni-Leena said. 'It would be a bit like watching two TV channels at the same time. That's why they make sure that the memories are erased.'

However, Rauni-Leena's understanding of her abduction differs from the American 'model': she believes that her physical body remained in her bed throughout the whole experience and that it was her astral body which boarded the spacecraft. This makes her story a bridge between the claims of out-of-body experience, and abduction. That there is a conflict between this claim and the physical removal of tissue and the leaving of scars is not of concern to Rauni-Leena. She starts from what she knows and searches for the explanations. One speculation is that 'damage' to the astral body can be manifested on the physical body as psychosomatic scars or wounds – such as stigmata. Abductee Barney Hill claimed that he developed a ring of warts when aliens clamped a device to his groin, and they flared up years later when he relived the experience under hypnosis – even though the aliens and their machinery were no longer present.

I was reminded of the claims of Australian Maureen Puddy. She had reported an apparently physical abduction while driving alone through the open countryside. Later she took two highly respected researchers with her (Paul Norman and Judith McGee) on a re-run of the event and was abducted again while they were in the car. She went through the whole experience apparently feeling the events physically, yet she never left the car. The researchers, however, were convinced that she was experiencing something real to her. An astral abduction perhaps?

Several other abductees have reported being drawn out of their bedrooms literally through the bedroom walls to waiting spaceships. Could this reflect a movement of the astral body rather than the physical?

Rauni-Leena describes the entities as having 'a big

head, no teeth or hair and with three or four fingers on their hands'. She believes there are different races of aliens, many more human-like, and describes the blond, blue-eyed, slim figures that have featured in the claims of contactees such as George Adamski. She also believes the aliens are highly intelligent and advanced, particularly in their medical knowledge. 'They cure illnesses by using energy, light and colours, and examine by using thin needles.' Bridging the divide between the 'accepted' medical profession and the paranormal would, she is convinced, bring tremendous results. 'Then we would gain greater understanding of psychotically ill people. They show symptoms which indicate that they have been in contact with other dimensions but have become so frightened that they have become physically ill.'

Rauni-Leena has tried faith-healing with good results. 'A good friend of mine had a tumour the size of three centimetres. I held my hands over the tumour until it became so hot that she could not stand it any longer. When she was examined by her doctor a couple of days later before the operation the tumour was gone.'

For some time I have believed that UFOs are an expression of the paranormal. For Rauni-Leena the connection is direct: faith-healing, clairvoyance, out-of-body experiences and other paranormal effects are 'everyday' matters for the aliens. 'If we are open to the signals from space we can also learn, at least partly, to practise these techniques. From experience I also know that those who have been in contact with aliens become gifted with rare physical powers,' she says.

I can't confirm that, but my research indicates that some positive effects do arise from these alleged contacts. And the effects – whatever the cause – are often as Rauni-Leena describes and as so many others, such as the English abductee Elsie Oakensen, have found.

'How would you advise someone to deal with what they believe to be an extraterrestrial encounter?' I asked her. 'Treat it as a wonderful experience and a chance to learn,' she said. I could have used it as a foreword to this book.

LORRAINE PARRY

Lorraine, whose close-encounter experiences are related elsewhere in this book, is a good example of a UFO witness who has also been exposed to the paranormal.

Slide – Street Lamp Interference

'About seven years ago I used to walk under a particular street lamp every day when I came home from work and every time it went off. Every single time. And so the council came down because it was off more than it was on. And they kept changing the bulb, but it made no difference. There were about six in the street and it was this particular one. [This was in] Sudbury, near Wembley.

'And [similar things happen] in the house. If I have a great intensity of some feeling, whether anger or joy or whatever, sometimes I switch on a light and it just goes [out]. I do that quite often, unfortunately. It's definitely linked with my emotions, definitely.'

Lorraine described a similar thing happening in a health shop in Hounslow where the assistant was using a vacuum cleaner. She warned him to switch it off as she got near, intuitively knowing that she would 'blow' it. He ignored her, saying, 'No, it's OK, nothing will happen.' As he said that he touched her on the arm and between his hand and her arm there flashed a spark and an audible 'pop!'. He jumped back and he looked really scared, asking 'How did

147

you do that?' And Lorraine said, 'I did tell you. Some-times I affect electricity.' He didn't believe her.

OOBEs

Lorraine told me of two out-of-body experiences that she had had. The first related to 'flying' downstairs and is related in an earlier chapter. The second was as follows:

'I was sixteen; it was my birthday. I'd had a blazing row with my parents and one of my brothers joined in and I felt totally rejected and I went into my bedroom, laid on the bed and just wanted to die, literally. Just wanted to die. I closed my eyes and when I opened my eyes I was up in the corner of the room looking at my body and it was on the bed and it looked asleep. Some-thing told me, I don't know, impressed me that I had been given the decision whether to stay or go now. You can go now or you can stay. Because I had actually said let me out. I want out. So I was out and I could have stayed or gone. It was terrifying. And I remember I didn't suddenly go back but I was suddenly above my body and I remember just the last feeling of just floating down. I kind of gently lowered my spirit down and again that slight little jolt and I woke up and I immedi-ately went to sleep. I was terrified that all of a sudden if any of my family had come in they would have thought I was dead. And I had a panic feeling to get back because I didn't want them to experience that. And once I had experienced that, would I be able to get back anyway?'

Garden Gnomes

Lorraine had seen other entities in her young life, apart from the 'classical' aliens that she reported in her 'dis-placement' encounters:

'I was probably about five or six and where we lived we had an upstairs flat and, at the time, an outside toilet. [This was in Strode Road, Willesden.] I had been on my own in the garden and I went round into the toilet, played about for a while in the bushes that grew there. And I was going back into the grassy area of the garden, walking along the bushes which obscured the garden until you got to the path. And I looked round into the garden, because I thought possibly I had heard somebody. I thought it might be somebody I could play with in the garden. I leapt round [thinking] that my brother had come down. And I thought, "That's funny, I didn't hear him come. He usually calls me." He used to call me when he came down; if I wasn't around he would call out my name. And I looked up to the top of the garden and I saw something. I thought it was him. And then instinctively I knew it wasn't and I got frightened and dashed back behind the bush and there I was peeping around the corner.

'I think [the figure was] blue-green, about three and a half feet high. I was frightened and I was peeping round the corner and I wanted it to go away. I was very frightened.

'When I first saw it it just seemed to be looking around or standing still. And I looked around (again) and it started dancing up and down. I thought it was dancing.

'It had a face like a "he"; a [male] humanish face. No, more like a gnome, I suppose, in a hat. A gnome come to life. It was a grotesque thing. [His eyes] were sort of quite closer together if I remember. The nose was quite small and the lips were quite full if I remember.

'I became aware of [him watching me] because I started to enjoy the fact that he was dancing up and down. And I started laughing, I clapped my hands, like, to the rhythm when he was dancing. And the more I laughed and clapped the more he did it. So I knew he was doing it for me. That's how I knew. And I got a very friendly feeling from it. I didn't go any closer, I stayed where I was. I didn't get close. I made eye contact, just once, direct contact.

'I didn't trust [him] And I turned, I heard my cat and I turned away to see what [the cat] was doing. And when I turned back [the gnome-like figure] was gone and I was really disappointed. It disappeared. It just went.'

Section 3
Research, Casebook and Possibilities

14 What on Earth Are UFO Researchers Looking For?

What is UFO research? What exactly do UFO researchers think they are doing?

The answers to these questions may seem obvious at first; we are investigating UFOs. But to what purpose?

Let us take a situation where a sceptical investigator is invited by a witness to examine phenomena the witness has reported and which he is convinced is of a paranormal origin. For the sake of argument we will assume that the UFO researcher does *not* feel that this is the case, and indeed at the outset of an investigation it is perhaps wiser if the researcher does maintain a level of healthy scepticism but at the same time maintains an open mind.

Supposing that the sceptical researcher investigates the phenomenon and accepts that it does indeed have a paranormal origin and constitutes proof of the existence of UFOs (whatever we take that phrase to mean). What have we then got?

In fact what we have then got is just one more person who believes in an extraordinary origin of UFOs. With a world population of 3,000 million or so and with many new people born even in the time it has taken you to read this, that is a pretty slow way of convincing the world of the truth of UFOs.

We might therefore conclude that what UFO researchers are searching for is evidence that can be successfully presented to others.

For the sake of simplicity, let's make life easy for ourselves and consider UFOs to be spaceships from other worlds. I am not saying this is right, or that I necessarily believe it, but I need an easy way of describing an 'extraordinary' origin for UFOs and that will suit the purpose; the point I am making will hold true for any explanation of UFOs other than 'they are all in the mind', which I don't in any case believe.

Consider then, a second scenario where our witness invites us to a pre-destined encounter where we will see the spaceships and meet with the aliens.

As a result of it, we come away with, say, sixteen hours of continuous videotape of the encounter; visually and audio-recorded conversation between the witness, the investigator and the aliens; and information from the aliens which can be verified in archive records in museums all over the world – something a touch Biblical in origin, perhaps.

We might also have photographs of the aliens and the spaceship, and video footage of the aliens doing something distinctly and unambiguously non-human. We can accompany this with magnetometer readings showing massive increases in magnetic field disturbances at the times when the flying saucer appears; positive (or, if you prefer, negative) returns on portable radar; appropriate film of thermometer fluctuations; and just for good measure a few working parts cannibalised from the alien spaceship's drive mechanism.

What then?

It sounds like the sort of evidence that any UFO researcher, or any investigator into the paranormal, would give his third eye for. As he was collecting it he could probably envisage a lifetime of praise from his colleagues and the scientific community for finally solving one of the world's great mysteries. He may even be envisaging the lecture shows, the books, the films, and – if he were of a pessimistic nature – the endless round of television chat-shows.

But what will actually happen when he presents this evidence to the world?

Firstly he will come up against the jealousy of his colleagues and the political in-fighting which endlessly goes on amongst all the researchers into the UFO phenomenon; his methods will be questioned and his honesty brought into doubt. Genuinely committed researchers will feel a grudging admiration but will probably still challenge the work on less than reasonable grounds, if past experience is anything to go by.

And once the material is presented to the world at large, the UFO researcher can look forward to spending the rest of his life defending himself against allegations of fraud, mainly from the scientific community, whose institutions have a massive interest in not accepting challenges to science, and partly from the media, many of whom have a natural tendency to say 'black' the minute anybody says 'white'.

But there is a whole world of difference between academic theory and spending the night in the company of a man or woman who perceives themselves to have been raped or bizarrely used by aliens from another planet. And a whole world of difference between sitting in an armchair and spending the night alone in the cold and dark in some snowbound Scandinavian wasteland seeking to understand what a witness went through in terms of isolation and sensory deprivation.

So UFO investigation is not solely about the collection of evidence, since that alone will not convince others. One thing we certainly are doing – or perhaps it would be more accurate to say *should* be doing – is attending to the needs of the witness.

In the case of those afflicted by repeater abductions – and we don't have to believe their claims to believe that the witness's fears are real – and whose main worry is to be protected from the excesses of the abductions, it is the UFO researcher's job either to help them or to bring in those other professionals that are necessary. Whether abductions are extraterrestrial, or the action of an earth-bound force, intelligent or otherwise; even if you believe them to be nothing more than the wanderings of fantasy-prone minds, no serious researcher should ever lose sight of the importance of attending to the needs of the witness in as professional a way as possible.

But important – paramount even – though the witnesses are, researchers also have a duty to what is called the Big Picture.

Presumably, all UFO researchers not only want to be sure in their own mind as to exactly what UFOs are but also want to share that information with others. Most witnesses have the same driving need to communicate their experiences, so there doesn't have to be a conflict in this.

Total unanimity will never be possible – many people will believe what they want to despite evidence to the contrary – but there are people who are open to evidence *of an acceptable nature*. So the UFO researcher is presumably looking for evidence of an acceptable nature.

We can be fairly sure – from decades of bitter experience – that recorded data of an event is *not* acceptable. There have been many videos, many photos, many sightings, but the collected evidence has not yet really dented scepticism of the subject to any measurable degree.

We have to consider for a moment the question: what is Science?

Let us consider that science is really no more than a way of measuring things, and a set of 'filters' set up to prevent mistaes and confirm reality.

The problem is that science has determined that the proper filter size for UFOs is totally closed: it has denied any possibility of the reality of UFOs. In the early and perhaps naive days of UFO research, UFO researchers set the filter totally open; everything was real. Warminster in the 1960s, for example, was a sort of hippy-skippy, happy-clappy UFO believers' club. On the hills around the town people would see starships and scout-ships and all the rest of the 'alien' paraphernalia. We know now that not all at Warminster was as honest as it seemed. The ufology filter was too open and it left researchers vulnerable to the ridicule which has charac-terised science and the media's response for the past 30 years.

We need to work with witnesses on a much closer and more open basis to find out the proper size of the filter. And the only way to find out what is true and what is not is to give witnesses a chance to prove what they claim on their own terms. This is the basis of 'witness-driven investigation', a term I coined in my earlier book *Perspectives* and which arose from my work which had been in turn partly inspired by BUFORA researcher Ken Phillips.

Witness-driven investigation has a different approach than that of conventional science. Science says 'I will set up barriers and if you get through them then I'll believe you.' But there is evidence – even scientifically accepted evidence – that paranormal events can be enhanced if investigators and witnesses work in positively reinforced atmospheres. John Hasted, professor of physics at Birk-beck in London, showed this with his psychokinetic experiments.

I can write with a pen on paper; science would confirm that because it could test my claim empirically. But what if during the test I had my hand clamped to the table? Would that prove that I could not write? No – it would prove that science had set me the wrong test. Science today has made the same mistake in approach to UFOs. It has failed to devise the reasonable tests, tests suitable for the subject. Clamping a prisoner's hand to a wall might be an adequate test of his escapology but not of his ability to write; insisting on repeatability might be appropriate for Boyle's Law, but perhaps not for UFO research. In order to be convinced of the reality of a phenomenon, science demands that the phenomenon should be capable of prediction and reproduction in experimental form. Spontaneous paranormal phenomena, including UFOs, obviously fail this test; science rejects them. Conventional science fails to acknowledge that there are many aspects of the world around us which cannot be understood within accepted terms of reference. In the end there probably is no such thing as spontaneous phenomena; but there are phenomena whose causes are *unknown as yet*. That is the definition of the paranormal: the normal we haven't got to grips with yet.

It is the UFO researchers' duty to collect the evidence, not only of paranormal events themselves, but of the conditions under which they happened. Their duty may include allowing the witnesses to – in effect – manifest some of the phenomena, if that is a part of the way this UFO phenomenon works.

UFO researchers should then correlate this evidence with as much other evidence of similar events as possible. In addition we should be drawing on work of researchers into other paranormal activity: there may be actual interaction between the two areas and, there may be lessons for each set of researchers to learn.

Let us suppose that a witness is one of those known as a 'repeater', somebody who sees many UFOs over extended periods of time.

Let us also, *for the sake of argument only*, suggest that the UFO in this case is appearing because the atmospheric humidity is z, the degree of copper and zinc in the surrounding rocks is y, the temperature is x and there are geological stresses underground corresponding to a strain of w; each of the witnesses has just undergone the tragedy of bereavement with whatever consequences that may have, at the chemical level in the brain and the emotional level in the mind; there may be a host of other factors. Such a scenario doesn't rule out the extraterrestrial hypothesis; maybe it takes a set of just such strict conditions to allow 'them' to interact with us, and in these circumstances it would be hardly surprising that the exact combination of factors would come together only on rare occasions. None the less the UFO researcher should be accumulating as much trivial data about each UFO appearance as possible, in order that some small facet of each case could give the clue to the 'trigger'.

Assuming the researcher correctly pinpoints *all* of the necessary factors for the sighting to occur, it should then be possible either to predict with a reasonable degree of accuracy when those factors could come together, or to recreate them experimentally. In either event it should then be possible to 'manifest' the UFO in a way that would satisfy sceptical laboratory conditions. Such an achievement would mark the beginning of the acceptability of paranormal phenomena to conventional science (though even then only with a great deal of struggling!).

It is obvious that for this to happen UFO researchers would need the full and open trust and co-operation of witnesses prepared to work with them in partnership. What witnesses bring to UFO research is a source of data; what we bring to them is a willingness and a structure to share that data worldwide in order to put the Big Picture together.

In such an ideal world, conventional science would also make some compromises. One of the 'laws' of science is that any experiment should be capable of being replicated under the same conditions by anybody with the same equipment. Studies of the paranormal *seem* to indicate that the state of mind of the researcher and the witness are a genuine factor necessary for certain spontaneous phenomena to manifest themselves. Therefore, if as has been suggested by such people as professor of physics John Hasted, the results of certain phenomena – in this case psychokinesis – are heightened by the witness being positively reinforced by the investigator and believing himself to be in a true partnership with the investigator, then science has a duty to accept that as part of the test conditions. Until we know all of the factors involved in creating certain phenomena, we must be very open-minded.

The question of partnership between investigators and witnesses is vital. Consider the analogy of a train-crash disaster. Someone involved in a train crash does not necessarily make a good train-crash investigator. A good train-crash investigator's strength lies in his analysis of the reports of a number of crashes, as well as his own, first-hand experience of the aftermath of a number of crashes. Of course he must also interview witnesses, but many witnesses are traumatised by their experience, and often don't remember even the moment of the crash. Many close-encounter witnesses are also traumatised, or have memory blocks. Investigators generally have neither of these problems, and they have the willingness and resources to go around and talk to many other witnesses, forming an overall picture of what has happened. The witnesses, on the other hand, will tend to focus on their own experience, not the Bigger Picture. Furthermore, frankly, witnesses don't make very good investigators because they see and hear all other cases in relation to their own, which is not a very sound basis for dispassionate research. This is why a partnership between researcher and witness is needed.

BUFORA is planning to train investigators to work with witnesses; Ken Phillips is heading up this work. Training in the past has concentrated on teaching people to measure angles and estimate sizes of objects, and a host of mechanical skills of that nature – all good and important stuff, but very basic. Witnesses are often not happy with the investigations they get. By joining in BUFORA's training plans, witnesses can ensure a higher quality of investigation, a better quality of understanding and a closer partnership for future witnesses.

As in every area of research there are going to be different standards of research and researchers. However – and this is where I get into a lot of trouble with UFO researchers both in England, indeed in BUFORA itself, and certainly abroad – *I am not going to pretend I could set that standard until we all know more.* Only when we know what the subject is truly all about can we begin to set out the criteria for a good researcher. Our conventional thinking suggests that a good researcher is a well-balanced individual, educated and intelligent, fair and methodical, and so on. Maybe so. But maybe the ideal researcher is a hopeless drunk with the IQ of a garden umbrella and for whom sound judgement is picking the right dog at White City . . . but who has that 'whatever-it-takes' to see what others do not, or even manifest what others cannot. The line between recklessness and radical thinking is a fine one, but researchers should not be afraid to tread it.

Throwing caution to the wind and allowing total openness of work with witnesses will leave researchers open to criticism from the general media, the UFO press and the scientific establishment. If researchers are too radical in their thinking, they also risk alienating those scientists who agree in principle with the concepts of UFO research but who worry about pressure from the academic world to conform, and withdrawal of grants. Such scientists have placed a certain amount of trust in UFO research; we in turn owe them some consideration.

UFO researchers have to walk a tightrope between what I believe we should do – open the field to new and radical thinking – and the damage so doing might bring upon ourselves and others.

How do we meet the needs of witnesses, serve the wider interests of UFO research, and maintain the respectability we have built up to date, all at the same time?

Answers on a postcard please.

15 Working with Close-Encounter Witnesses

In the previous chapter I touched on the importance of allowing close-encounter witnesses to prove what they claim *on their own terms*. Such witness-driven investigation aims to ensure a higher quality of investigation, a better quality of understanding, and a true partnership between witness and investigator. However, methods of investigation have changed over the years, and this chapter aims to give a history of alternative approaches to dealing with witnesses.

THE ANAMNESIS STUDIES

BUFORA conducted its first serious study of witnesses as a group over a decade ago. It was formulated with Austrian psychologist Alex Keul. Keul began his academic career in astronomy and meteorology, but in the late 1970s he entered the fields of clinical psychology and psychoanalysis. He later developed an interest in Jungian psychology and shamanism. He had been the Austrian representative for MUFON (The Mutual UFO Network, the world's largest UFO study group).

The study was started in 1981 when Alex Keul visited Ken Phillips in Milton Keynes, where Ken then lived. Keul was proposing to study UFO witnesses as opposed to UFO reports, which until then were the main thrust of examinations. The proposed method was a questionnaire of over 60 questions called the anamnesis (Greek for 'life memory'). The anamnesis is a culture-free, time-invariant study. Because of this it can be applied to witnesses at any stage in their ongoing UFO experiences. The prototype questionnaire was used in the Milton Keynes area and surrounding districts – the counties of Bedfordshire, Buckinghamshire and Northamptonshire – for its sampling.

Ken Phillips used this prototype for around a year; the response was positive. He found that witnesses were only too keen to discuss events in their lives, apparently finding the process meaningful. In other words, it helped them to put their own UFO experiences into perspective. The witnesses came through the usual channels: the BUFORA national investigations network, personal letters, telephone calls, reports in newspapers, and so on. No advertising was used. When the witnesses reported their experience to BUFORA or the media, Ken would make contact and get the witnesses to fill in the usual BUFORA 'sighting report form' (form R1), which deals with physical parameters of the sightings. Once this was completed, Ken would then explain that he wanted to carry out a witness-centred survey in order to profile the witness within the overall UFO experience. A total of between twenty and thirty witnesses completed the pilot survey.

In 1983, due to the success of the pilot scheme, Keul decided to modify the anamnesis with the introduction of further questions and deletions of others which he came to believe were irrelevant. For example, he brought in 'Did you or did you not like school?', which was thought to reflect on the subject's wellbeing during early life. Another addition was 'Did you have a happy childhood?' Omitted was 'Do you consider that your personality has changed since your UFO experience?', regarded as meaningless since it was too subjective for analysis. This survey ran until early 1992.

During that time anamnesis questions were applied to over a hundred subjects. These subjects were found in the same way as in the pilot study. However by 1985 the emphasis had shifted its geographical bias to London and the immediate surrounding areas, because at that time Ken Phillips had himself moved to London. The anamnesis was applied not only to close-encounter and abduction witnesses, but also to witnesses of other classifications of UFO phenomena. The subjects came from all levels of the social spectrum but there was a bias towards the so-called 'working-class' population simply because that was the way the reports came in. This could mean that close encounters happen more to 'working-class' people, but the sample is too small to be sure to be rid of other bias. For example, it may be that so-called 'middle classes' resist involving researchers for a variety of reasons, even though they have an equivalent number of experiences. Of the hundred or so people involved, around ten to fifteen per cent were non-close-encounter types.

One result of the study was that self-reporting such other phenomena as ESP increased with the nearness of approach of the UFO. The study also showed that there was a tendency towards 'status inconsistency' in witnesses – and this also increased with the closeness of the object to the witness. Status inconsistency refers to a situation where witnesses hold jobs that are not consistent with their intelligence or social status – usually holding a lesser job than would be expected. It is not a new theory, and was first proposed by D. I. Warren in *Science*, 6 November 1970 (p. 599). When it was first introduced 'mainstream' UFO research rejected the proposal; the anamnesis has shown it to have validity.

The control sample that was used was not accepted as statistically significant, invalidating the controls scientifically. It was the best that could be done at that time, however.

The project seems to have temporarily discontinued because of the changed circumstances of Alex Keul. He had been appointed Research Assistant to the Department of Psychology at Salzburg University, a demanding post that has prevented him working on the anamnesis documents. Because of that, the work was actually carried out by Professor Streichardt at Freiburg University's Parapsychology Unit. However, after Keul's withdrawal from the project, Professor Hans Bender died and his demise was closely followed by the closing down of Streichardt's unit. Applications have been made by Ken Phillips to re-start the project with others – the Koestler Chair, the Society of Psychical Research and so on. So far, there has been no take-up.

However, an American group, CUFOS – the Center for UFO Studies – is doing similar work. It is to be hoped that BUFORA will now continue its work under CUFOS's project; Ken Phillips is currently co-ordinating that work in the UK.

There were faults with the anamnesis, admitted to by all parties. The main disadvantage was the fact that the survey was restricted to a population of witnesses and that, beyond the ten in the control sample, there was no good basis for comparison with the general population as a whole. In short, we know a lot about witnesses but we do not know if similar trends exist in the public at large.

Ken proposed that BUFORA should allocate funds to a survey of non-witnesses, but to date this suggestion has not been taken up, due mainly to lack of available funds. There are also some doubts as to the expertise available to ensure samples are statistically significant.

Another interesting group to study would be the UFO researchers and devotees themselves. As a test Ken Phillips took the anamnesis; he came out in the 'normal' range, with no leaning towards the factors detected for close-encounter reporters.

The summary results of the survey were as follows:

(1) Close-encounter witnesses have a high rate of self-reported ESP.

(2) Close-encounter witnesses also have a high rate of self-reported UFO and 'flying' dreams.

(3) Close-encounter witnesses tend to be status-inconsistent.

There is some material to be considered within these results.

Those witnesses exhibiting status-inconsistency also exhibited severe difficulties in adjusting to virtually all areas of life – marital, social, business and professional. Status-inconsistent witnesses also displayed some tendency towards isolation in their communities, even in their marital lives. Those witnesses with happier lifestyles dealt with or assimilated their experiences better.

Another interesting outcome was that a reasonably high number of witnesses reported having religious or mystical experiences. They also attached emphasis to 'spiritual quality of life'. However, there were few 'establishment' church-goers. What seems clear is that close-encounter witnesses are following the trend of the general public in turning away from the 'conventional' church, or at least that they are finding that mainstream religion is not meeting their personal needs.

As Ken summed up: 'There seems to be evidence, from the close-encounter witnesses themselves, it should be stressed, of an ESP-prone, close-encounter UFO witness who self-reports precognition, telepathy, out-of-body experiences, clairvoyance and other conditions

167

whereby information is received outside of the normal five senses.'

THE WITNESS SUPPORT GROUP

Ken Phillips also co-ordinates the witness support group (WSG) with BUFORA, the British UFO Research Association. The group is a product of witness-driven investigation, a method of approach that I created based on earlier discussions with Ken over his work, and is, as far as we know, unique in the UK. Ken emphasises that he is its facilitator, not its leader. It is independent of UFO researchers and indeed of BUFORA, although I have been privileged to be asked to attend it on several occasions. The following is a synthesis of my interviews with Ken. 'The group is turning out to be a very unpredictable affair. It was formed in October 1991, and we all first met in north London at the house of one of the witnesses. It was highly successful and seemed to be the right sort of format for the witnesses. It is a forum where people with similar experiences can discuss their experiences, the problems arising from them and other issues in an open and unafraid way. The witnesses have no fear of comeback, ridicule or scepticism.

'As a result of the success of the first meeting, another meeting was arranged a few months later at the same location. Bi-monthly meetings have been held ever since.

'To begin with many of the witnesses were not convinced of the validity of other witnesses' experiences; they found other people's claims hard to accept. This is something important for readers to realise. UFO witnesses are often presented as a unified group who have "experienced something" and who are either believed or disbelieved by "the public". This is not so; they are not unified and have to deal with other people's belief systems themselves.'

UFO reports vary a great deal and Ken, with some difficulty, managed to convince the witnesses that despite the divergence of their stories, there was a common thread linking them. This common ground was one of the reasons why the group was formed in the first place.

'After a few teething problems were overcome the group began to settle down to its bi-monthly meetings, and the individuals were exposed to ever-widening vistas of experiences.

'Basically the witnesses wanted to demonstrate to the UFO fraternity how, until now, they were simply not being listened to and/or believed. The group has moved on from trying to demonstrate the reality of their experiences to ufologists, and is now seeking a more creative method of expression.'

The witness support group has developed its own newsletter, *The UFO Witness*. It is very important because it contains raw material, written by the witnesses themselves – opinions and viewpoints have not been filtered through researchers. This may be the first time that the public has had access to the minds of witnesses without the clouding and damaging opinions of writers – particularly the highly opinionated and self-important 'in-house' magazines that abound in the UFO 'industry'.

The WSG see all of their efforts as a blow against the domination of the UFO fraternity by sceptics. The group may lead UFO research where it has not been before, and thus to answers. They might become an unacceptable fringe. Precisely because the group is so dynamic, its future is hard to determine.

However, in 45 years we have not found any answers to the UFO phenomenon. I believe that at this stage any alternative route of investigation is to be considered. I support the WSG fully because for all the time I have been involved in UFO research (over half my life) I have recognised that whatever UFOs are, ufology itself is about *people* and their responses to those UFOs. As such, witnesses *are* UFO research. I am the first to agree that the approach of the WSG is not scientific, but it could be the rudimentary start of a form of research using intuition rather than science. However, it is interesting to note the views of those not so persuaded. When Ken Phillips took over for an interim period as editor of BUFORA's 'main' magazine, *UFO Times*, the Director of Publications and former editor said that allowing witnesses to have their own say was acceptable, but it shouldn't be allowed to go too far in case we upset our readers.

In the end the scientific community will – and should – have its day. However, we might find that our radical study can provide them with a few avenues of investigation other than the extraterrestrial hypothesis they long ago rejected. There are problems with witness-driven investigation and with the group. I have noticed that the need not to criticise can mean that radical, even ridiculous, views are allowed to be stated; if unchallenged, they can even gain a certain acceptance. However, the openness of communication is similar to the technique of brainstorming used by businesses all over the world to develop radical thinking in executives and operatives. It can be confusing, but it usually sorts itself out in time. I feel that the WSG will come through that in time as well.

However there is also a tendency towards paranoia within the group; almost everybody believes that governments are conspiring to cover up UFO-related material. Such unanimity tends to enforce everybody's views. Government conspiracies are, however, a very common theme in UFO research generally, and therefore it's not surprising that they should surface here.

There are other, probably short-term problems: the WSG has not yet formed coherent goals, though they are beginning to emerge: the magazine and the UFO roadshow, where members creatively express their experiences through music, dance and other forms of art, are examples. There is not yet much team-building going on, though that might prove necessary or useful. However, some teamwork is emerging in their projects and this may develop. So long as the group meets its own needs, it will find what team dynamics it requires.

There is no leadership as such, Ken Phillips rightly not wanting to be seen as anything more than a facilitator. In my view natural leaders always emerge and I believe I can see them in this group. Leadership will develop according to goals and effort needed.

The biggest fear is that the WSG could become a cult; cults are rarely constructive in the long term, except perhaps to their leaders. Certainly the WSG has the potential to throw up a cult leader. I believe that such a person would be rejected by many of the down-to-earth types currently in the group but changing dynamics means that this could develop.

They are highly motivated as individuals but not yet as a group. For this they will need a common purpose and the one that seems to be emerging is to become the platform that will legitimise UFO experiences and become a voice for openness and debate.

THE WITNESS SUPPORT NETWORK

The WSG was not the first attempt made by Ken Phillips to provide for witness needs. The first major attempt was, however, pretty much an unmitigated disaster.

Known as the Witness Social Network (WSN) it was created in 1987 at the request of Alex Keul, the Austrian psychologist who assisted in the anamnesis studies. Its only redeeming feature was that it was short-lived. Keul had visited Ken Phillips and suggested that, as a result of all the problems suffered by witnesses, it would be a good idea to establish a Witness Social Network. Such networks had apparently been organised in other countries to deal with other social issues: rape, abuse and so on. Witnesses did not meet face to face; rather, the WSN was a telephone-link network. This, Ken Phillips believes, is the main reason why it fell to pieces.

However, at Keul's request Ken (who was at that time a BUFORA investigator and council member, also the national investigations Co-ordinator for ASSAP – the Association for the Scientific Study of Anomalous Phenomena) contacted a number of close-encounter witnesses and other paranormal self-reporters and established a network between them. For the first few months everything seemed to go well. I will let Ken explain the failure in his own words:

'One evening I received a mysterious phone call from a BUFORA investigator explaining that he had been contacted by a London-based psychic who had explained that important meetings of the WSN group must be convened as soon as possible. The psychic named a person through whom the meetings should be convened. However, when the investigator phoned that person, severe interpersonal difficulties developed. The investigator accused this person of "fraud". This, in turn, led a relative of the person concerned to suspect the whole call was a hoax and/or troublemaking. From then on accusations were made from one member of the group to another as the word spread. It culminated in severe accusations and a serious breakdown of relationships between members of the group. Consequently I pulled the plug on the WSN in order to restore some semblance of normality. I phoned everyone and asked them all to back off from each other. However the rift left a deep scar in those witness relationships that remains to this day. ASSAP decided as a result of complaints from the group to hold an enquiry into the matter. I admitted that I had naively handled the situation and resigned as NIC. Eventually I departed the ASSAP organisation.

'Ego and paranoia were strongly involved with this group, and this surfaced too easily after this trouble. The main reason for this problem was that the network was only on the telephone – there was no personal interaction which might have made matters easier. The new WSG is a much fairer and more sensible way of dealing with problems. The person-to-person basis enables any misunderstandings to be clarified and put right.

'There was, I think, no difference in the types of people involved – it was simply the wrong dynamics for these particular needs.'

It is also interesting to compare the WSN and WSG with the very loose 'network' that I found in Sweden on one of my trips there. This network was centred on a witness, a Mrs Andersson. There were no formal arrangements or meetings and the group, if group is the word, sought no identity through newsletters or the like. Mrs Andersson worked in the local supermarket and anyone wanting to chat about their experiences went to see her. If asked, she would set up a 'coffee-meeting' at a house so people could share views. Very informal and easy. At the time of writing the group seems to have suffered no ill effects, though it is not taking up any particular direction of research. (Nor, to be fair, does it seem to want or need to.)

16 Regression Hypnosis: Research, Therapy or Both?

It is very clear that hypnosis, and regression hypnosis, are valid and useful tools of therapy. However, I have always been unhappy about the use of hypnosis as a tool of research. It seems to me that it is one thing to use this tool to relieve pressure in people's minds about the experiences they are undergoing; it is quite another to believe that the images they construct to explain those pressures and stresses should be taken at face value.

In my previous book, *Perspectives*, I spent a good deal of time demonstrating why I believed this to be the case. I received some criticism as a result – mostly from the United States – because I made clear that while I believed witnesses were experiencing *something*, I did not accept that recall under hypnosis necessarily revealed accurately what that something was. In particular I was criticised for not accepting the explanations for the UFO phenomenon constructed by researchers such as Budd Hopkins. Budd himself proved to be a good deal less critical and at our first meeting we finished off a fair chunk of a bottle of Bourbon, swapped a lot of stories, came to respect each other's positions and ended still holding pretty much the same opinions as before!

In the years since we have met a few times, to my educational gain and, I hope, to his. It is a pleasure to be able to use this fact to set a few points straight. I still believe that Budd's acceptance of the claims made under hypnosis is premature, and I do not accept that the abduction accounts he produces are objectively accurate. However, I have always believed that the work he has done is genuinely intended to be beneficial. I believe Budd is honest in his approach to the subject, and of course he sincerely believes the accounts he tells.

DEBBIE TOMEY

I was able to speak to Debbie Tomey ('Kathie Davis' from Intruders*) while I was in America and she made it quite clear that Budd's therapy had probably saved her life. She had many pertinent observations to make about her experiences: telling me in interview:*

'If there weren't so many damn people to talk to about this, if it was just me, I would be down to The Seven Steeples right now – that's the local madhouse. When I started working with Budd I started getting into this network of people like me that had had the same memories and stuff. I can't say that I got better, I guess you never get better from anything, but I changed. I grew. I could cope even better and the anxiety was gone. After therapy for a year I feel like I must have been on the right track because something certainly made a big turn-round in me. If you knew me six or seven years ago and you knew me now, ask anybody that I know, I am not even the same person. I must have been on the right track with Budd, and everybody [else] must have been on the right track.

'Things are still happening. Different things. It's like in some ways it's moved up [to] a different level. I was interested when you and Budd were talking on that panel last night [we were both speakers at a UFO conference in America] about creative and artistic ability.

I've experienced that, you know. Like Budd says he doesn't know whether it comes from within us or may be external.

'But it is as if you develop, I guess, because of the traumatic experience, you develop a heightened sense of awareness of what goes on around you which kind of bleeds in and affects other things. I developed a heightened sense of what goes on inside me and in my head and in my heart, you know. And it continues to grow. It's like somebody put a seed there and now it's grown, you know. And I'm not saying they put the seed there, maybe it was already there. There's, like, poltergeist activities going on, I don't know how to describe it, things going on, flashes of light, things going missing. I think [the wider paranormal] is all connected; and there is one other thing that's begun. It was happening a little bit in the beginning during the first investigations with Budd. Budd and I talked about it; he decided to keep it out of the book. I would get words and little images flash in front of my eyes, like I would see something. Do you know what I am saying? I'd see a face or a piece of machinery or a landscape or something or an animal flash before my eyes and I'd have little funny sounds in my ear, it was more like in my head. And then I'd maybe get a word or something, I got a whole list of words in the beginning. None of them made sense, they were out of context. And then I had a real weird . . . something happened. I had just gone to bed after getting off work, I had just shut my eyes and this zap like a flashbulb went off in my head. And it scared me so bad I thought I had had a stroke. That was my immediate reaction and then I thought, no, everything works. I [thought] maybe I had a brain tumour. After thinking about that a minute I thought no, I have just gone nuts. I've got UFOs up to here and I'm out of it. Then I started hearing a man's voice, something I never heard before, and I couldn't understand what it was saying. It was like another language or something that I didn't understand but then I suddenly got a little glimmering of understanding and I understood a little piece of sense and then lost it, but what I understood was "Prestigious listener in November" which makes no sense. It was in October when I heard this. I got all upset, I jumped out of bed. I told my husband, "I'm going crazy, I'm going crazy." He calmed me down. He said, "Maybe you should write down what your hear." So I went into the other room to get paper to write this down but as I was coming back I had this swirling feeling all around me, and it wasn't like an adrenalin rush, I have had those. It was like static electricity. The hair on my arms stood up and it started at the top of my head and went down like a swirl, real hard swirling all around my body. And I went back into bed and then I looked at my husband. I said, "God, I feel strange." And he said, "Well, write this down and come to bed." Well, I went to bed and as soon as I shut my eyes I heard the man's voice again and he said: "Still feeling strange?" Just like that. I came off the bed again and then my husband and I talked and then I laid back down and shut my eyes and then I heard him. I said to my husband before I closed my eyes, "This is not funny." And as soon as I closed my eyes I heard the man's voice one last time and he went, "Ha, ha, ha."

'I think it's going to be OK for most of us. Everybody I talk to I tell them that in Budd's book he has this theory of what is going on and why. Everybody has their own theory as to what's going and why. I don't have a theory. I feel like shit's happening to me and my family and I don't know [what it is], so how can these guys know?

'I'm not here to shove anything down anybody's throat, but if somebody feels they're in the same shoes I am . . . I feel like I have something I have to do. I feel like there is something I should be doing to help. I feel like if I can just talk to one person and just let him know that you are not going to die, this isn't going to kill you, you'll be all right, maybe you'll even be a better person for it in the long run, just hang in there, you're not alone. I feel like I should be doing stuff like that.

'I stood up and spoke in Connecticut for the very first time, used my real name and everything. When I got up there on that stage I thought I was going to die. My heart was beating so hard that it was skipping in my throat. I nearly passed out and my mind went blank. I looked at the crowd and I said, I am scared to death; please hang in now with me.'

I asked for Debbie's opinions on Budd and the therapy:

'Oh, I love him. I mean he's like almost second family after all this time. He's been very good to me. I feel like he has helped me to get control of my life for maybe the first time. He has opened doors for me, you know, and he has helped me learn things. His whole family has treated me and my family so good and I have a tremendous amount of respect for him. I know how hard he works and how emotional he gets about everything. I don't always agree with his opinion of something, but that's cool. He's a wonderful guy.'

More recently I asked clinical hypnotherapist Lucien Morgan whether or not he believed the uses of hypnotherapy as a tool of research and of therapy could ever be reconciled.

'One hundred per cent definitely they can be reconciled. There should be a structure and a responsibility to abductees,' was his answer. A meeting of selected abduction researchers in America resulted in the formation of a code of ethics drawn up by a team under the highly respected David A. Gotlib MD. The code is still in consultative draft stage at the time of writing, but if readers want details of this please contact me at the address at the back of the book. Final drafts should be ready by the time this book is published.

Lucien continued: 'There should be therapy done all the time; never take people into a trance unless it is for some form of therapy. Never brainwash the person, but it is ethical to "trap" the unconscious into opening up. Like "You say you don't know yet but when will you be ready to know; one month, two months?"'

Lucien believes that hypnotherapy has great potential for research, so long as *therapy* is the main aim. Lucien does not believe, however, that the 'grey aliens' explanation of UFOs is likely to be valid, and has other views about the claims of abductees. I asked him why he thought there was a growing acceptance of 'greys', almost a consensus reality of 'grey' aliens.

'I think we have a consensus reality of the "greys" because the colour grey can be anything. People can project [anything] into the image; not good, not bad; not black, not white. It's something [people] can put their fears into. The image is a feeling image, an image of feelings and memories that we had when we were in the womb, or just very small. With frail arms and a head large in proportion to the body. To me it looks like a human foetus development. It's a communication device, for communication with oneself.' That sounded a bit like the birth-trauma theory that had been popular a decade or so ago, I suggested to him. 'I am most definitely not saying that [abductions] are [the result of] birth trauma or birth-trauma memories. I am sick of having to put people together who have been with other therapists and have been damaged by reliving their birth trauma.

'I don't think that it's a good thing if people put their positive energy into the "greys". I think it's a good thing if people don't lose the locus of control and [remain] aware of the energy, love, power, ability, talent that may lie inside them.

'The creation of an abduction experience by the "greys" can have positive results for the person . . . using a sub-personality [which we all have – it's quite normal] . . . it can be exactly and precisely what that [person's] soul, mind and body needs. That sub-personality can be like the governor in a steam engine, to let off pleasure, or re-balance the ego, or give the personality the difference and strength to carry on with life. It can be very positive for that time. But there may be inherent dangers in letting a sub-personality get out of control: memory loss, the sub-personality can totally split away, and creative energy can be misplaced – and this type of experience can create a lot of creative energy, as you and I both know.'

I asked why Lucien thought these experiences he was hearing about were not objectively real, as presented.

'The responses people make to me under hypnosis are not correct for that situation. The terror is a different type of terror. The personality reacts in a totally different way when I'm dealing with abductions. I need to do more work to be able to comment with authority, but so far that is my conclusion. And I'm very used to dealing with strangeness. The "something" that isn't real is that the person doesn't feel it as vividly as reality.'

Given that Lucien had confidence that it was possible for hypnotherapy to work as a research tool, I asked what technique he used:

'I deliberately split the personality, disassociating the

part that causes the bulimia, self-mutilation, the bad habit, or whatever. I isolate it, split that part away, do therapy on that part, I can even regress that part [alone]. I communicate with the unconscious, getting permission from the ideo-motor responses [IMR] to split that part further. It can go on and on and on like Russian dolls if we need to. My job as a therapist is to make absolutely one thousand per cent certain that every part of that personality is put back together. I use various techniques: bringing the levitating hands together in the air, strong visualisation, making the personality come together as in a ball, the person bringing the ball back inside themselves. It's a fairly standard kit, I haven't developed these myself but I have elaborated on them.'

Keeping contact with the hypnotised subject is important, and ideo-motor responses, already mentioned, are useful:

'This is direct communication with the unconscious mind. Never regress anybody unless you have got the co-operation and permission of the unconscious mind – the unconscious mind always protects the conscious mind. It is shown by outer signals: finger movements asked for and received, and so on.' I have seen Lucien use this technique very successfully.

Lucien also brought up the subject of 'missing time', according to some researchers the key to 'discovering' abductions:

'Everybody has missing time every single day,' he pointed out. 'Could be minutes, could be a few seconds. There are times when we disconnect ourselves with our surroundings. Familiar road journeys, train journeys and so on. Go into a trance in a lift, watching TV. It's totally natural. Can be a little fantasy; fantasy produces endorphines which release stresses. Missing time is probably very healthy; it is a stress release, another governor on the steam engine.'

Getting to the more intricate details of abductions, I asked Lucien to reconcile his theories with the so-called physical evidence, such as the claims of implants:

'I do not believe in them,' he said emphatically. 'They don't exist. I think it's codswallop. People can create sensations in their body if they believe there is something there. Then you can "be aware" of where that implant is. The more you believe in the implant, the more you can "feel" it.'

Why then, I asked Lucien, are we seeing a standardisation of the abduction phenomenon? My own opinion had been for some time that researchers were carrying the abduction stereotype around in their heads, and unconsciously directing witnesses' recall. Lucien agreed this could be the case.

'They use embedded commands like, "But what if *it was real*?". This is a command to make it real. And don't underestimate the effect attention, the care of a loving and famous person, author and so on, can have. When in a trance witnesses can access their own creative resources themselves, they will become creative. You cannot believe everything people say in a trance.

'I'm a modern hypnotist, a connectionist. Connectionism holds that the memory doesn't lie in a particular locale in the brain but is stored all over. Emotion colours the picture constructed from all over the brain. Emotion triggers off the memory response, not the other way around.'

Lucien has joined me in a series of experiments where we wanted to discover just how easily a witness could be led. These experiments were videotaped throughout, and the first subject was Tony. He was put into a very light trance state, just enough to free his imagination to be creative.

Tony had been part of a team that had 'learned' from

the researchers the totally fabricated details of a race of tall aliens from Jupiter. Under hypnosis he was able to recall an abduction by these aliens, with graphic details of their encounter at Canary Wharf, on the River Thames, and a medical investigation by the aliens. Impressions from the room seemed to affect him: the aliens he described turned out to be wearing cowboy boots, and one of the people in the room was in fact wearing cowboy boots.

Another, later, experiment attempted to see how easily a witness could be 'turned around' in their recall. Again, the 'witness' – Annice – had 'learned' the details of a false race of aliens. She described them as evil, doing bad things. With slight encouragement, prompted by my written suggestions, which Annice could not see, Lucien indicated a religious overtone to the event, and a benign reason for the alien intervention. Very easily Annice adopted the view that the aliens were friendly and became quite comfortable with the abduction.

'We've shown how easy it is to lead the witnesses,' Lucien concluded. 'And how easy it is for the witness to lie under hypnosis.'

17 Not Always Painless

The effects of a UFO encounter are not always up-lifting, however. This case concerns a man who had an experience shortly before he became a teenager and who could not discuss it for the next fifteen years without tears and distress. He was helped enormously by James and Lorraine Parry, who introduced him to me. By the time we got together he had a more positive attitude towards his life; nonetheless he was frank about the suffering the experience had caused him. Throughout my long interviews with him he was always passionate and tense about the sighting, particularly whenever he forced himself to search in his memory for details. The sighting might not seem too dramatic – at face value it is nowhere near as extraordinary as many cases in this book – yet the effects on 'Mark' were all too dramatic. Close encounters are always complex experiences to come to terms with; this case shows that better than most.

'MARK'

The witness was 27 years old at the time of our interview in April 1993. The primary incident he related took place when he was around eleven or twelve years old.

We are using the pseudonym name 'Mark James' for

him. His case has been touched on in other books where another pseudonym was used; I have changed it because the other people involved in the other release of the material have since decided that they do not want further public exposure and both Mark and I wish to respect that.

'It was the summer of 1976, around July, I think. Prior to the sighting I was with a friend [pseudonym "Charles"]. I used to live along —— Road which [overlooks] a primary and secondary modern school in ——. I was walking up through the school grounds to get to my house. [Where] I lived, I had a view of the school. [When I got home I went to the kitchen] to get a drink of water. My friend was outside in the driveway and I can distinctly remember staring at these [window] blinds and my friend shouted to me, "There's a UFO outside." The kitchen window faces away from the school, by the way. So I put the glass of water down and instantly ran out. I had no thoughts of UFOs, flying saucers or anything at that time so I basically went out to discredit [his claim]. And, over the school, there was a hemisphere. It must have been quite big. It had three windows in front of it.

'[It was] right over the school building, above a box [like] construction on the roof.'

Mark and I discussed the shape of this for a time and decided it was probably something like a central heating vent, or cooling tower. This was the name we adopted for ease of discussion. There was one on the roof of both the primary and the secondary school.

'I asked [my friend] two years afterwards: "Did we actually see something? What did we actually see?" I wanted to know if he saw it. He said "yes", [but] he saw something different to me. He didn't see a hemisphere or anything like that. He saw a white light. [But] I saw a specific thing. This sighting literally blew away everything in the space of about two minutes, one or two minutes. Everything. I never had any belief in flying saucers before and this is why [the event] traumatised me. I was seeing something which I couldn't comprehend. Still can't comprehend.'

I asked Mark why he thought he and Charles did not see the same thing.

'No idea. I felt, in a way, let down because he just saw a white light [but] I saw something much more "fleshed out". I saw something much more; I saw three entities inside it as well. There [were] three windows. The two entities in the middle window were indistinct but I knew they were moving, I knew they were figures. But one figure in the first window was actually staring at me and this is what [traumatised me].

'The thing was over two hundred yards away. It was hanging over the school and must have been about forty or fifty feet in the air. It was about twice the size of the cooling tower, [which] would have been about twelve feet.

'There was no distance between [me and the entity]. I could see the face up front in detail. There wasn't a "zoom effect". I knew there was distance involved but I could see it as [clearly as if] I was looking through binoculars. There was no distance, I could see it like I'm staring at you.'

This was interesting. In our discussions Mark made it clear that he was experiencing a kind of 'double' perspective. He was seeing the face right up close while still knowing he was 200 yards away. Mark had been introduced to me by Lorraine Parry, and she had made an exactly similar claim in her story [related in this book]. Yet Mark had been unaware of that, and it was not something I had commonly heard of. At an appropriate time I mentioned Lorraine's report: 'I have known Lorraine for a number of years, since about 1987. James [then Lorraine's friend] has known of my sighting for fifteen years. I didn't know of Lorraine's sighting at all [and] Lorraine didn't know of the sighting that I had.'

Mark seemed pleased to hear this. As he said:

'I just basically want reassurance and confirmation that it does happen to other people as well.'

We went back to discussing the sighting:

'[Of] the actual craft that was over the school, there were two things about it which I picked up on immediately. One was the actual face which was very close; it wasn't invading my space, it was at a comfortable few feet from where my vision [seemed to be]. The other [thing] was the fact that [on the outside surface] I think the left-hand [side] was [a] graduated red colour and on the right side where the windows [were] I think it was a blackish colour. In the middle there were colours which were the most brilliant colours I have ever seen in my life. And they were merging into each other. And that mesmerised [me], that was the thing that struck me the most. I saw the colours first before I actually saw the entities inside. That was the thing I picked up on. When I met James for the first time he picked up a glass figurine of a chicken which had different colours in the glass, and he held it up to the brilliant sunshine. That was a way of describing it. It was almost like that; a vivid colour, almost alive.

'The only other brilliant colour which I have seen like that lately is in the last few years [when] I have had about six migraine attacks. The actual colours of the migraine attack weren't as intense as the colours on the UFO but that's the closest that I can pick out with the same kind of dazzling brilliance.'

I asked the obvious question, whether Mark thought that a migraine attack could have been a factor of the sighting:

'No, I don't. The migraine aura is different to the colours on the UFO, I was simply making a comparison. It's only recently that I have had migraine, I have never had it in the past. The first time I had it, I think, was in 1989. I have been to the doctor's. I'm not sure [but] I think [the migraine] is because lately I am beginning to get more active creatively. I'm very creative; I'm a professional drummer. I draw and I write as well. This may sound [at a] tangent but I'm [also] left-handed.'

I asked why Mark had chosen to point these things out to me; he would not have been aware that this was an area I was studying:

'James said, "You must have seen it for a reason, it must have been there for a reason, and you must have been there at the right time at the right place to see it." I said to him, "I think they made a mistake with me."

'I personally think I was the wrong person at the wrong time to be there to see it, because it led on to other sightings as well. For a period of three years I was receptive. I was seeing [things] on a regular basis; it almost became like a requirement, I required to see different visual things. It was almost like I was addicted to the sightings, but I was frightened as well. Once I met James – who wasn't scared of them, I was scared – the sightings went completely. James was integral in helping me accept my sightings and not be so scared of all the bizarre things I was seeing.'

Mark made it clear that he connected his creativity with his sightings, but he wasn't necessarily grateful. He said:

'I have talked to [a close circle of] my friends about this. I said to them, "I want to be a mundane person, I want to be ordinary. I want to have a nine-to-five job. Nothing strenuous and nothing over-exciting to happen. I was denied that by my sighting and subsequent sightings, my first sighting completely denied [me] that. That's why I am angry. It seems strange, like reversed psychology, but I would have preferred not to have seen anything, I would have preferred to just go on my blinkered way. It was shown to me, it seemed, in a very brutal way [and] I didn't want it." '

Mark took up the details of the sighting again:

'After I watched the light display on the surface of the craft, my eyes went to the side of the craft and I was running up the road to avoid losing sight of it. [I forgot earlier that] I didn't describe it as actually moving along my line of sight. It went over the second cooling tower of the other school. At that time I was running up the road to see it. I passed two girls on the way. I think they [saw it, but] I wasn't concentrating on them at the time.

'As I was running [I made] actual eye contact, very, very briefly, with the entity. Although [it was] brief, I made a very detailed examination of the face, eyes and upper torso. The eyes were large. They were oval-shaped. They weren't the shape our eyes are; they were almost circular. And the thing is they [seemed to have] a very tiny dot of an iris. It was a pinkish colour. I don't know if the pinkish- colour iris was an optical effect caused by a reflection of sun on glass or its natural eye pigmentation. The skin was like a nondescript battleship grey. [It was] very thin, a spindly token musculature. It had a large head on such a thin neck.'

Mark again mentioned his amazement at the 'double perspective' he had had; it seemed almost to trouble him. I asked if he was thinking that he might have been on board the craft:

'No, I don't think I was on board.'

We discussed out-of-body experiences and whether or not he thought he could have been 'taken up' in that way, perceiving through his real eyes and 'astral' eyes at the same time.

Kenneth Arnold, the man who launched the 'flying saucer' into public consciousness

Betty and Barney Hill, two of the most famous abduction witnesses of all

Artist's impression of the
Adamski landings, the
first publicly claimed
encounter with alien
life. Accounts of this
event created the now
stereotypical images
of flying saucers and
Nordic-type aliens

Klaatu and the flying saucer
from *The Day the Earth
Stood Still*, a film which
did much to shape public
perceptions of UFOs

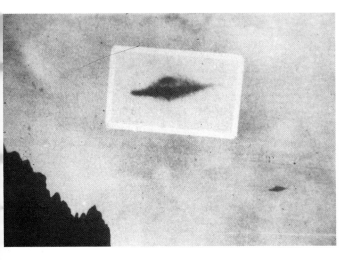

The Trindade flying saucer, attested to by over 50 witnesses. This photograph was released to the press by Joscelino Kubitschek, the then President of Brazil

The author (*at left*) with Roger Hooten who, after 26 years, admitted that his famous 'Thing' photograph from Warminster – which led many into UFO research – had been a hoax

The Mandelbrot corn circle appeared ten miles outside Cambridge in August 1991, intriguingly close to the site of the formulation of the Mandelbrot set, a fundamental principle of chaos theory

Kathie Davis (real name Debbi Tomey) has been the subject of a lifetime series of abductions

Peter Holding's art frequently imitates the swirling patterns which were a strong feature of his UFO sighting. Peter and his father (*above*) indicate the spot where they saw their UFO

Janice Georgiou (*pictured with author*) underwent an extraordinary blossoming of creativity, apparently as a direct result of her UFO experiences. Her quilted portraits of Elvis Presley and James Dean are rich in detail

Elsie Oakensen, who experienced a startling development of healing powers after her close-encounter experience

Ken Phillips, facilitator of the Witness Support Group, which helps witnesses come to terms with their experiences and increases understanding of the UFO phenomenon

Many people suddenly become more creative after a close encounter. Bryan, who had never drawn before his sighting, is now a commercial artist (*see above*). Rohan Hinton also became interested in art after her experiences; her drawings appear below

'It wasn't like an out-of-body experience. I knew I was on the road, looking directly at it.'

The passion that characterised most of the interview returned:

'I find it very hard to cope with this sort of thing. Those eyes were alive, they were living. They were cognisant/intelligent, they were completely aware that I existed.'

I made a note at the time, not discussed with Mark, that this was another thing that Lorraine Parry had said of her sighting.

'[This is] something which I find very hard to deal with. These entities were things which I never wanted anything to do with and suddenly I'm seeing something which . . . It wasn't an animal I was familiar with. I think animals are aware but a dog can only behave like a dog. But these things, they [had] intelligence. I thought they were very exquisite, they had an exquisite intelligence.

'I don't think for one minute that [the object] was a spacecraft. At the time, after my initial sighting my first taste of ufology was unfortunately ETH, but in retrospect, and even at the time I was viewing this thing, I didn't say, "Oh, there is a spaceship there." I couldn't think of it in those terms. I didn't have the mental vocabulary to describe it but intuition told me it wasn't extraterrestrial. I don't know what it was.'

We agreed to use the terms 'aliens' and 'spaceships' as a useful shorthand to avoid tortuous descriptions. However, Mark is very clear that he finds ETH, the extraterrestrial hypothesis, cumbersome and outdated.

'Even when I was exposed to my first encounter with "aliens" I felt deep inside that they didn't come from outer space.'

Mark went on to describe his period of sightings as an education.

'I had an education for three years through what I was seeing.' *I asked whether he thought he was being deliberately educated or whether he felt he created his own education from the experience.*

'The education process was my safety valve. I don't think for one minute that I was undergoing a deliberate and systematic educational schooling by "aliens". I was merely attempting to "make sense" of apparently "senseless" experiences. I was attempting to second-guess the next experience – which, to be honest, failed hands-down. Each new experience always consisted of elements not previously seen before.

'Please understand that my use of the term "education" quite literally translated means second-guessing!

'I didn't like being surprised by each novel experience, hence I tried to out-guess the next sighting, based on understood elements from the last.

'I do believe humour was involved in my sightings, albeit a very bizarre humour. This has to be stressed, because I can only make that presumption on the evidence I have witnessed, reluctantly. I don't mean our comedic or theatrical humour – please don't infer that – but just a potential for humour.

'I was getting that [for] myself. I didn't know the rules of the game so I decided to make a few myself so [that] I could comprehend what I was seeing. The aliens denied [education] to me. They didn't tell me who they were.'

The problem with repeater witnesses is that there can be a tendency to start believing everything is a UFO. It was Mark who brought up the point that people had asked him whether he could be confusing some of his sightings with airplanes, satellites and so on. His answer was very honest.

'I've said to them, "Goodness yes, I probably have.

One or two. I probably have." And I completely accept that. I have got nothing to hide about that. Of course I'll have mistaken one or two. Distant objects or whatever.'

But Mark did not put all his more distant sightings into the 'possibly mistaken' category. There was sometimes a quality which marked them out. He described:

'But other sightings I have had, like balls of light in the sky, I know when it's going to happen. It's almost like a mental thing. It is almost like it suddenly "twigs". For example, years later I was in the bedroom and I was drawn to open the curtains. As soon as I opened the curtains there was a ball of light, I saw it straight through the clouds. And that's happened on every occasion when I know it's a sighting, when I know it's real. It is almost like a calling card in a way.

'And also they move differently; they move differently to any aeroplane. Aeroplanes seem to move in almost like a jerky fashion, I know what they look like. I also know what helicopters look like as well. But the balls of light which I have seen [have] more of a smooth [motion]. And [these lights] are more intense than aircraft lights. If it's a white light, it's almost like a firework light, like if you see a white phosphorous. They go from A to B in a very purposeful way, a very, very fluid motion, a very fluid motion.'

I asked whether he felt the compulsion to open the curtains was a deliberate message to him, as several contactees have suggested.

'No, I don't take [these compulsions] personally. That's something which I have grown up with now. I don't take them personally. When [these lights] are in the neighbourhood, I think that when they become solid, they can use whatever material is available to become solid. I don't mean just blinking into existence

193

because they were undetected, a proto-UFO, [but they get their] mass together; they convert energy into mass. It's that process of solidifying that I think I pick up on. That's when I notice it's going to happen; I don't think it's personal whatsoever.

'When the mass/energy conversion is operating, a receptive person will perceive it happening. *By accident.* It will be perceived like hearing a car engine starting in an empty street, or switching a light on in a dark room. You cannot avoid hearing an engine starting in an otherwise quiet neighbourhood, or avoid seeing light generated from a switched-on bulb.

'*That is what I meant.* When I hear a car starting, I don't think: "I am interacting with the car"; it is just that I come equipped with ears, and thus am able to perceive it and experience it.

'Given that, a proto-UFO is a very loud experience waiting to be "picked up" by the person with the right visual/cortex/psychic qualifications.

'Migraine/left-handedness/epilepsy *do not* cause people to see UFOs – not in a million years. That implies that UFOs are just biochemical apparitions stimulating the perception centres of our brains [which is an incredibly wrong assumption, it implies that UFOs are hallucinations].

'But whatever is causing migraine conditions in the brain is just one of a list of conditions that make that brain more open [receptive] to a completely new and completely inhuman "alien" external force.

'I think [the lights] are living things. I think they are purposeful, they know what they are doing. When we see them we just get on with dealing with them in any way we can. [But] they don't know the mistakes they make; that's the one thing which I bitterly hold against them.

'I think there is a relationship. [Just as] dolphins are drawn towards humans for some reason, [so] there is an affinity [with these living things]. However these things create themselves they are drawn to us. I think they get as much out of it as we do. The thing is, it can either be constructive or it can be destructive [but it just happens]; I don't think there is any choice in the matter at all. With these things I feel a relationship there. They certainly changed my life although I didn't want it.'

I asked Mark to fill in detail on some of these comments; why he hadn't wanted it, why he had been scared, and what he meant by 'the mistakes they make':

'I was scared of the fact that I was seeing something which throughout my early childhood I was led to not believe [in]. I was led to not accept them. Suddenly I am seeing aliens, suddenly I am seeing a UFO. I was incredibly frightened. There was nothing there to worry me, I wasn't under threat. And then my other sightings reinforced that I couldn't cope with [it]. But I want to see lights like [I saw on the surface of the craft] again; they didn't frighten me at all. [But] I was mesmerised by the lights; they were almost, like, drawing you in. It was the most lovely light display I had seen in my entire life. I have never seen anything like that. [Like] the surface of a cuttlefish. You know how they [the colours] blend in together. You know, it's on the contours of the body. That's what I was seeing. But it wasn't as if on the surface there was an independent light effect; it was almost like the actual light effect *was* the surface. The surface was actually responsible for it; it was almost like it was generated by the thing itself, by the craft itself. It wasn't incidental, it was a very essential part of the ship.'

Mark commented again on the education he felt he'd received:

'Because each sighting I had after that, after the first

sighting, it was almost like I was thrown in the deep end and for my own sake, for my own peace of mind; because I had nobody to turn to, I had to jerry-rig a framework based on prior UFO experiences. I had to go and do it on my own; to make sense [of it]. I didn't understand what was happening so I had to learn from it how I reacted to it. When it was happening I was remembering past sightings so I could look back and say, "It's scaring you again. OK, if it happens the next time like how far can it go? How far, how different can it go?" I was just basically trying to learn not to be frightened of them. That's the education that I meant, it was like picking up things from an earlier sighting to take with me to the next one.'

I asked if Mark thought that his experiences would have continued if he hadn't told them to 'go away'. Had he stunted his development by 'turning them off'?

'That was kind of on my mind, but I hadn't vocalised it before. That would make sense, actually. That would actually make a hell of a lot of sense because I think I must have put out such a strong reaction to the first sighting. I was raw and my emotions at the time were extremely red raw. I was reacting naturally to something I was seeing which I couldn't make sense of. I must have been giving a strong signal back, I must have been giving a hell of a signal back as big as they were giving me. A psychic scream. Yes, that would actually make a hell of a lot of sense. That's brilliant. That's something I couldn't have thought about. And something else I discovered was that each sighting is different. To me there was no common trend. If there was a common trend I would have been able to [deal with] the routine but even that was denied me. Because I couldn't see the same thing every time. It would have been great if I could because I would have been desensitised. I could have ignored it.

'I think there will be a time when it will come back. I think this has been building [up]. In a way just talking to you now is part of the process, like James said; it's a healing process for me. The reason why I have decided to speak to you is because I want to get it off my chest. And this is something else; I have got a responsibility to pay back now. I have got to put in now. I have got to contribute. Just by talking to you, I'm contributing. I'm paying my share back now. There's a debt in me which I have to pay back. It's an odd concept that. I have only discovered that recently.'

Mark wanted to explain some of his indignation about his sightings:

'It's impossible to ignore because that option has been taken away from you. You have to see it. There is no getting around it. If I'm having a sighting, it's visible, it's very immediate, it's very responsive and it's happening in the present and there is no way of ignoring it. But at that stage when it's just prior to happening, when it's about to happen, if I shut my mind to it it would harm me. It's like once the pin has been taken out of the grenade and you put your hand over it to suppress it, it's going to blow your hands off it, you can't stop it. It's almost like that. It's like something that's being set into motion. You have to see it to the end. If you interrupt it just as it's bubbling, [just as] it's about to explode, it's damaging. That's what I felt.

'I don't know if it's had a beneficial effect on me whatsoever. I see the world differently now. I have to see it differently. I never had an interest before. I like the [UFO] subject and I'm completely absorbed by [it] but, before the sightings, I could have studied history or something. But now I have got this interest. I still haven't found the answers yet but I am looking, and I think one day [they] will come.

'I'm making connections nowadays which I should have made then. I've got no pet theory. To me everything is valid, [including] extraterrestrial spaceships, [but] it doesn't have to be [that] at all.

'I read a hell of a lot of books during the three years after my first sighting. I could sympathise with the people I read [about] in the books very much, but they were having different sightings to me and I wanted something which I knew I could relate to. I didn't find that in a lot of cases. *Close Encounters* helped me through it. Since that came out it did me a world of good. I even bought it on video. It gave me a reassurance that others have these sightings – I am not the only one, I don't have a monopoly on UFOs. And the visual effects as well; they are very accurate. Douglas Trumbull, who did the actual spacecraft effects, actually with the lights, was very accurate.'

I asked Mark again what he had meant when he had earlier said of the aliens that 'they make mistakes':

'I think I'm one prime example. I am living proof of the fact that they made a bloody big mistake and that is the fact that has had such a powerful effect on me. They made a bloody mistake. They shouldn't have picked me.

'[But] it's obviously helped me, it has helped me. I think the creative side of me [wouldn't] have come about if I hadn't had the UFO sightings. I think it's indirectly linked, it's because my mind was expanded by what I saw. That's why I became creative.

'I think we share the same chemistry, [we have] certain things in common. I think we have been seeing each other for a very, very long time. I think they are very aware of us. They must be aware of us, of course. They are just as quizzical as [us]. They must be as curious about us as we are about them, and that's been going on for years. I can't name a date, I don't know, thousands of years, millions of years. I probably think it's millions of years. Mankind developing in tandem. I certainly think our ancestors saw them.'

Mark went back to describing his first sighting:

'When it [the spacecraft] was actually moving across the school it retained the hemisphere shape. But as it went close to the road at double the height of a lamp post, maybe sixty feet, it changed shape. As far as I was concerned by the time I registered it, it was a different shape. It was a different shape now but I hadn't noticed it changing. It became more of a dumb-bell sort of shape; smaller [one end] and larger [at the other]. But I think that was to do with perspective, I don't know if [one end] was larger than the other, maybe that's perspective because that [end] was pointing further away from me. I'm not entirely sure. And as it shot away it went darker, a lot blacker. I don't know if that was to do with the fact that it was moving away, but I think that it wasn't; it was a factor of whatever the surface was made of. It was caused by that.

'I remember distinctly as it shot away, that it covered that [very long] lane in the space of about two seconds. I was running along with it trying to catch up but it's like running after a train [that's already gone]. I just couldn't keep up so I stopped.

'Something I distinctly remember: once the sighting had finished my tension went. I was relieved, then I got excited by it. And then a day [or] two later I began to think "God, I think I'm becoming unhinged." I thought at the time, "I can't be mad because I'm too young to be mad." That was my logic at the time. I told my Dad about it as soon as I walked in straight after the sighting [but he had] no time for [it].

'I go back [to the site], [but] not to see [them]. I don't

go out to see UFOs because when I used to go out to see them I never saw them. It was just like I was trying to re-live the scene, trying to go over it in my own mind. What I was learning from my sightings was the fact that I wanted to observe, I wanted to behave in a [certain] way, I wanted to know how to behave. So I [am] basically [re-living] the sighting to calm down, to know how to bring myself down. So I go along the lanes, I have a nice walk and I play it through my mind and I try to talk myself down. I have to do that, I have to show myself that I can actually walk along that lane again, they are not going to frighten me off.

'After that, I have put a lot of the sightings that I had out of my mind. I have forgotten, because I don't think of them now. I have learnt not to think about them. I like this; if I want to I can forget them and it's natural to forget. It's what shows me they were real, that I can forget them.

'I had further entity sightings but I don't remember them. I only remember one: there is a stream, it's further up —— Road. There is a brook, two large meadows on either side. On the left-hand meadow the grass disappears into thickets and trees. I was walking down the lane, I turned round and at the moment I turned round I saw, just going into the trees, a figure bigger than me. I saw it as a giant because I was small. But it was obviously over six feet. As I turned round it turned round as well, to see me. But the thing is it turned its head back and just went about his business not caring about me. I didn't interrupt it. I was just there. I saw no UFO. The only way I can describe [the entity] is [that its face was] very reminiscent of an ape face, but it wasn't an ape. Imagine an ape's face made out of some sort of flexible metal, or a bust made out of something very, very smooth which gets all the contours. [It was] very,

very slender. If it [had been] a person he would have been in very bad need of a diet. It was very thin but proportioned, it was proportioned very well. It was painfully thin [and] tall with it, very, very tall. It was a different figure to a human. It was human-shaped; it had two hands, two legs and a nose. I can't remember if it had ears or not.'

Mark returned to his chronology of sightings; he described the next 'phase' as 'cones'. It was about the strangest shift of gears I had heard of:

'It was just basically large cones in fields. Just standing there. It wasn't an artistic structure or anything like that. It was something in the field that I was walking past. These are the quirky things, you see, these are the ones which are almost deliberately quirky. Large cones in fields. They didn't look like a man-made thing, like a traffic cone or something. They became commonplace; these are probably the only things which I saw which stayed the same. I didn't go into the fields and touch them or put my hand against [them]. If I had they might not have been there, my hand might have passed through or something. But certainly from the roadside they appeared quite solid.

'[I can think of] no purpose [to them] whatsoever. If it was to irritate me it didn't work because I wasn't irritated by it. I wasn't frightened by it. It's almost like a joke that you can't pick up on; it was like a kind of a feeling. I don't think [they were] a permanent structure in the field. They were medium size, like a medium-sized tree. Some of them were even smaller.

'They looked like tiny things, tiny cones, whatever. Very, very slender, drawn out. Almost like a glass. They weren't glassy, almost like a stretched glass. Very smooth and very polished. It was not the sheen you get from metal but more of a plastic. You get like a sheen, like a plasticky . . . It didn't look hard or metallic.

'And then I was gradually seeing less and less UFOs or lights in the sky, entities or cones. I was seeing less and less. And it was almost like in a way I was seeing less of things related to the sky. I was seeing more things related to [earth mysteries].'

Mark went on to briefly describe a variety of paranormal experiences; blowing out lightbulbs by thought, seeing auras, and so on. He assumes that the experiences were 'changing tack':

'I was focusing differently. It was the same thing, I think the same thing was there. It's just that it had to come through [differently]. I was expecting it through one door [so] it had to come in through another. It was exactly the same thing. I wasn't seeing it from a ufological angle; I was now seeing it like a paranormal thing.

'I had nobody to turn to and nobody to look up to and I needed a shoulder to cry on. I had none of that. I had to keep it all contained but I was like a bloody champagne bottle that had been shook up for two years. I had to keep it to myself so long. When I was given an olive branch my first reaction was relief and out of the relief came tears. That was my first reaction because I had somebody to listen to me who wouldn't laugh at me. That was something which I was wanting. [Mark was referring to James Parry and the members of the family he was spending time with.] Now I was in environments where people were listening to me, for once they were listening to me and I was scared. I was blocking it out. With every ounce of strength I had I was resisting it. I wasn't going to let it in. And then it began to be unhealthy for me, being in the —— family. It's almost like they were leading me astray. I don't mean it in any bad sense. [What] was bad for me was the fact that they were almost dictating the terms. [But] they weren't laying down rules or regulations or anything like that.'

Mark had great difficulty explaining exactly how he felt; clearly the experience had been a two-edged sword. It amounted to the family dealing with their own needs and Mark being unable to deal with his as he fitted in with them:

'I was shutting myself off from my own experiences. And to also be in an environment where other people are doing that as well – it had, like, a treble effect or a quadruple effect. It was almost like I was wearing a suit of armour and another suit of armour was being built around it.

'James understood that and he was the one who snapped me out of it. Very understandingly. He knew what was happening. I had a breakdown, I had a nervous breakdown. I was fourteen and I had a bloody nervous breakdown. I was approaching a point where I would have gone mad or something. I don't know what I would have done. I was reaching a flashpoint. James saw that and before it happened he took me back and said, "Don't go over that edge." He was the one that stopped me going. I would have been a mental case if I had gone over. He stopped that.'

After a short break we discussed some of Mark's other paranormal involvements. We started with the PK, blowing lightbulbs and such:

'It was never easy. I could do it on railway trains better than anywhere else. They used to have old carriages, the old rolling stock. It's almost like flexing. What I used to do was concentrate, not look at the object, but look at a point behind it. Never look directly at the object, look behind it. And what I used to do was, I can illustrate it better with the tennis balls, look behind the ball but think [back towards yourself]. And the ball would move. I was doing that with the lightbulbs. I was thinking of the direction towards me. And – bang!

'James reminded me that I actually hurt somebody by [doing] that as well. I actually felt very angry. Somebody was threatening me physically and I didn't touch them. But I felt like I would have and [they went down, hurt].

'I don't really draw but when I draw I have to be in the mood to draw. And it's the same thing with smashing lightbulbs. You have to be in the mood to smash lightbulbs for some reason. So it's almost like, it's such a big concentration that you can't go into it half-heartedly. You have to do it the whole hog.

'I think the state of epilepsy, migraines as well, is related. I'm not saying that a UFO encounter is an epileptic attack or a migraine attack. I just think that migraine allows you [to experience these things].'

Mark was keen to point out that he had wanted to speak to me after reading an article I had written about letting witnesses lead investigations. This attitude gave him the courage to come forward. I was glad to hear that witness-driven investigation was going down well somewhere – it doesn't always with UFO researchers!

Mark commented on the opinion of a friend who knew of his experiences:

'He said, "Well, you must feel very privileged." I could have thrown a chair at him. I really could. "Privileged?" I said, "It must be a use of the word privileged I have never come across before."'

18 A Toy to Play With?

W hy do most divorces arise during or shortly after family holidays?

Why do people all too often die shortly after retiring from work?

Why was there less civilian paranormal research during the years between 1939 and 1945 than, say, 1969 and 1975?

What have these questions got to do with corn circles and what, in any case, has any of it got to do with UFOs?

Read on . . .

Psychologists I have worked with in many fields agree that human beings need stress, and we need challenge. I have worked with several in paranormal investigation and experimentation, and they have seen how the paranormal can represent that challenge.

Psychologists in industry and training are agreed that eliminating stress is undesirable. They realise that 'good' stress can be a positive thing, a driving force. Bad stress causes irrational behaviour and withdrawal. Bad stress usually reflects a no-win or no-advancement situation. Modern training is not only about eliminating stress but about channelling it, understanding it, using it, and even enjoying it.

'Classes' held by companies for people about to retire always put great emphasis on not vegetating. Retiring people are advised to take up a hobby, join local societies and so on; indeed they often become more active after retirement than before! Most of the fatalities that arise within one year to eighteen months of retirement arise because the person vegetated, spending all day in front of the TV, and so on. Retirement can represent the end of challenge – with fatal results.

The divorce problem is slightly different. There is always strain and stress within families, but individual family members have their own 'space' – time alone or with selected friends – to work out their own feelings. Psychologists have recognised that desirable though family holidays seem to be, they are an artificial world where everyone is expected to play together in a way they normally do not. The result is usually that the holiday becomes a time when pent-up aggression comes to the surface – often with fatal results for the marriage. It boils down to the fact that people have no time to be challenged by their own desires, they force each other to face each other's problems. People do not just need challenge, they need challenge of their own making, or in which they have control over their own lives.

Why did we have less paranormal research during the war? Obviously because people had other things to worry about. When you lived with the possibility that your house could be a smoking ruin when you returned home (a greater fear than a reality, but it is our fears that we respond to, after all), when your children had been evacuated to strange homes in the country, and when your future was very uncertain, then you had little time for worrying about less immediate challenges. Equally, less paranormal research takes place in drought-ridden Africa than in the technological West. The answer is the same.

A motivational theory known as the 'hierarchy of

needs' insists that there is a ladder of needs all human beings have, as follows:

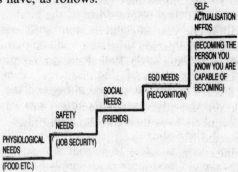

The rule is that you have to satisfy the lower-level needs before you can move to the next level; in other words you have to meet people's lowest-level needs for food and shelter from the elements before you can motivate them in any other way. (You cannot, for example, expect starving children to worry about their social relationships and to play with other children when they face a high probability that they will be dead tomorrow!) Having met basic needs, then people seek longer-term safety – usually in the form of job security – and so on up the ladder.

In the western world people's lowest-level needs have largely been met; the provision of food, shelter, job security and social needs. People now need to be recognised for their contribution to society, and so on – a higher-level need. In the technological west we are searching for ways to stretch ourselves to our full potential, physically, intellectually and spiritually.

That is where I feel UFOs came in.

Their extraordinary attraction came about because in 1947 the war was over, the Allies had won, and UFOs represented a problem, a challenge, that for a time allowed interested people to develop themselves intellectually. Germany and Japan were out of the way; there were alien invaders to deal with next!

But there is little challenge in constantly admiring distant blobs in the sky. Intellectual and spiritual challenges were needed. Intellectual challenge was provided by the development of the 'saucers' themselves – they got closer, they disgorged aliens and the aliens got threatening. Unfortunately the threat was very non-spiritual and suggested a need for 'Rambo-like' tactics to 'sort out' these aliens.

Attempts by contactees to introduce a spiritual dimension failed to meet inner needs simply because many found the claims hard to accept at any level, physical, intellectual or spiritual. So for a while the mutation of the UFO phenomenon thrashed around looking for something to turn into.

And in the 1980s it may have found something: patterns of circles in cereal crops.

Many questions about corn circles remain unanswered. The viewpoints of cultists are unacceptable to science but are important here. Many believe that the elaborate pictograms of the circle formations are a form of message. If this is a possibility, then these messages are complex; so complex that they are a challenge to our present understanding.

What seems fractionally more likely (though still pretty improbable) is that this unspecified intelligence is laying out Rorschach tests; certainly they have been interpreted in dozens of different ways, according to the predispositions of UFO researchers.

The last possibility is that, like the UFO phenomenon before them, corn circles are a form of intelligent message placed in front of our eyes so that something else can be done in the backs of our minds.

Unlike UFOs, crop circles stay around for weeks, even months, and despite opportunities for studying them everyone sees in them what they want to see. But established science is failing to 'make them go away' or explain them, leaving a clear field open for radical approaches that might offer a new lead to 'traditional' science.

Intelligent direction to the circles has been suggested by some researchers, such as Colin Andrews, Pat Delgado, George Wingfield and so on, and hinted at by others. We must work on the circles as we do on all areas of the paranormal: believe what is provable, do not jump to the exotic simply because it is attractive but do not put up so sceptical a barrier that the more exotic possibilities are filtered away from our studies.

Colin Andrews is one of those who believes there is intelligence behind the circles. In a video of his work, *Undeniable Evidence*, he points out that people have benefited from the circles. They have come together and developed friendships around the circles, they have been challenged by the patterns, and have developed personally as a result of directing their attention to the patterns. I suspect that Andrews believes the circles have some sort of non-terrestrial origin, but he's keeping his options open. The most important thing is that, wherever they come from, corn circles are an intellectual and spiritual challenge. Andrews finds his theories at odds with those of 'traditional' researchers, but both views and approaches are valid and important.

The circles may all be man-made; they may be natural and still a puzzle to be solved; they may be new energies we have yet to discover, which will perhaps assist us in our energy crisis in years to come; they might be a message from Gaia-Earth telling us to take care of our planet; they might be a message from the stars.

Research wants to know which, of course, and I hope that radical and traditional thinking can apply itself to find a solution without being too bogged down in 'traditional-only' thinking.

But it is the journey to the answer – not the answer itself – that is helping mankind to learn new ways of thinking. That is at least one 'message' of the circles. It is a message shared by UFOs.

This question of development can be illustrated with a couple of cases from paranormal experience.

'JAMES'

James and his wife were camping in Dorset near the Chesil Beach. In the middle of the night he had a call of nature and he saw what he thought at first was a farmer working in a field with orange lights. Thinking that that was unlikely (on the basis that the farmer would not be able to get lights into a field without power) he looked more closely and saw that the lights were moving off the ground in what he described as up-and-down motions. The words he used were 'balls in the sky'.

James called to his wife to see them. The time was 2.55 a.m. His wife said that she would go and get the camera and that they should make some tea, and then said there was a light behind him. When they looked they saw that the sun was coming up. It was 5 a.m.; some two and a half hours had passed 'just like that'.

His wife also noticed there were eight cigarette ends in a pile in front of her: the number that she would have probably smoked in two and a half hours. This would seem to indicate that whatever happened – 'missing time', or an abduction – her body was not only physically still present where it had been at the beginning of the experience but continued performing certain autonomous actions, i.e. smoking, throughout the time.

'These things make you think more deeply,' said James.

Janice Georgiou, whose case is outlined in this chapter, described how her experience made her develop personally: 'I have been reading and learning avidly since the event.' She added: 'This thing is supposed to make you think, it is supposed to aggravate you.'

Perhaps suppression occurs because a witness cannot put an experience into words. By reading and extending their vocabulary the person can then formulate expressions to describe the experiences, relieving the suppression and perhaps starting on the road towards better understanding. This may be a more effective research approach than hypnosis; certainly it suggests a possible explanation for the sudden burst of enthusiasm for reading, knowledge and expression that UFO contactees such as Janice often display.

CHARLES HICKSON

Charles is one of the celebrated American abductees. His case received worldwide attention when he and a companion, Calvin Parker, reported being abducted during a fishing trip, when strange, virtually non-humanoid creatures took them aboard a landed vehicle.

During an interview in July 1990 at the Florida International UFO Conference I asked Charles whether or not he had had any similar experiences since that 'main event' in October 1973.

'Yes, I don't know how to say this but these things know where I am and what I'm doing at all times. They keep track of me. Evidently they must have planted something on me or in me whenever I was first carried aboard that craft. Of course I don't know it all, you know. I've told the doctors about it [but] they don't know what to look for. But a daily communiqué was made – off and on – all the time. Mental telepathy.

'I have no way to contact them. In fact, all I can do is receive, I can't transmit. But all indications are to me that they are going to [reveal] themselves openly, they are going to come down openly within the next few years. There will be no doubt in anyone's mind that there are other worlds out there with life on them.'

I had heard that Calvin Parker had suffered rather more from the effects of the experience, and asked if he had had the same reaction.

'Oh, when one of those things took hold of Calvin he fainted. And he told me that he was sure – he'll tell you – that he believes he died. They frightened him to death and they brought him back to life. Now, I don't know. But they've done something to his mind. He has had a few nervous breakdowns since then and he is not all himself now. There is a time he is OK and there are times he is not.

'I don't think he had any real religious experience. His belief is he is a Protestant. He believes in God but I don't think he had any real [faith]. The way he tells me is that maybe it'd shrink his belief in God. I don't know. It did me. I am also a Protestant. Our family believe in God. But he did have some nervous breakdowns afterwards. And it wasn't fake, it was real.

'I am not afraid any more. I was truly afraid then because I didn't know what they were going to do with me. I had no idea. In fact I have never been as terrified in my life as when I was aboard that craft. I was afraid it might carry me away and probably no one would ever know whatever happened to me.

'Calvin was young; he had never known any kind of

real fear. Now, I have known fear, I had known fear many times. I was in the Korean war, I was twenty months and sixteen days in combat. And that's normal fear. Many times I have known fear. But this wasn't normal. This was something that just wasn't supposed to be. I guess that's why it frightened me to death.

'I wish I could talk with you to give you the overall picture of the way this thing has come to me. In fact just a few short years ago I talked with a lot of people. They recall now that I had been told then that communism was going to be a thing of the past but they laughed at me. Because then we were expecting war almost any time with Russia but it's all coming to pass now, you know. Oh it's good, there's peace coming back into the world. It's a moment for peace. [This was recorded over a year before the start of the collapse of the Soviet Bloc was evident.] I also stated that it was told to me that there would be a worldwide organisation that would begin to do something about the environment. That's beginning to happen.'

'We had to do this too because what has come to me is that when we were almost at war with Russia, we had all that nuclear power and the weapons in Russia also. What we have done, we have created something that we can't control. We have created something that would literally blow this world apart from its axis. They couldn't allow that to happen.

'So when they come down it's going to be peaceful. They are going to let us know that they are out there. There's another world up there with life on it. And you know back when this thing first happened to me people were even afraid to talk about life on other worlds out there. Now it's beginning to be a common thing. They have brought it out in the open. I think what we are doing now is preparing this organisation for this meeting.'

I wondered what the after-effects of the experience had been; had the event caused a bond to form between Charles Hickson and Calvin Parker?

'Yes, it has. It's hard to explain what kind of bond it has created between us. I don't know, it seems like at times I can feel what he is doing. And that's strange. He'll call me or he will come out and see me. I feel when something happens, small things, some things happen to him sometimes, I feel it. I get in touch with him and those things happen. It's something that I can't explain, but it's something there. There's something else. I know you are familiar with [the case of] Betty Hill and Travis Walton. I went to New Hampshire when this happened to me and met Betty Hill and spent about three days [with her]. It seemed as if I'd known her all my life.

'I think [this experience is uniting people]. Travis Walton: when I met him, the first time I met him, it was the same way. Like we are brothers, we are real close like brothers and sisters. Something really happened to us.'

I have two young daughters. When they were around three or four years old they were highly competitive and did not play well together. Their conflict was fairly normal for that stage of development, the first stages of asserting themselves.

To encourage them to learn social interaction I tried a ploy.

One of their favourite television programmes at the time was *Thomas the Tank Engine and Friends*. The central characters of the programme are four train engines: Thomas, Henry, Percy and James. My children loved the series and frequently played games, acting out the stories. I did not tell them they had to play together; I gave them a toy to play with. I bought small models of each of the four engines and I gave two to each of the girls.

The trick was successful (as far as one small trick can be). My daughters were forced to play together if they wanted to act out the scenes from the programmes.

Consider the toy engines from my daughters' points of view. They were small train shapes. I know from my childhood that when I had toys like that I could smell the smell of the smoke-puffing engines; when they clattered over the floor I could hear them clatter over points. The trains were real.

What did my daughters learn about the trains? They probably *thought* they learned a lot about how real trains worked: how they turn on turntables, and so on. But what did they really learn about trains? Practically speaking, nothing.

What they *really* learned was social development. They learned interactive skills: generosity and sharing. They learned how to 'manipulate' others to make them compromise and trade, and in doing so they learned how to accept being manipulated while retaining personal dignity.

What would have been the result had I chosen a direct course? Suppose I had sat my three- and four-year-old girls down and said to them: 'You don't seem to play well together. You must learn to share, and to trade with each other; you must learn generosity and you must become more socially interactive.' They would not have understood or learned anything. For one thing they would have had no real concept of the terms I was using. They had not developed to a level where such terms were valid concepts. Particularly as children, we learn by *doing*. Secondly, my daughters would have no reason to shift from the way they were to what I thought it best for them to become. I could not have demonstrated the benefits of becoming socially interactive without them experiencing it for themselves. Not knowing how much fun sharing can be, they would have missed out.

As a trainer in management development for industry and commerce, I know that it is only recently that training organisations are have begun to copy principles which my partner and I understood many years ago. The many books that 'teach' you to change your behaviour ask you first to change your 'inner self' (attitude, emotions, et cetera) and promise that you will then change your behaviour. It doesn't work that way. People leave such training courses feeling good, but asking the question – albeit subconsciously – 'But what do I do today that is different from what I did yesterday?' Our training reverses that idea. We teach people how to change behaviour; the 'inner transformation' automatically follows. Teach someone, even just mechanically, to speak in front of a group of 500 people, and you never need to teach assertiveness training – buy one, get one free! By teaching my daughters to change their behaviour their character change was natural, and permanent.

Of course my girls would have learned such skills eventually, probably when they went to school; but I was able to accelerate the process by my intervention. I was also able to prepare them better to handle such situations when they arose at school. This demonstrates a very important tenet of learning: for effective learning you do not teach, you develop in your students the desire and the ability to seek out the answers *for themselves*. Further, you let them have the thrill of *discovery* for themselves.

Perhaps most significantly for this analogy of the UFO phenomenon, you teach people to *want* to learn by *developing their curiosity*.

Has the UFO phenomenon given us a toy to play with?

Are we being presented with a tantalising series of

toys? Are we being left to do with them whatever we will, while subliminally learning to develop skills that will make us a more developed people? Skills which we presently have no real concepts for, and so cannot understand? Skills a vague inkling of which arouses in us concepts such as 'cosmic vision', 'wholeness with the Earth', 'oneness as a race' and others?

And what of the toys themselves?

Are they sometimes physical, as the toy trains are and as some UFOs seem to be?

Some toys are not physical; television programmes are electronic images created for sending messages directly into the brain. Are some UFO sightings images for transmission directly into the brain? Some certainly seem to be.

And are all toys nice? Or 'good'?

The answer is *no*, even though they are presumably all designed to be. I am again able to draw from an example with my children. In one case I bought them a ball; they played with it and one of the pair got smacked in the mouth and was hurt, and cried. The toy hurt her, but it wasn't designed to; it just happened that way. Many people have suffered, or seem to have been hurt, by UFOs. Perhaps that was never intended. In some cases people seem to be more afraid of the phenomenon than is reasonable, given even the anecdotal material on offer; that is no different to many children's reaction to toys. The unknown is always scary – but overcoming our fears is what makes us develop.

JANICE GEORGIOU

Janice Georgiou has experienced an extraordinary range of paranormal events that have had both positive and negative effects on her life. Her first encounter took place at the age of thirteen.

'It was around 6 or 7 p.m. one evening in November 1962. It was dark outside because it was wintertime. I had a strip electric fire high on the wall in my bedroom. It was switched off at this time as I was only allowed to have it on for half an hour while changing for bed . . . And I had already done that and remembered switching it off.

'As I was not allowed to have my light on either, the only light in my room came from a street light outside which was not close, as my bedroom backed on to other houses.

'I kept a small torch that my parents were not aware of and often used this to read under my covers at night.

'This particular night I was a bit fed up due to a misunderstanding with my father and also a bit cold so I climbed into bed with a book and went under the covers for a read.

'After a short time while still under the covers I had a strange feeling that I was no longer alone. I was gripped with fear. "Maybe it's Dad. He will find out about the torch, take it away, I'll pretend to be asleep." I quietly switched off the torch. Carefully stretched out, pushing the book under me but remaining still with my face covered by the sheets, I could still feel a presence. Eventually curiosity got the better of me as it always did and I had to take a look. As I slowly poked my eyes out of the cover I noticed the fire on the wall to my right seemed to be lit up blue on the bar. It seemed to fill the whole room with this funny kind of blue light. There was a sound that seemed to come from it. The light appeared to glow brighter and brighter until it looked as if it would explode and then suddenly it was gone.

'I then noticed on the ceiling on my far left there was what appeared to be a reflection of water in a glass moving around but there was no water, mirror or anything else that could have created that effect and it could not have come from outside.

'As I watched it some silvery kind of liquid appeared to be falling from that patch. It fell lightly, never touching the floor, until it formed the shape of what appeared to be a seven-and-a-half-foot man covered in some kind of artificial skin. There was no sound, I don't know how I thought it was a man because there were no features that I could see. He then spoke directly into my mind: "Don't be afraid, I am your guide." I could not move apart from my eyes and my mouth; I was frozen at this point and not from the cold. I don't think it was fear because I remember not feeling frightened, only curious. Maybe whatever it was had somehow put me into this state. When he spoke I remember thinking, "How come it has taken you so long to come back?" So the thought crossed my mind that somehow I had encountered this visitor at an earlier stage of my life and could not remember it at all. I felt very angry at him for leaving me for so long. I did not say this verbally, I thought it but he picked it up.

'With my movement still restrained he continued to speak into me. Then something else happened which did not seem logically possible. [Janice drew me a sketch of her room.] The bed seemed to change position, and either the bed became smaller or the room larger, but we know that isn't possible, don't we? Then a large circle from a beam of light appeared on the floor straight ahead of me. It manifested into a miniature city under glass. It reminded me of the glass dome ornaments with snowflakes in them that you shake. And all the time I was being told by the entity that this was the first part of my lessons and he was showing me something that I should recognise. I was still unable to move and I did feel at one point like shouting out but although I was able to open my mouth no sound would come out of it. I think I actually felt a tear in the corner of my eye at that time. I don't know if it was the cold that caused it. I was able to see and I could see everything that was going on. I then saw a tiny head pop round my door which had been ajar: it was my younger sister. Then she was gone. I don't remember the entity going away or the room retaking shape, I must have fallen into sleep. I woke up thinking it must have been a dream, but so real. When I went down to breakfast my younger sister asked me, "Who were you talking to in your room last night and what was that toy on the floor?" I told her I was not talking to anyone – we were never allowed friends in the house. Although she persisted, saying that she had heard a man's voice and that it had woken her, I suggested that she must have been dreaming or sleep-walking or something. It was then that I began to realise that something real had taken place and I was looking forward to the next visit. As the events of the night before fully came back to me I had to stop her from talking about this to my parents, I was so scared that I would get into serious trouble if they found out.'

Janice describes some detail of the contact with the entity as his visits become more regular:

'He wanted to discuss "The Book", the Bible. He told me that it had been written by many people over much time and that it was not the work of one man, each person giving their own sometimes theoretical view of what had happened in the past and things I did not even know about then. For example the cloth that covered Jesus when he was placed in the tomb [this was long before Janice had ever heard of the Turin Shroud]. He said it was an item of truth for the future.

'The entity and I had this sort of learning game we'd play. It began by my writing a list of twenty questions that I could ask him. If there were any that he was unable or not permitted to answer then I could ask for the same number of visual explanations to the questions he could answer.

'He would then ask me twenty questions related to all kinds of things and for every question I could not answer he would not visit me again for that amount of days.'

Janice is sure that this was a very real teaching experience. Others might argue that it was a way that she created of teaching herself. Either way, it is the clearest example I have seen of how contact with the paranormal can become a toy for self-development.

'These visits and lessons continued for quite a while. I left school at fourteen and home at fifteen. I never learnt anything at school. Any knowledge I have gained has been through my experiences. In fact without the experiences I am quite sure I would be illiterate. I would not have any interest in maths, history or anything like that.'

Janice went on to make her first comment about needlework, which is now one of her major forms of expression:

'At school I was an absolute disaster in the needlework class and in art, I could only draw stick insects. I am no good at drawing even now. But I can transfer any picture into cloth, any size, completely accurately.'

Janice confirmed that this needlework ability arose from an experience shortly after the death of Elvis Presley. This is a facet of Janice's story we will come to later.

Janice told me that these contact experiences continued but she has never seen the dome again and has had no contact with the male entity for about the last ten years (prior to my interview in 1993). Although she had not

*been in contact with her guide she confirmed, however,
that he had been replaced and that her experiences continue to the present day and that they continue to be
beneficial to her:*

'Say I'm doing something and I can't find a solution,
I want to know which way to go. I ask, "How shall I
do this? Which would be the best way for me to do
this?" And then I am questioned as to the reasons why
I can't work it out for myself. Now a lot of people might
say, well, that's you answering yourself.'

*That was my thought too. I thought it almost humorous
that while some contactees get knowledge given to them,
Janice – who admitted she was argumentative – got an
argument. I asked Janice why she did not think that would
be the case.*

'Because of all the contacts I had had for so long. I've
gotten used to them on a daily basis. They are like close
friends to me. They have names which I did not give
them and if I had the answer to the questions I had to
ask, I would not ask the question. When the advice
came back to me I acted on it. Sometimes I don't even
need to ask for advice. I am simply told to do something, and even though the suggestion is sometimes so
ridiculous I still do it and maybe after a few months I
find out the reason why it had to be done at that time.
One Christmas I was preparing the meat ready for
Christmas Day dinner. I was advised by my contacts to
prepare and serve an extra dinner for the Christmas Day
dinner table. I did as I was asked and just as we sat
down to eat there was a knock at the door. It was a
friend we had not seen for some time. He was amazed
when we invited him to stay for dinner to see the plate
in front of him ready prepared ... Everyone was
amazed.'

I pointed out to Janice that this could well be imagin-

*ation. She agreed that it had been suggested by others,
however, she was certain that it was not imagination
because the contacts had a quality of reality she has confidence in.*

*Janice then went on to describe her contact with three
female entities with which she has had contact since the
last visit from her guide.*

'They all have names and they all have places where
they reside. The first of the female entities that I had
contact with is known to me as Orthena (she says the
name means all things). She told me that there was a
planet on the other side of the sun where she resides.
The second is her half-sister Thethronne (her name
means The Throne). Both of these entities are very human-looking but without ears; Orthena has black hair
with highlights that make it look almost blue and
Thethronne's hair is very long and gold in colour. The
third entity is Christy, she lives on a huge vessel about
three hundred miles long. I've actually been there in a
visual lesson, I've been underneath it. I've seen ships
and planes clinging to the under-chassis. It reminded me
of a scrap yard. Actually there was a battleship that was
underneath it. I don't know how it stays there but it is
just stuck to it. I have seen the inside also. Many things,
many stories.

'Christy is the most interesting. She isn't completely
flesh. She has body shields underneath her surface and
the joints in her body are not bone. I don't think she
has bone. She is the one that I daily talk to because
she has a great way of helping me work things out. To
talk to her you would think she was a little girl but
she has great intelligence. I ask her lots of things. I still
have the ability to ask for a visual lesson. It's easy, I
just lay down on my back and close my eyes. On one
of these occasions I wanted to know about what was

on the surface of Mars. As I can go there in my mind, I can be taken there, I can sit on that planet. I can look around me and take in everything . . .'

Something of Janice's recall was reminiscent of the way 'Bryan' (another case in this book) describes his contacts. Janice was also giving me a fairly clear description of remote viewing, a paranormal claim under test in many areas of the world. Janice also had a visual lesson relating to the city that will come down out of the clouds, reminiscent of the Book of Revelations.

'I wanted to see it. I wanted to know what it looked like. I closed my eyes and I was there, I was outside this building and I saw it. There was no earth below nor sky above. I saw the entrances. I saw what it was like inside. I went up inside it, I was spoken to in there. I asked what it was for and I was told what it was for.

'All my female contacts are connected. They talk to each other. They are all very close. Christy talks to me about Orthena and she tells me where she is and where Thethronne is and what they are doing even though she is not with them in the same place.'

I asked Janice if she enjoyed having these contacts and if I could make them go away, would she want me to.

'Sometimes I feel frustrated by it because it's a part of me that I have to live with and I don't want to get rid of it because there is a reason for it. I know it can't be got rid of, I don't want the contact to stop. I have always felt I am living a double life. My contact told me right from the start that I was related to them and that I have been purposely misplaced in time for a reason. I must finish my education to the point where I will open memory banks I did not even know I had . . .'

Any psychologist would recognise in this at least one alternative explanation to Janice's contact. The entities could be sub-personalities she has generated to develop herself. Her struggle to regain her memory would be a struggle to re-connect all the strands of herself. I do not feel that I want to challenge Janice directly with this interpretation, though of course I have discussed it with her. So long as the entities or sub-personalities continue to be beneficial then it would seem harmless. She is now working with Lucien Morgan, a clinical psychologist, to try to understand more about the experiences, whatever their origin.

Janice also describes how paranormal experiences helped her to develop artistic expression through appliqué, and a link to the late 'King' of Rock-'n'-Roll, Elvis Presley.

'When I was young I was always into rock 'n' roll. Obviously Elvis was a great singer, but Cliff Richard was my favourite because I knew him. When I heard Elvis for the first time I got a funny sensation inside. I felt related to him. I followed his career.'

I pointed out that the world is full of fans who have expressed extraordinary closeness to that particular singer.

'Yes, but not in the same way.'

Janice never actually met Elvis in life but she felt for him and had been concerned about his wellbeing when he was cloistered in Graceland with the friends who became known as 'The Memphis Mafia'.

'I'd go down to sleep and I'd feel that Elvis should have someone with him to take care of him because he had got real problems. Somebody could stab him in his sleep. I used to really lose sleep over that. So I was, in a sense, obsessed. But it wasn't like an obsession, I didn't worship Elvis Presley. In fact I didn't really have a great collection of Elvis records either. I bought Cliff Richard records and The Shadows and stuff like that. But as the years went by I became known by the rockin' crowd as Elvis, they used to call me Elvis. That was my nickname. Then, not now.

'When I heard that Elvis had died I took it very badly and I kept thinking to myself, "I never got to see him." I suppose I became what most people would describe as a recluse. I locked myself away. I was in one room and I had experiences and dreams where I spoke to Elvis. We walked in a garden and talked to each other and he made suggestions to me about things I should do. I told him that my life was so wasted, I do so many things but I don't get anywhere.

'I felt like one foot was nailed to the ground. He said, "Well you know, Elvis sells." That's what he said. I said, "I can't make money out of you." "Everyone else will," he told me. "What difference does it make?"

'So I said yes, but I would not know where to start. He said, "Well, you deserve something back for all you have given over the years." He was talking as if he had attended every one of the birthday parties that I had had for him. He even described the huge cakes I had made depicting him and more, so I said, "Well, I wouldn't know what to do." But I had been working on some small appliqué designs. It was a graphic design of Long Tall Sally in a square, ten inches by ten inches. I had made a long "L" crammed into the rest and then transferred the whole messy picture into appliqué using textiles. After doing more of these designs (all different) I joined them and made a bed cover. One night I put it on my bed and in my own way I asked Elvis what he thought of it. The next time I dreamed of him he told me that what I had done was good but he would like to see it much bigger. The next thing I made was Elvis life size in cloth. And I made many of them, wall hangings.'

Extraordinary appliqué wall hangings of Elvis hang all around Janice's walls; some are shown in the photoset in this book.

'It was in 1977 that we got the news of his death. By

1984 I had actually been a recluse for six and a half years. I just totally cut myself off and during that time I produced forty wall hangings depicting Elvis. Just as I think I was coming out of it I also did James Dean, Marlon Brando, and other legends of the 1950s.'

Three of Janice's artworks have been published in art books related to Elvis and Marilyn Monroe which have been distributed all over the world.

'Then things started to turn a bit weird for me. I had all these wall hangings. What the hell was I going to do with them? A neighbour suggested that I have an exhibition of my work. I'd never had an exhibition before, I was not sure how to go about it but where there is a will there is a way and I arranged two exhibitions, one in London and one in Toronto, Canada.'

I wanted to be sure that these very different experiences that Janice was describing were related. She assured me they were.

'I was told and have later read in a biography that Elvis himself was a witness, that Elvis was a descendant. They did not say of what, they just said a descendant. And that he had been special and gifted. I asked why I felt so close to him most of my life and I was told that I did not need to know the answer to that question "yet" so I did not pursue it any further.'

Janice described a 50th birthday party for Elvis where she had baked and iced a huge cake in five segments, spelling out his name.

'A TV crew were interviewing me and Dave ["Screaming Lord"] Sutch. We were standing over to one side of the hall. There was something going on on the stage, an Elvis "soundalike" competition. I have never been keen on Elvis impersonators and try to avoid them, so I wasn't really interested in what was going on. But then suddenly the competition was over and they

227

put an Elvis record on. As soon as they put this Elvis record on all the camera crews rushed to the stage as if something had happened. We then all rushed to the stage as well to see what was happening. It was then that I realised that the competition was still not over and that the song I heard was not a record by Elvis, it was Billy [now a client of Janice's] and he was laying on his back singing on the stage. You could not see him because he was laying on the floor. It was phenomenal. People were on their seats, they were screaming, women were crying. I looked at Billy and thought I saw something. There was a moment there when he was on the stage that something happened.

'Something definite happened. He looked at me, I looked at him and I felt something good. I felt that I knew him. But I had never met him before having come to London from Wigan. As he was leaving the stage I approached him asking him if he had a manager. He said, "No". I said, "You are going to need one." I gave him my phone number and address and told him to give me a call. He arrived at my house the next day insisting that I manage him. I did not want to become his manager – I had no experience – but he insisted. I invited him and his friends to stay for a few days. On the second day Billy came to me and asked if he could speak to me privately about a problem he had. "It's my voice. It's not me." I said, "What do you mean?" He said, "I can't sing any other way, even if I sing a song that isn't an Elvis song I sound like Elvis singing it." '

I asked directly if Billy thought he was channelling Elvis vocally. Janice didn't know, but clearly believed that it was Elvis's voice Billy was using. She told me that if I heard Billy singing I would be stunned. I asked if we could do just that and Janice was delighted to set it up for me. For over an hour I listened to Billy singing Elvis songs in

*a small recording studio on their premises. I have a lot of
Elvis tapes and CDs and frequently play his music in my
car so I am fairly familiar with the sound. I wouldn't want
to put an interpretation on it but it was impressive. For a
while Billy sang while the same song, by Elvis, was playing in the background and there seemed to be no vocal
separation. I had to touch Billy's throat a few times to
make sure he wasn't just miming. But, to be fair, the
world is not short of Elvis soundalikes and his voice is so
distinctive that copying is easy.*

*Janice went on to describe something like channelled
songs from Elvis:*

'I wrote a song which is supposed to be a message to
Elvis fans, from Elvis, if he could have given it. It is the
kind of message that Elvis would have given to his fans
if he could have done. I don't know how I wrote it. It
took just a few minutes to write, and since then I have
written sixty songs for Billy. All given in the same way
via dreams of Elvis. I suppose what I'd like to say is that
if Elvis had lived longer I think he would have done
those songs.'

*The implication seems clear: Elvis was somewhere in-
side Billy, and he was channelling his voice while Janice
was channelling his song-writing. I asked if Janice thought
that Elvis brought them together.*

'Yes, I really believe that he did. I'd be lying if I said
no.'

Just how much of Janice's story related directly to an
alien intervention, even by her own interpretation, is unclear. What is clear is that these 'other' areas are a vital
part of the fabric of her thinking. No understanding of
her alien contacts is possible without considering the
whole.

There are parallels in the claims of Swedish abductee

Gifts of the Gods?

Lena Backstrom, who has experienced a series of paranormal events in her life. 'It was after my close encounter that my ability became real strong and I turned into a psychic,' she said. Like Janice, Lena also 'used' the contacts to 'educate' herself. 'I call them frequently now because they have given me answers to many of my questions, and I don't know what would have happened to me if they hadn't contacted me.'

Time and time again witnesses have experienced a sudden blossoming of creativity or of psychic ability as a result of a close encounter. Peter Holding's experience, related in Chapter 22, is a further example. BUFORA's Ken Phillips, founder of a witness support group, is so convinced by this that his group is currently organising a roadshow demonstrating the UFO experience through art. Witnesses express their feelings through music, poetry and other artworks. 'These are very dynamic and creative people,' says Ken, 'constantly looking for ways in which to express their inner feelings, to share them with others, even if that means circumventing what they see as a conservative UFO fraternity.' I strongly believe that this is a phenomenon which demands investigation.

19 Alien Intervention

This chapter looks at four more cases of perceived alien contact. The claims of these witnesses are very similar to others in this book, and hundreds worldwide.

If aliens are coming to Earth, we might ask why they choose to contact the people they do. I can understand that aliens would not necessarily seek out politicians, whose power is short-lived and usually abused; in the West at least they would be lucky to find the totally non-corrupt. But such people do exist. Mother Theresa and Gandhi would, I think, be good examples of people with whom the aliens would have little trouble working, who might be well respected if they substantiated claims of alien contact. That such people do not claim contacts must indicate they have not been contacted. The pro-ETH lobby will argue that clearly the alien's game is beyond this reasoning – possibly true but a handy excuse also. Bertil Kuhlemann suggested that 'good' aliens would not want to hamper the work of people such as Gandhi, that it would have turned him into a cult guru which he would not have wanted. (Indeed, he shunned even the title 'Mahatma').

So let us accept that if aliens are involved, their game is subtle, and let us look at some of the people they have contacted. One thing becomes clear; the range of alien contacts is much more varied than 'abduction-lore' in America would have us believe. The various experiences of these witnesses show also that they are having a variety of paranormal experiences referred to elsewhere in the book. Are these experiences linked or does a sensitivity to the paranormal allow the witness to experience various types of sensations?

The first case relates to a young Englishwoman, Rohan Hinton, whose whole family has a long history of alien intervention.

ROHAN

'I have always been aware of UFOs. My mother says she saw cigar-shaped ones years ago and my uncle Chris talked about an experience that happened at the age of nineteen when a UFO stopped and he spoke to the occupants. He learned that this wasn't his first experience.

'I've always had a feeling of being creeped out, being spooked out, but then I have had other psychic experiences which have upset me in a similar way.

'We were on a beach in Delaware. It was August 1987. I was sixteen. I had gone out with one of my uncles and his wife; the rest of the family had gone off to the beach.

'I went to the beach with my uncle and his wife and I just had this strange feeling that someone was watching me over the ocean and as we were walking away from the beach I had to keep turning, looking back over my shoulder because I was convinced someone was watching me. There was nothing there. We got back to the house and the rest of the family came in, which was about six [or] seven people, and they had all seen an orange triangle with green lights. I hadn't seen it, but I had felt someone watching me. [And I thought] "Oh no, I didn't get to see it. I have never seen a UFO."

'The next evening my mother and I were out on the beach. My uncle Chris and his wife were going to meet us. We were scanning the sky for [meteors]. One of the stars started to move at quite a fast speed. I said to my Mum, "Mum, I think that's a UFO. Mum, that star is moving." She [said] "Don't be stupid," and looked up. Then she said, "Oh, my God, you're right."

'And I got up and started running. I was so scared I ran off the beach. I left my Mum sitting there. And there were people around, people fishing. It wasn't late – eleven o'clock or so. And I found my uncle and we went back to find my Mum. [When we found her] she said, "Well, there were other people around, I guess we were safe enough."

'I was completely shaken by it. We sat on the beach but with my uncle Chris around I felt safe. A feeling really, I don't know why.

'And then we saw a tumbling disc; quite low down. One side looked almost luminous and white and the other side was like a matt, dull silver. My uncle Chris said, "That's what they call an unmanned probe." Whether he believes it, whether he really is that know-ledgeable about them, I couldn't say.

'That night I had a strange dream of being in a me-tallic place. But was it a dream or was it an experience? It wasn't really anything I could put my finger on.

'We had the same experience every night. We would be on the beach and first of all we would see the star that would move. And it was quite definitely a star; we could see the difference [from] an aeroplane. And then it would be followed by the tumbling disc. And I felt such a thrill like, "Wow, I'm one of those people, I've seen a UFO. Instead of [just] reading about it in the paper, it's me." And I also felt a warmth towards them [UFO pilots], and grateful in a way. Singled out, special.

'But a couple of days later in the afternoon I got very

angry at an incident that happened. The house we had rented was on the bay. People were fishing for crabs, which I didn't like – I was vegetarian at the time. [But] they were letting them go. But a couple came to visit us and they took a load of crabs and they proceeded to boil them. At which point I walked out of the house and I was crying and very angry, very emotional and [asking myself] "How dare they do that?" We had just eaten dinner, there was no need [for that extra food]. And I said to them, to the aliens: "Do you agree with that, do you think that's right? I think that's disgusting. What do you think?" And I was sitting on the step and a silver cylinder, completely flat, no wings, no tail, in a nice bright blue sky, came along, went ahead and I felt – it wasn't a voice, but it was a feeling of "No, we don't agree with that. We don't really think that was a very nice thing to do. You are right to be upset."

'[I called out] "Mum, Mum quick. Quick, there's a UFO." She said, "Oh, yes. Wow! That's a nice one." And my Auntie Pam [said], "Yes, great." Then it just disappeared; it came over, swept behind us and disappeared. [About] ten minutes later it reappeared; my uncle Chris saw it this time as well. Then it went again. But I felt it was as though it was in response to me, I had asked them and they'd answered me.'

I commented on the suggestion that a UFO potentially visible to others could be 'specifically' addressing one person. This was a claim Rohan was making, yet also one I had heard many times: contactees and witnesses in Sweden had made the same statements, and Elsie Oakensen in England had seen a UFO over a major road during the rush hour, yet which had not been reported by others; she felt it had 'selected' her. Rohan pointed out that others had reported her sighting – she had read reports in the local papers shortly afterwards. But she added:

'I believe that we have our own mentors up there. We don't get picked up by a different crew every time; we are specifically in tune with one [alien] person. [We have] a guide, that would be another description [of that alien person].'

I tried another tack, to be sure I was understanding what Rohan was telling me. I made the point that similar 'contact' or channelling claims are made by yogis, but there is a belief that you are 'getting in contact with your own higher self' – another level of your own consciousness. Rohan did not think this applicable:

'I can only say that people might believe that. I don't know. I don't believe it. I have always believed in aliens [since I was] a little girl, even though I hadn't actually seen anything. I think it's arrogance to assume that we are the only living things. There has got to be other people out there.'

I asked Rohan when she thought these aliens first made contact with their human 'targets'. The prevalent belief in America is that these abductions are a lifelong experience.

'Well, there are theories that they [the humans] are [selected] years before being born. My mother feels that maybe visits I had as a small child [of a grey lady] were them asking "Hey, we'd like you to be part of us, will you give us permission now?" and being a gullible infant [I had said] "Yeah, sure." Perhaps then it was no problem and only later I developed fears and inhibitions.'

There is a reaction against that feeling in America; abductees are protesting against implications by researchers that they have given permission for aliens to manipulate themselves and their children. Abductees feel this is making them unfairly guilty and that this is akin to blaming rape victims for the crime. Rohan knew of this and had read a report from an abductee who had said, with anger: 'I don't recall giving anyone permission to mess with me,

*my mind or my body.' But she was sure in her own mind
that while some 'single-event' abductees might be 'victims', the multiple-event witnesses had 'made a deal with
the aliens'. She believed that she herself had made such a
deal early on in life. She was not unhappy about that
although she admitted that when she was alone in her
home, late at night, there were times when she felt less
comfortable.*

*I asked Rohan about her sightings of a grey lady. It
seemed to me that here was some overlap between 'normal' contactee claims and the claims of ghost sightings,
though I didn't mention that connection to her.*

'I have vague memories of people coming into my
room at night when I was a small child. We lived [then]
in Herne Bay. My mother said I used to talk about a
grey lady very matter-of-factly. Maybe it was a ghost, I
don't know.'

*Rohan currently shares a flat with another woman. I
asked what her flatmate's views about this were, and
whether she was involved:*

'She was possibly part of just one "thing". I don't
know. She is not a non-believer – she doesn't disbelieve
what I say – but having never experienced anything to
her knowledge says, "I'll believe it when I see it." She
doesn't disbelieve. The opposite of my father; [he] gets
very angry. He [tells] me, "People will think you are
mad. They will have you put away. I won't talk to you.
Shut up." ' [Rohan's mother and father have been separated since she was very young.]

*Having got Rohan's background I asked her to take me
through more specific details:*

'I can tell you my first definite [contact] sighting. It
was in the summer of 1988, the year after I first saw a
UFO. We were again at the beach and it was just my
mother, my aunt and myself and we were in a motel

room. We were only there for a couple of nights. I was going through a stage of being completely horrified and terrified of the whole thing. I just couldn't sleep at night. I was terrified that they were going to come and take me.

'We had gone to bed. In the hotel room were two double beds. My aunt and I [were] in one bed and my mother was in the other one. I was sort of in the middle of the three of us.

'As I was going off to sleep the voice that I talked about before came into my head and said, "Don't worry. We decided that you are far too young and you obviously can't deal with it emotionally. You are getting too scared. We are not going to bother with you. You can live your life. We are going to let you get on with it." And it brought such an instant feeling of calm and relaxation that I just felt so soothed. I [said] "Thank you."'

Given several possibilities to account for this I asked Rohan whether she felt the voice could have been from somewhere in her own mind. She was sure it was not:

'No. It's very hard to explain. There is a definite difference between your own thoughts [saying] "Don't be stupid, go to sleep" and [this] voice appearing in your head. I instantly went to sleep and I felt really good.

'Then I woke up in the middle of the night and I was floating above the bed. And I could see red lights from the balcony French windows and the moonlight was coming through into the bedroom. I could see the hotel room quite clearly in the moonlight. It was dark but I could still see enough. And I was floating above the bed and I floated off and felt as though someone had hold of my arm. And then . . . it was like [a] jump . . . and I was lying on a metal sheet in . . . I don't know what the room looked like because I was surrounded by the grey people. A light was in my eyes and it hurt. [I kept asking] "Who put the lights on, who put the lights on?" And I was blinking because it was really hurting me. They were standing there and one [had] the expression of how you look at a child. It wasn't laughing, it wasn't openly smiling but it was a kind of smile, and [it was] warm [and] tender.

'It was real. I know they were around me. It was very bright and very sterile. I'm pretty sure that it was like a metal sheet table that I was lying on. I [knew] that they had taken me up now [into a UFO]. Then I got missing time [because] the next thing I knew about was floating down. I remember floating down in the room again and again there was a difference in the lighting. I was falling on to the bed and all I could think at that time was the light, the light. And [there was] just this feeling of "they lied to me" [about leaving me alone]. And then I went straight to sleep. When I woke up it was so vivid, more so than a dream. But on the other hand it wasn't that bad, [I wasn't] frightened at all. It was so weird.

'Maybe I made it all up, and it was a dream. The mind is a very powerful thing, I don't deny that. But I believe they gave me that waking, definite memory to soothe me, to stop me lying awake at night.'

Rohan went on to tell me about what she referred to as her next definite contact.

'I [was living with] my boyfriend who was my fiancé at the time. He used to get up about five o'clock in the morning to go to work. It was winter. It must have been November, December or January because it was still dark. He had gone off to go to work and I had gone back to sleep, or so I thought. My bedroom door was open. I heard someone moving around in the hallway and the hallway light was on again. So I assumed he [my fiancé] had come back because he had forgotten something. I yelled out: "Is that you? Is that you there?" And this "thing" came into my bedroom.

'I [was] lying on the bed, looking up. And it was there. Being flat on the ground I couldn't tell you how tall it was but from that perspective it looked tall and thin. It came towards me and my heart was pounding. All I could think was "Oh, my God. This is really happening. This is really happening." And then it came forward, it bent down and it touched me somewhere [on my neck] and I just felt as if I was falling backwards into darkness.

'The description [of the entity] more or less fits the greys [the picture of the Adamski alien]. I didn't really get a look at its face and head whereas when I had the other experience of the greys it was their faces – and of course, their eyes – that I was really drawn to. But this [perspective] was more [due to] the angle [I was at].'

I asked if Rohan was sure the creature was really there in the flat.

'I'm fairly certain. Of course it could be a dream [but] I think it was physically there. I [had] heard the noise of somebody moving in the hallway and the light going on. I think the noise woke me first, [then] seeing the light was on I assumed it was Andy, having forgotten something. Then it came in. I wouldn't even say it walked, it shuffled.'

Rohan does not remember discussing the incident with her fiancé, and said that at the time she hadn't felt able to discuss it with anybody.

The next incident Rohan related was 'classical' in abduction terms in that it seems to indicate a medical involvement, and an apparent 'operation' on her ovaries. It had happened approximately a year before our interview in early 1993.

'That [incident] was really weird because . . . I didn't

have any feeling of an abduction. I had a bath, I went to bed and everything was fine. Tuesday evening I was going to my friends and I was having a wash, getting changed and [then I saw] that there were these marks. And I knew as soon as I looked at them what they were. [But] I didn't have any memory.'

Rohan indicated the area where marks on her body had corresponded to the position of her ovaries.

'As I have got a hormone imbalance I have had hormone replacement therapy so I don't ovulate. I stopped taking it from December through to April. So I was ovulating from about January and this happened in early March.'

Coming nearer to the present time Rohan related an incident that had happened the previous summer.

'I woke up in the middle of the night, sat up in bed wide awake and thought, "Oh, I've just been somewhere." And a voice, not a feeling but a voice, said, "Lie down, roll over, lie down, go to sleep, you are all right." And I did. I went straight to sleep. I wasn't scared. [Usually] when I wake up in the middle of the night and I am scared, it doesn't matter how many times I tell myself, "Don't be stupid, roll over, go to sleep," it doesn't happen. This was very different.

'The last thing was a Sunday evening in November 1992. My flatmate had gone out to the pub with her boyfriend. I felt very tired, I felt really like I just had to go to bed. I had gone to bed about half-past nine. I've got a telly in my bedroom and I went through a stage where I'd fall asleep with the telly on. I was watching the American football on Channel 4. I must have fallen asleep about ten to ten because the football was still on and I didn't turn my telly off. Normally if I am falling asleep I turn my telly off and leave it [on standby] with a green light on. [Then I would normally] get up in the morning and the green light would be on. And even if I fall asleep with it on I normally wake up in the middle of the night and turn it off. But I didn't remember turning my TV off and I fell asleep about ten to ten.

'I also have kidney problems [we have already noted that many witnesses have a history of medical problems] and I tend to get up to go to the toilet during the night. I didn't get up that night, didn't move, didn't stir. I slept very heavily. And I woke up in the morning aware that I had slept strangely and I felt grotty. I had had a good night's sleep but I felt really grotty and ill. I didn't feel right, I didn't feel comfortable. So I got up, went to work and as I [was] driving to work a thought came into my head like a flash – "the aliens took you last night!"

'When I came home I realised that my TV was off. Properly off. It had been switched off and I know I hadn't switched it off. So I asked my flatmate, "Did you switch my telly off when you came in last night?" because I felt maybe she had heard the TV and looked in when she came in from the pub and switched it off for me. She said, "No." She said, "When I came in you were up. Your light was on and you were moving around in your bedroom." And I said, "No, I wasn't, my light was off before I had gone to sleep." I said to her, "I felt grotty this morning and I knew the aliens had got me." She sort of looked at me rather uncomfortably and we didn't really discuss it after that.'

Although it would prove little, I thought it right to confirm Rohan's statement about her flatmate's slight involvement. Lucie Butler told me: 'I came in about three o'clock in the morning. There were lights and things, I could hear things in Rohan's bedroom. I assumed it was the TV and went to bed. That was my interpretation of events, Rohan's interpretation was very different.'

Rohan's most recent sighting was a 'simple' UFO

*sighting that had happened a few weeks prior to our
meeting, around half past six on a weekday evening. She
had, however, felt connected to the object. The sighting
had been from the window of her flat.*

'It was like a red acorn-shaped light, it is not one I
have seen before. It was in the sky [Rohan pointed out
the location to me, above buildings on the opposite side
of the road]. It seemed to move around. I felt very cas-
ual about it, I watched it for a while and then I just felt
"Yes, that's great but I have had enough now," and I
sort of said, "OK. Thank you. I'm going to sit down
and watch telly." And then it went. And I really felt it
was a treat for me, like a little reward. [It was saying]
"Yes, hang on in there." '

*Rohan clearly attributes personal involvement to her
experiences; I asked her to elaborate on that for me.*

'It sounds crazy sometimes when you say it, even
when you think it, [but] I have always felt, even when I
was a little girl, a sense of destiny. I am a firm believer
in destiny anyway. I think if something is meant to be,
it will be. I have always felt a sense of purpose, that
something is going to be there in my life. I remember
[talking] with my uncle Chris about aliens and he said
to me, "Do you ever have the feeling that you are meant
to do something?", and I refused to answer the question
because it was too close to how I did feel.

'I wasn't really interested in getting in touch with
BUFORA or anybody else. I don't keep records [of my
sightings]. And although my mother sort of made this
initial contact before she went to the States I didn't have
any need to follow it up. I didn't feel the need to see
Budd [Hopkins – a prominent American abduction researcher.] although he has expressed an interest in seeing
me and I've got his address.

'Around November I kept drawing the greys at work.

I've got a compelling urge to keep drawing them. [The drawings are] just little doodles of their faces. I don't keep them. I have this real problem [that] I cannot get them exactly right. I'll be sitting at work and I'll just [start drawing]. I'll draw their eyes and then I'll draw the nose and I'll try and draw the heads. Then I look at it [and think] "That's wrong" and I try and draw it again. It becomes a real compulsion.'

I pointed out that she was describing an artistic compulsion that had been illustrated in the film Close Encounters of the Third Kind. *Rohan told me that she had never made the connection, but she then remembered the scene where one of the characters, Roy Neary, feels compelled to build models of the Devil's Tower in mashed potato, shaving foam and so on.*

I asked Rohan directly about any artistic talents she had. She told me that she was herself pleased with her art though she did not consider herself especially talented. She pointed out that she had been given an 'unclassified' in her art 'O' level examinations. When I saw her drawings I felt that this reflected more on the marking than her talents, which I thought were very good.

I admitted I was asking a leading question, but I wanted to know if she connected her art to her experiences. She commented:

'Well, part of me feels, how could I draw them if I don't know what they look like?'

We discussed phobias and the belief that fear of animals may be a 'screen memory' covering a reaction to the aliens.

'I suffer from arachnophobia which is a common fear. Budd [Hopkins] feels it's [related to] rats and spiders. Rats because of the eyes, spiders because apparently one of the types of aliens up there is quite insect-looking. This is something that I have been told. But you can use it as an excuse for anything.

'I also have a very strong reaction to pictures of the planet Earth taken from space. I have had some hypnotherapy on that; my mother did a bit with me. She bought a new shower curtain for the bathroom that's attached to my bedroom in the States and it was a massive picture of the Earth taken from a spaceship. And I completely freaked out so she did a little bit of work with me on it. My mum used to say that she would love to go into space if they ever made that possible. But I'd say, "No, I want to keep my feet on the ground." The view of the Earth from a spacecraft gives me a feeling of panic. When Mum did the hypnotherapy with me on my reaction to the shower curtain she tried to anchor it for me so that I could have a pleasant thought of using that shower curtain. But my feelings were: "It's wrong. I don't like it. I want to go back. I shouldn't be here. This is wrong." And I've always had a funny reaction to seeing [the Earth from space] on TV [or in] pictures. [Maybe] I witnessed it through a porthole into space . . . I don't know. I remember even [when I was] small I used to say, "Oh, suppose you get trapped out there. Suppose you get trapped and you can't come back." That was always my reaction. This is way before I considered myself an abductee.'

I asked Rohan if I should use her real name or a pseudonym. Her answer made it clear – as so many other abductees have done – that her 'coming out' was a part of her belief about the meaning of her experiences.

'This is something that I have decided. Like I said, I didn't have any need to contact BUFORA to talk about it and then I started drawing the faces and I thought, something has got to be done. And then eventually I went to the witness meeting and as I said, I feel like it's started me on a path, something that I didn't want to do but it had to be done.

'I have my suspicions about what [my purpose] is but I'm not certain so I'd rather [not say anything about that]. I do feel there is a purpose. I don't know if I'm imagining it or not. I have an idea what mine is, it might just be [my] projection, or maybe they have implanted something in my head which I am using. But like I said at the [witness support group] meeting, doing the camera interview, this interview [and so on], it's the start of the path. Maybe part of the purpose.'

Rohan believes that abductees are becoming more willing to open up. I had felt this too, though I had not discussed it with her prior to her mentioning it.

'The air of anticipation is also felt. I know when I spoke to my mother she said, "Yes, that's the feeling we've all had and it's building up." It's becoming more intense, more reports, more sightings, more contacts. It just seems to have taken a step forward.

'Though I have to admit I feel very ambiguous about the idea of them landing here and it all being out in the open. Because obviously there will be change. I know one woman, I read the transcript of one of her hypnosis sessions when I was in the States. It was quite frightening, and very nightmarish. She had met the children, the [human-alien] hybrids, and she was able to describe them. She was also talking about what they told her about what the future holds. No old people, no this, no that, and sometimes I feel quite resentful that they are going to come here and change [our world]. Sometimes I look at the world and I think about pensioners being raped [and so on] and it's so diabolical that it needs to be changed but I [still] feel quite resentful.

'Like I said, I've got no answers and I [sometimes] feel very bitter and frustrated. Why haven't I got any answers? Why don't they appear and tell me the answers now? I want to know. And then I calm down and go

back to my feeling of kinship. I don't feel angry about
the situation that I am in, I feel comfortable with it.
I feel kinship with them, I feel a kind of warmth, a
kind of kinship and so I am prepared to let things
go at the pace they dictate. Like I said earlier, when
it's time for me to know I'm sure I will know. And
that's OK. I don't know if I could live with the knowledge today.'

*Knowing that Rohan's mother works in America with
abduction researchers who fear that the underlying meaning behind these encounters is malign, I asked Rohan if
her belief about the meaning of these events was positive
or negative.*

'My general view is that although some of their
methods are dubious and some of the effects are very
dubious they don't have bad intentions. But as in any
situation, people will abuse it. And you are going to get
that in any situation. People do abuse it. They abuse
their power. I would say that they abuse what they do.'

*Rohan and I discussed several cases by way of expla-
nation that she had heard of by being in group meetings
in America. I can make no mention of these as it is a rule
of such meetings that material discussed is not made public. Rohan, incidentally, maintained confidentiality by not
giving me the witnesses' full names.*

*I asked Rohan what her family 'history' of UFO experi-
ences was. She also gave me permission to include the
following entry which she was sure would be acceptable to
her family:*

'My mother has definite sightings of UFOs and possible abductions. She is fairly sure she had one recently.
My uncle Chris is a definite abductee; he thought his
first abduction was at nineteen but hypnotherapy has
proved it was around the age of three. Grandmother has
seen UFOs but hasn't really talked about her children's

childhood experiences. My uncle Joe was with Chris when the abduction took place when he was nineteen. My uncle Joe refuses to acknowledge UFOs exist even though there would be eight of us had witnessed one. He is very anti, very, very anti. And his wife Cathy, she is very cool about it all and just ignores it. Pam is married to Chris. She sees UFOs; I've been with her, we've all seen UFOs together. [Aunt] Veronica has seen UFOs, I have been with her. I don't know whether or not she has had any abductions. My other [aunt], Joanna, again has seen UFOs. She's a scientist, has a PhD in biochemistry, and I don't know if she has had any actual experience.

'They are possibly changing us. When we go up there we see the light maybe and we come back down and try and sort it out but I don't, I know my own experiences, I don't seem to have been set on a path to sort things out in a big way like that.

'I sometimes get this obsession that people need to know. I don't read many books [about UFOs]; I don't know the history of the subject and so on. But people need to know. I was with my Dad in Sheffield in a book-shop and I saw there weren't any books [on the subject of UFOs]. I was very angry, I was running round the shop like a madwoman, cursing the shop because they didn't have any books. I feel that's part of my purpose; to say "Hey, let's face this, let's deal with it, let's make it available for everyone to know." '

I discussed Rohan's medical history more fully with her. Some American researchers have placed great store on the medical state of their witnesses.

'I do recall at the beginning of *Intruders* that [the witness, called Kathie Davis] has a history of illness which is common [to abductees]. Both my mother and I are quite ill people; she has had problems, I have got problems. Who knows?'

Janice Georgiou

Janice, whose close-encounter reports appear elsewhere in this book, also has a history of illness which seems to be related to her experiences:

'Quite a few years ago I was told by Orthena [one of the "aliens" who visited Janice] that with my permission they could use my body. If I left my body they could actually come into it. They could communicate just like I do with anybody else. I was told that once I gave permission my body would be processed for about twelve years and that through my life I would feel certain discomfort because of it. I have certainly felt that since I agreed to it.'

Janice has had several illnesses, including fevers and migraine. Many abductees are illness-prone; Rohan Hinton made the point to me and also commented on 'Kathie Davis' being an unwell person. Kathie Davis is the name given to the principal subject of Budd Hopkins's book Intruders. *She has now 'gone public' in her real name of Debbie Tomey. A short interview with her is also included in this book.*

Janice also described a different and unpleasant experience she had had. She started by telling me that she had once witnessed somebody else being abducted. Janice did not know who she had seen, but thought that it might have been an abductee she later met.

'I saw this man having something pushed into the back of his ear and he was quite frightened but he was not able to scream. You could see the look on his face. He was very scared. I asked someone "Why are they doing that? Why are they putting something in his ear?" I was told they were removing tissue from inside that prevents a build-up of something or other. They have got to be able to travel through space at speeds they can't comfortably travel at. There is pressure-building tissue that can damage the ear, so they remove it to prevent this from happening. That's what they told me anyway.'

Janice has basically had what are called 'contactee' experiences but she told me of an abduction encounter that was quite unlike her 'other' contacts. She does not connect the two types of experience, feeling that the latter is 'bad'. I speculated that her bad feelings about the house might have contributed to the experience, as negative feelings often generate poltergeist reports. But she had no firm feelings about that.

The occasion was in November 1991. Janice had gone to lie down for a few hours' rest at 2 p.m. but after thinking she had slipped into sleep did not surface until 9 p.m. – a gap of seven hours which was unusual since she would normally only have rested until around 4 p.m. Feeling only slightly strange due to the long sleep but at this time no other effects she went back to bed at 10.30 p.m. and slept all night. The next day was a Saturday and she was not sure if she would feel up to going to her bi-monthly witness support group meeting so decided to have a refreshing bath before making a final decision. She recalls:

'I first went to the sink to wash my face. When removing my hands I felt a strange burning feeling on the wrist of my left hand, I noticed a line of burn blisters . . . Five of them, I did not know how I could have got them. I climbed into the bath. There was no other problem anywhere else. But when I stood up to get out of the bath I felt a burning on the right side of my navel. I looked and there was another line of about nine burn blisters running upwards. They really hurt. The next few minutes are still a bit vague but I know that when I called my daughter to come up that I did so in an angry way, which was so out of character for me. When I shouted I had flashbacks of something. I realised that shouting was giving me vivid pictures so I went to my room and did some more ... I eventually remembered how I had received the burns and decided to attend the meeting that day and have them witnessed by Ken Phillips, who is an investigator with BUFORA. I recall seeing a figure of a man standing 'through' my bed. Two figures behind him gave me a command and led me out. I found myself lying on a table. I could see figures standing over me with instruments, one instrument was a prong full of needles which was pushed into my stomach. I felt semi-paralysed but asked the creatures what was happening to me. I got no response. Then they were going to use a long rod on me, it looked white-hot. Somehow I found the strength to reach out with my left hand and push it aside but it caught me across the stomach resulting in another blister. During that abduction I remember being questioned about something. I remember that they were talking to me. I heard somebody say something to someone else about me – "She does not belong here" – and I did not fight them. I actually thought, "I did ask why was I abducted. Why did they do this to me? Who are they?" and I was told that the abduction was carried out by something that is semi-terrestrial.'

At the witness support group meeting Janice showed Ken Phillips the marks, a fact which Ken confirms.

Janice did see a doctor a few weeks later but the doctor said her burns were nothing to worry about (Janice did not tell him how she came by the injury). Five weeks after this there were no scars, no traces.

(Note: at the time of writing Janice is having further similar experiences, one of which has left a line of marks on her skin on the left side of her body in two places. I was able to examine these and photographs of them are included in this book. Janice is working with me and others to examine her experiences for herself. She is de-

termined to know why her experiences seem to have taken a turn towards the negative.)

While some abductees are certain that they are contacted by extraterrestrials several have admitted to me that they use the term 'alien' as a form of shorthand and that the origin of the entities is a mystery to them. I asked Janice for her comments on this:

'I know that some of them do come from outer space. But I also know that some of them don't.'

BRYAN

Bryan was, at the time of my first interview with him, a fifteen-year-old schoolboy living with his aunt. He is an intelligent and sensitive person who is very gifted artistically. He tends to be introverted by nature, presumably a characteristic partly created by his early life experiences.

His childhood was marred by severe domestic problems which included abuse by his stepmother who, he stated, tried to drown him in a bath of water. His early family life was somewhat chaotic.

It is probably worth mentioning that at the time of my first interview, 25 January 1991, his mother (who was at the interview) was just about to move to Switzerland for professional reasons, although at the time she knew that her son was undergoing trauma related to his real or imagined experiences.

Bryan's quality of life at that age was not the best, though his aunt was doing a great deal to care for him and made considerable effort to understand the nature of the phenomenon affecting her nephew. Indeed she even attended a witness support group meeting with Bryan on 2 February 1991.

Gifts of the Gods?

The First Interview

'[Things started for me] when I was about four. I woke up and it was very bright and I went downstairs. This was at nighttime. I thought it was morning. I thought I was waking up in the morning and it was like I remember voices, feelings, [telling me] to go downstairs and I remember picking up the cat and it running away and then suddenly the lights went out. I remember managing to get to the bottom of the stairs and starting to cry.

'I was, at that time, on my own with my father but shortly afterwards he met my stepmother. I [now] don't speak to my dad. I was beaten up a bit by [my stepmother], she was a drug addict, but I came through it.

'When I was [about] five I was extremely hysterical about something. My stepmother and my dad came in, one after the other, and smacked me, my dad left the door half open and the landing light on and I was in bed. My bed was by the window across the room from the door and I was on my side propped up with one arm. I don't know how much time passed, it didn't seem like much, but I was calm, I stopped crying and I was looking behind the door, and then, I think three beings came into my room. They [had] large eyes, almond-shaped and slanting, and they seemed like they had claws and sort of three fingers. They were very angular and fierce-looking, their chins went down [pointed] and their fingers were bone-like. They were between three, four, five feet tall, reasonably tall, taller than me at that age anyway. And the way they moved they were just extremely quick, they were sort of all over the place, sort of in and out of each other; almost in a blur. Slowly they were coming towards me as they moved around. It looked like they were dancing or something. I hadn't [got] the courage to move. I sort of pulled the covers over my head and lay on my side and the next thing I remember was like a dream, like what's referred to in Whitley Strieber's book [as] "screen memories". It was like I was in my bed and the covers over me were like rocks, like I was in a cave.

'Now I was on my back and I was wearing the clothes of the fifteenth or sixteenth century; knickerbockers [breeches], little buckled shoes and a shirt with frilly cuffs. And down by my foot I was looking at a little man – about two inches high; he was human-looking and was also wearing the same sort of clothes. He had a wig, a scroll of paper and a quill pen and he was looking and writing, and then I heard the creak of a door, and to my left up on this "rock-face" or whatever, there was this door opening and shutting and another man of the same description came down some steps and he walked to the other man by my foot and then they talked and looked at this scroll and then walked to my knee and that's when I woke up.'

We discussed the books that Bryan had read; it was obvious that he knew most of the classic cases and had been somewhat 'taken' by Strieber's Communion *which he had read; he had also seen the film. I pointed out that the* Communion *film showed the aliens 'dancing' in one sequence, very much as he seemed to be describing.*

'I don't like what they did in the film.'

Bryan also added that he enjoyed reading science fiction, books by Michael Moorcock for example. I made the point that his 'cave' description seemed to owe a lot to Gulliver's Travels; *Bryan had seen the cartoon version of that film and agreed that he, too, had come to that conclusion years later:*

'When I was younger I was more into ghosts. I was into spooky stories and that sort of thing.'

Bryan went on to describe how he had told his

experiences to one friend at school, who had had similar experiences:

'It sounds like they're checking him out or something, possibly because of me, but I keep an open mind. He had [experiences] three times. He said that it happened over a space of a week and a half. He'd lie down to go to bed and he wouldn't actually fall asleep but his eyes [would be] shut. He said that his vision was [of] a white wall or a piece of paper with very small text running across it. He said that he couldn't read it. And he said that to [one] side [of him] there was a face. He said that it had really big eyes and they were black but they were like they had been polished.'

Bryan agreed that this, with other details he related, seemed to be the same face he had seen – the 'Strieber alien' face. Bryan told me he had had other paranormal experiences:

'I had an out-of-the-body experience when I left my dad and came up to live with my mum. I was staying at my grandmother's and one weekday morning I was in bed. I had, like, a dream, but it wasn't really, it was more than a dream; I wasn't sure. I went downstairs to the kitchen door and more or less went [physically] through it, then I was inside the room. My grandmother was sitting at the table and there was this other woman I didn't know. (They didn't see me of course.) I went to my grandmother and she said: "But it says in the Bible the sea will give up its dead." And I wanted to ask what she meant. And then that was it. [A week later] I mentioned [this] to her. And she said: "Yes, I remember, that's the day you slept in that morning. I remember saying these words to a Jehovah's Witness in the house. And the Jehovah's Witness's friend said, 'Yes, obviously something has happened,' and they gave me a book and they said that the Devil's in here . . ." From what I can gather the Jehovah's Witnesses said that it was the Devil working his way through me.'

We discussed the origin of the 'aliens' and Bryan randomly speculated about extraterrestrials, other dimensions, and so on. He admitted later that he uses the term alien to mean 'non-human' and that he has no real idea where these beings come from. Bryan said that sometimes the experiences scared him, and he offered examples:

'Well, one night [when I was about twelve or thirteen] I was in the house when I became very scared that something was there in the house with me or [something] was going to happen. I had the cat with me because I thought she would [act as a warning]. When I switched the light off I was lying on my front, on my "good" ear – because I've got a bad ear. (Sometimes when I don't want to hear anything I lie on it.) My hand was pretty close to the switch of the lamp, but I daren't move. The cat started to really miaow and she started to jump and dart about because things were falling off the shelves and it sounded like things were getting knocked over. I didn't hear a door open or close but then everything went quiet, then I was absolutely tense with fear. Then all of a sudden the cat [fell] down on to the small of my back. When the cat jumps at something it doesn't leap into the air and fall. Something, a being or a force or something, [had] lifted the cat and dropped it on to me.'

We talked a little about his ear problem. Bryan thought it might be congenital though he wasn't sure, but he could not remember a time when he did not have the problem.

I also discussed with him the similarity between what he was claiming and poltergeist reports; he agreed that it was something he had already identified.

Bryan wanted to tell me about his UFO sightings:

'I was camping out with [a] friend, I was thirteen or fourteen at the time. It was a summer's evening [and we were] at the back of my friend's house in Letchworth [where] there was a field. And we walked away from the [camp] fire and we walked to the end of this field. We were looking at these houses and I turned round quickly and over the houses, at treetop height, it came over. It wasn't rounded, it was more of an oval, an intense bright light. It went from [one spot] to [another] just like that and it sort of left behind [light trails]. There were two of them and they ran parallel with each other, the outside edges went out so that they were bigger at the ends. They then caught up with the light before the whole thing disappeared. I turned quickly and told [my friend] to turn round, I turned back and saw it disappear and he [didn't see it].

'One time I got into the tent and we heard somebody walking near the fire and of course I got very scared. [My friend] went out of the tent for a few minutes to have a look and then he came back and said that there was nobody there. I'm not sure if it was the same night as I saw this UFO light.

'[At] another time, I can't remember my age, I was probably about ten [years old], in broad daylight on a hot day I was going swimming. I was walking up a road and I looked up and saw [what] I can only describe as a missile. [It was] not too high but moving quite slowly, it was just like a greyish-brown sort of missile, no wings, no tail. It just moved across the sky, slowly.'

We discussed the expression 'missing time' since it was obvious from our earlier discussion that he had read of this. He did not know if he had had missing time or not, but he felt that hypnosis would be a useful way to search for this possibility. We agreed that we would not get into that yet as there were pitfalls and Bryan was keen to avoid them. Bryan did, however, also consider the use of hypnotherapy to cure him of his fears:

'I'm scared of waking up in the night and seeing this face or whatever. [But] the reason I wouldn't want to get rid of [the experiences] is because I feel one day I'm going to get over this fear and that maybe it's exciting, that it might be something from the stars.'

I asked Bryan how he would react if he had the chance to go on a spaceship to a star, but wouldn't be able to come back. Would he go? He agreed that he probably would.

I discussed with Bryan's mother, who was at parts of the interview, whenever Bryan felt it correct to have her there, her own experiences. She had had something akin to a ghost experience at the time of death of a boyfriend, and she had seen a UFO once.

'In 1979 I believe I saw a UFO. I was driving with a friend of mine, along the A1 from Grantham to Peterborough, and I remember looking out of the window and seeing this oval sort of light just in one position in the sky and I was saying, "Stop, stop, I want to look, look at what's out the window!"

'But [my friend] didn't stop, he kept on driving and driving and then [the light] would disappear, it would be away for a few seconds and come back again. Why it couldn't have been an aeroplane was because in the dark they have the red and green lights that flash at the end of the wings [but] it was too big to be anything else. Well, this thing just kept on coming and going, it stayed sometimes longer than other times, like sometimes it was just for a few seconds, sometimes just for one second and then [it would] go away. In the end it just disappeared; it just went.'

We discussed the film Close Encounters of the Third Kind *which both Bryan and his mother had seen and were fascinated by. Bryan's mother particularly latched on to the sequence where Roy Neary, a character in the film, had felt compelled to build a structure in his house. She described what she felt about this film sequence:*

'He was frantic. He was trying to get to know what was in his mind and this vision he kept on having, he just had to . . . you see, I'm like that with drawing. I have a vision and I have to draw.'

Bryan is also an accomplished artist; some of his work is reproduced in this book. (Three years after this initial interview Bryan had left school and was at art college.)

Of the intruders into his room, Bryan commented that he also heard three voices in his head:

'I used to put the three figures in my room and these three voices that have always been in my head together, but now I believe that they're totally different; the three figures are possibly an encounter with another race. These voices I believe are just auditory hallucinations due to my needing someone to talk to when I was younger.'

I made the point that that was a very considered thought for a fifteen-year-old. All our discussions showed me that Bryan is very well read in paranormal subjects, and highly intelligent. I asked him why he thought that:

'They don't tell me anything practical – they speak like I speak. The strange thing is they've all got their own characters; two are like men, and they are sort of lazy, and one's like a woman, very active, telling you what to do. There was one time I remember [the "female"] actually went and I was frantic all day asking the two males where she was but they said "we can't say". Apart from that I'm inclined to believe that they're just created by myself for company.'

Bryan was clear that he meant only the voices, not the entities. He believed the visions he had seen were too complex and too strange for a child that age to have created. I did not take the point up with him further.

He was less inclined to attribute gender to the entities:

'I can't tell. I feel that some of them are male – I think it was mixed, I'm not sure. It's not easy when they look the same.

'I don't know if this would mean anything but the [paternal] side of the family are mediums, faith healers, my dad nearly went into it when he was a kid.'

Bryan and his mother both agreed that they would connect these paranormal phenomena to UFOs. Bryan also commented that he had seen a ghost:

'I've seen the ghost of my grandma from my dad's side; she died just before Christmas. The following year, around the same time, I visited the house, I went upstairs and suddenly I was ... overcome with ... emotion. I turned round, attracted by a light. The whole thing lasted for only a second. I saw her standing there, sort of surrounded by light. I was sad, she smiled at me [as if to say] "I'm fine, don't worry." I'd lived with her, I think, for a couple of years and I'd spent a lot of time with her.'

Bryan's mother knew of this story, I asked her what she thought of it. She said:

'I believed him because I believe in that sort of thing anyway. My parents have had a house on some land in Derbyshire – this was an old orphanage at one time and it was massive, a really big house – and every time I went up there with Bryan, as soon as he entered the door he would scream and he wouldn't sleep at nights. That worried me as he was usually a good sleeper, but in that house he would not sleep. My brother was only five years old at the time – he's [now a] really down-to-earth sort of person – and he actually said he was scared out of his wits because he went downstairs to the bathroom and as he was going [back] up he [said he] was being followed. And then my sister who is five years younger than me was with her boyfriend – and she's also very down to earth – she actually saw a ghost in that house. So I believe. Also, I believe, I have seen a ghost myself.'

Bryan went on to fill in more details of his experiences as he relaxed more:

'I think [it was] the same year as the [incident] with the cat. I was in the house, on my own. I was reading a sci-fi comic when I became scared again. All of a sudden, a scratching started on the door, which isn't totally unusual because the cat sometimes [makes a scratching sound] on the door. It sounded slightly higher up, though, just under the middle of the door and it wasn't like her paws doing it, it was like a clawed hand; that's the image I got. So I got up because I was going to confront it. The door was pushed in but it wasn't clicked in; it wasn't totally shut but had been pushed. The moment I pulled it open, nothing was there. [To] my mind the cat would have had to suddenly jump and leap to the stairs and round the corner very quickly, but I tried to make myself believe that. I shut the door firmly this time. I went back to my bed, which is by the window – my head was near the window – the curtains were very slightly not shut and in the light of my lamp I suddenly caught the eye of my cat, because the cat was sitting on the windowsill. At this stage I thought, "What the hell's at the door?" and at that point it started again. I was looking at the cat then and on the other side of the room there was this scratching on the door. I got into bed, tried to read the comic, I was shaking all the time this scratching was going on. I put the comic down and kept the light on and just lay there with my eyes open. Eventually, after about an hour, I fell asleep. If something had come that night why [were] they just content with scaring me? Is there something I haven't remembered? Did they come in and do . . . whatever?'

Bryan, aware of the possibility of missing time, commented that he had no watch with him at that time and so could not know if he had a time lapse to consider or not. Bryan's mother commented: 'Bryan has mentioned he seems to feel that they're getting nastier.'

Bryan took up this point:

'Maybe they are collecting fear or something. Thinking about why they do it, it's either they're nasty, which I don't really think they are, [or] the only other reason is more . . . scientific.'

This was an interesting point. Budd Hopkins, in the United States, had mentioned to me earlier that he had cases where it appeared the aliens were 'testing' human psychology by making abductees go through unpleasant experiences. He gave the example of one man being forced to shoot another, though the 'victim' afterwards turned out to be an alien. Hopkins thought it was a scientific study rather than any viciousness on their part. Bryan's comments were pretty close to that. However, Hopkins had not yet released any of that information in his books. In any case Bryan was only vaguely aware of Hopkins and hadn't read his two books.

Bryan described dreams he had had:

'Recently I've been having chains of dreams where I see a UFO in the sky and then I'm panicking and running, waiting for these things to come. I've had loads over the last week – I had one last night. They don't scare me.'

I asked Bryan if the images of aliens had any detrimental effects. He told me that although he had never needed a light on to sleep, he had taken to needing one:

'I never used to [need a nightlight], but I've started to now. About two weeks ago I couldn't sleep, I awoke, I've got this bedside light. *Film '90* came on, and I saw these aliens dashing about. They were talking about

Communion and it was such a big shock to the system I had to sleep in my auntie's room – I couldn't go back into my room – after that. I [later] got into my room again but with the door wide open and the next room light on, it was just a landing light with the door partly ajar, but that [brought] back memories of . . . the time they came [to me], like in the film when the thing pops half its head around the door. I can get in the room [now], but once I've switched off the light and I'm in bed I can't get up – I'm there until I go to sleep.

'This week I've heard [something] like a humming noise in my head which is really weird. I woke up after this strange dream about two weeks ago, and it sounded like outside there was a noise. A sort of electric noise like a keyboard. I've never heard it before, but [it was a] big shock and I heard it really in my head.

'About two months ago I think I observed a UFO with a friend who's a next-door neighbour – we went out into the garden to star-gaze and saw a UFO. In the stars you get very faint white dots moving slowly across – satellites I presume; we were following one of those, it was an extremely clear night, and as it went past a set of stars which we recognised (so we knew where we were looking – it was like a triangle of three stars) suddenly, right above it there was this huge flash, but really high up – higher than aeroplanes usually go. And shortly before an aeroplane had gone past and the flash from its light was dull. This light was up very high; it was so pure. And it sort of went out, and then I said, "Quick, look at it," and it did it again. Then it moved, and the next time it flashed it [had] moved up quite a distance away and then it was up again and it flashed and then down here. So we ran inside and we got a torch to see if it would flash in sequence back. We were flashing at another area and then it started again in the same area.

Every time it flashed it was moving very quickly, but it was in a line; it was going somewhere. It seemed like it was responding to us.'

I asked Bryan for his opinions on what he was experiencing:

'I just want to know what it's all about and what's happening. [Maybe] when you get older you go through changes and maybe become them, sort of thing. I want to remember it and feel sort of more involved and then know why perhaps we're involved.'

The Second Interview

Three months later I re-visited Bryan, with Ken Phillips, as promised to see how he had felt after our initial meeting. Bryan explained:

'You [JS] said that memories would emerge and I've had some memories or extra bits added on to the other ones. I've remembered a different entity, something I've never read about. It started off when I was having trouble sleeping and I'd go to bed and close my eyes and I'd keep getting sort of images, just my imagination. Suddenly I got this strong image and it sort of shocked me for a bit but I forgot about it. About a week later I remembered [while] doing some sketching. The alien is a sort of off-white colour but I coloured it in grey because I wasn't sure.'

Bryan showed Ken and me his sketches. They were artistically very good, and – at that time – all of 'grey'-type aliens.

'I was just sketching one day when I sort of felt [something] very familiar about [it] and with [this] came the memory of a room. I did try to draw it; it was like a hospital ward more or less but it was rectangular and along the walls there [were] bits that came out [as if] you cut down the middle wall of the house and left the bits at the side, creating one room from two adjoining ones. Well, there were lots of those and in between each was like a bed. I closed my eyes. [There was] this thing sort of moving across and things sort of moving together and [speeding] away . . .

'Around this time I saw an image on television that brought back a really old memory of a book. I don't know why but I associated this memory with this new type of alien [the one Bryan had sketched]. It was nothing strange, it just sort of puzzled me. I [asked] my uncle, who comes round here, about this book and he said, "Oh, I remember that. I read it to you once and I remembered the whole night." And he was looking [at my sketch] and he said: "I've seen it." [Meaning the face that Bryan had drawn.]

'The creature scratched its nose. And we both remember it as though we were both there or something. I don't know, I used to live with him when I was about three or four [years old]. And it would sort of stand there with a white face, as far as I could remember, and lift up its hand and gently scratch the bridge of its nose. And that's all I can remember.'

Bryan confirmed that his uncle remembered this creature as real, and pointed out that his uncle is a very down-to-earth person:

'I used to dream about walking to [the entity]. [There's] a big green lawn with trees and they're there [waiting] for me, these things, and they're sort of standing there.'

The Third Interview

After Bryan's second interview with me he spent a couple of years attending the witness support group sponsored by BUFORA and co-ordinated by Ken Phillips; we spoke briefly from time to time. In 1993 Bryan said he had a number of things he wanted to discuss with me – what he called 'new developments' – and we had some interviews in February and March of that year.

'It was like you said, from [our] meetings: "The brain's going to go over and over it and things [might] emerge." You actually said that possibly [they would emerge] in dreams. And shortly after I had this dream.

'It [involved] me and two friends driving to the country in a pick-up truck. We were going to a friend's house, a big country house. It was his Nan's, but apparently she lived sort of in the top corner of the house and it would be ours really for the week. We could shoot cans off walls and things. We'd got rifles and went out to the field.'

I confirmed that this was not the sort of activity that Bryan was involved in in 'real life'.

'We went back to the house and [we were just] sitting in the rain with a can of beer each. All of a sudden the dream goes really, really strange and it's like my friends are all sucked against the wall, crouching in the corners, sort of screwed up and they are really, really scared of something. And I look out of the window and there is a mass landing of UFOs. They were all coming down and landing around the house. I went outside and there was like a big tree, it was growing all crooked out of the side of the house. Sort of bent and grooved, horizontally. I climbed on to this and stood there. The UFO came down right next to me like this. The widest part – it was like two bowls on top of each other – had port-holes. It was right next to my face and I was just watching the portholes spinning past. Behind the port-holes there was a face, not spinning with them. The ship was moving, but there must have been a corridor inside that was staying still. That face there stared back at me.'

Bryan handed me a drawing of the face he had seen, and which is reproduced in this book:

'The portholes stopped and this is when the dream seemed to fall away. I think – because I am sure it happened – that it had a completely different quality from a dream, it was like a memory. And this is where it goes very strange. I am standing in front of this creature in like a circular corridor that goes around the edge of the UFO. There is a door behind him and he moves. It's very strange because I'm obviously very heavily sedated. My eyes are like there are a thousand images of [the creature] on top of each other all shifting about. It's blurred and I can't stare for long and it's changing. I seem to move into a room and [the creature] is standing next to an operating table that's on its left. And on the operating table is another one of him, identical, lying on its back, its head towards me and apparently dead. Behind all this there is a window on the wall, a square window with rounded edges I remember. Lined up behind that were three more of those watching for my reactions, sort of in the central circular ring of the UFO. Behind them is a much taller "grey" pacing backwards and forwards like a sentry; it seems like some guard patrol. The funny thing about his moving is like it's floating. I can only see it from chest upwards. Its head doesn't move from side to side like it would when you are walking. So at this stage I am sort of staring for a few minutes thinking what's going on and can't work out why this scary situation isn't really scaring me. It seemed like my brain was three seconds behind itself, everything took a while to sink in. The creature standing by the operating table moved his hand in a gesture pointing at the dead alien and words came into my mind, touch it. I seemed to take a step to the other side of the table but I was, like, instantly there. I really didn't

266

have much control over my legs. And I stand across the table from this doctor alien and I press my forefinger on this creature just above the knee of its right leg and it's stone cold. And I am really, really upset at this stage and then close to tears. And I was thinking Oh my God, it's the first time I have been near a dead body, and I felt really, really sorry for it, even though it wasn't human. I looked up again and the thing was just quite placid, staring at me.

'All the other "doctors" had turned their heads and were watching me, I think the sentry was even having a look and then the creature sort of moved its arm again and we both walked from the room. I don't remember how I got on to the UFO, how I got to that room, what happened after I left the room, or when this was; I haven't got any clue. One thing I did notice was these aliens were white and appeared to be absolutely hairless but when you actually touched them, because I moved my finger upwards, it was like going against a very fine layer of white hair. Very short and very flat so you wouldn't notice. You could just feel it like bristle.'

Bryan admitted that he felt this was more than a dream, that it represented something he felt had really happened to him. He did not know when this might have happened, nor could he visualise his own body, which might have given a clue to his age:

'I didn't see my own body. I think I was fully clothed, not naked or anything. I was roughly the same height as one of those [creatures], I'm not really sure how high. I assume they are three and a half to four feet tall.'

This indicates that Bryan believed it happened when he was very young; he is presently around six feet tall.

Bryan had commented in our first interview that he thought the beings were 'collecting emotions'. I asked if this was, in his opinion, another version of that:

'Yes. I think it was seeing how would I feel about one of them. Would I not care because it was one of them? I remember [before] talking about fear-tests because I was talking about the time when they were outside my door scratching and tapping and doing silly things that were driving me out of my mind. I mentioned it was like a gauge measuring fear. The two events scared me half to death. I couldn't really see a point to it. It certainly didn't feel [as if] it was for my benefit, and actually it's probably made it worse for me because I am still pretty scared about bumping into them again. There was just absolute confusion in my mind. They certainly tampered with my mind, I suppose they had to. If they tried to get me on to one of those things in a normal state I'd be clinging on to the walls.'

I reminded Bryan that in our first interview he had told me that he would be prepared to travel on a one-way trip to the stars. I asked him if he viewed these experiences differently, given that he was saying he didn't want to be taken on board this 'spacecraft'.

'It's just their physical appearance, the whole thing, it's grotesque.'

Bryan and I talked about fear for short while, somewhat in the abstract and theoretically:

'I've got a horrible fear of insects as well. I don't know if that's related but it's the way they sort of dart and move, like wasps or, as Whitley Strieber said, praying mantis. Tiny money spiders I don't mind, anything bigger than that I can't stand. Wasps, I'm terrified of wasps.'

Bryan mentioned some of his UFO-related reading. He was becoming somewhat interested in 'crash-retrievals'. I asked him how this fitted in with his experiences, and his beliefs:

'Sometimes I think they would be too clever to get

caught. It's like the time when me and my friend were camping. You knew for certain that we wouldn't have seen them if they didn't want us to. I'm [also] sure they can see through my eyes and they can hear all my thoughts. They are perceiving everything I am perceiving in this room if they want to, I am sure. Sometimes that bothers me. It would bother me if I got a chance to steal something from the UFO because they would obviously know about it. I know I can reverse it: I can't see through their eyes but I can call them down, which I have done before.

'I've only actually done it twice, I think. Asked to see a UFO and it happened. I did it with a few people a few months back and it worked. In quite a big way. Not far from here. It was October [1992], I think, around the seventeenth I think it happened. Dad lives a few streets away and he had a lodger, a young man called Justin, and Justin is very much into bizarre, strange things. He draws pictures like I do. He is all into mystical beliefs, strange theories, that sort of thing. He said that he had got relatives out near Shillington, near Pegsdon Hill. He was driving with his auntie one night and he saw a massive orange light like a cloud, it was as though an orange light was behind the cloud. It was going across the road, not low but quite high up. Below the clouds though. His auntie pulled the car in and they got out and they watched as it slowly went away roughly in the direction of Pegsdon Hill, they thought. A week later he was driving along the same road with his uncle this time. He [his uncle] is a bit sceptical. But even his uncle was forced to stop the car and they had to watch as this thing did it again. That night friends of his came round. They had been in the same area but the other side of Pegsdon Hill, and said that they had seen these orange lights. So Justin told me about them to see if I was interested and we decided to go out there. A week prior to the talk with Justin I had decided in my mind that I was going to progress with this. It has been a long time and nothing has really happened. I wanted to meet them or something.

'Justin got in and I was thinking I should name a place where I should go to see them. And I thought: Pegsdon Hill. I thought maybe inadvertently I had been told where to go. So we arranged to go up on a Saturday night if a friend could give us a lift. So Friday night I was thinking, right, tomorrow night I would be there and somehow I tried to communicate that I will be there. The lift didn't come, we didn't manage to get a lift, so about twelve o'clock Saturday night I was walking home when it's just outside here. I dropped my keys on the pavement as I was pulling them out of my pocket. I bent down to pick them up and as I stood up I looked into the sky above and there was this *massive* white flash and a white trail shot away from it and disappeared. It sort of faded away into the sky. So I think they actually heard me thinking and came. But of course I didn't get to Pegsdon Hill; they had followed me on my walk back and realised I had made it home [so they] departed. So I thought then that tomorrow night for definite I'd be there because my Dad's girlfriend had offered to give us a lift the following night. So at ten o'clock the next night Dad, his girlfriend, me and Justin drove up to Pegsdon Hill. It was a clear night and you could see, there wasn't any mist or anything, but there was cloud. We stood at the top of Pegsdon Hill; after about half an hour I started to think, "Oh, they are not coming, it's a waste of time." It was freezing cold up there. I walked away from the group and as I came back I noticed Justin was standing on his own looking out towards Hitchin. I went over to him. As I was looking past him I could see a huge orange light over Hitchin: really, really big. I went, "Oh, what's that?" and he said, "I don't know. I've been watching it for five minutes. It hasn't got bigger or smaller, it just like remained where it is." I thought, "That's strange, it should be diminishing or growing larger if it's an aeroplane coming to or [going away] from us." And we did see quite a lot of aeroplanes. You could tell the difference. It was below cloud level so I don't think it was a shooting star. I shouted across to my Dad – half jokingly – "Flying saucers at twelve o'clock" and he shouted at me, "Yeah, I am watching it. I saw it blink on five minutes ago and they walked over." They were all standing there watching this thing. Dad's girlfriend was sceptical, she said, "No, that's an aeroplane." But we stood for another five minutes and there was absolutely no change. So we were all pretty sure it wasn't an aeroplane. All of a sudden it started to grow bigger and then we felt quite disappointed that it was an aeroplane. But it wasn't moving towards us, it was just getting brighter. It got actually to the point where it started to hurt your eyes. And then it went back to its original size and then it started to grow again. All of a sudden a huge spotlight turned up from the ground and went to the object. [The spotlight] blinked out as soon as it hit the object. I don't know what's got one of these lights; I can only think it was possibly in the area of RAF Henlow. I don't know if that can be checked out. [I made enquiries to Nick Pope at the Ministry of Defence, naturally without mentioning details of the case or Bryan, protecting witness confidentiality. When he replied, he was sure that there was nothing happening in that area that related to military movements. He suggested enquiries to Knebworth House, a local site of several rock concerts and other events. Nick was of the opinion that laser effects from a show could have caused the sighting. Certainly there have been many of those recently. Enquiries there had not been replied to at the time of writing.]

'I think the craft must have blown out that spotlight as soon as it touched it. As that happened it started to move away towards the south. Dad and his girlfriend said, "We'll go back to the car and wait for you," because my Dad believed I would have more chance of seeing something if there weren't all those people there. So they went: me and Justin started to run in the field following it. It was sort of going above a line of trees where it stopped and hovered by a group [of them]. As we watched it was swaying in the wind or something. It was there for a few minutes and [then] started to move on. Suddenly it went down behind the trees and was lost out of sight. We thought, there's another field over there across the fence; we'll make a run for it and see if it comes out that side. This we did. There was nothing there apart from a big passenger plane coming up from Luton Airport towards the direction of this object. So we went back to the field, and watched as the aeroplane came over the area where the object had been. Then [the plane] went away at a distance. When it had gone a sufficient distance away this big orange light blinked on in full colour. So I presume it took evasive action to avoid being seen by this aircraft. Then it turned on its side or its front, I don't know, but it displayed a pattern of lights. It was like two orange lights next to each other, showing it was probably long. To the rear next to the two orange lights were two smaller orange lights. Therewas a blinking white light near there. They started to move the way they had been going. We ran back to the original field. [The UFO] wasn't there. We stood there for a few minutes. We decided to try and go to the large trees where it had been. To get to this other hill we had to go down a dip, through hedgerows and all sorts. We climbed on top of this hill and I said, "I'll bet now they're back where we were." We turned round and they were. This time there was more than one of them. It was where we had been, but not on the hill; behind that across another valley on the ridge of Sharpenhoe. It was like a huge orange light, and there was one that kept blinking on every few seconds. And this one came on, it's really bright. And I said to Justin, "What do they want us to do? Is there any message in it?" He said, "I don't know." I said, "What about a signal or something?" At that point they flipped around and three formed a triangle while the other one started to blink in the centre. A few seconds later another triangle came on, a smaller one down to the right of [the first]. Now we were getting really excited; we thought, let's run back to the top of Pegsdon Hill because we could see better from there. This we did. We had got to the top of the hill and they were still there. On the north horizon there was another triangle of orange lights. At this stage there were near on twenty objects flying about. One was coming up very quickly on the original flight path of the first one we had seen, almost on a head-on collision course with another light which was coming towards us. As they got closer the orange light dipped behind the trees again and the first one turned towards us. It was actually a plane from Luton so this one had to go again. This had all taken about two hours and we were only supposed to have been there for a few minutes. A few of the lights went out, there were still a few on the ridge of Sharpenhoe when we decided to go because they [Dad and his girlfriend] were waiting in the car.

'All four of us saw the first one. Only me and Justin saw the others afterwards. It was quite strange. Absolutely nothing has happened since that night. [This was now February 1993 – JS] It seems as though things were coming to a head and I bailed out at the last minute. It seems like there must have been quite a bit of effort to send all these craft down for my benefit. Since then Justin has seen them a few times.'

I assured Bryan that if he felt he could 'call down' UFOs again he should call me and I would try to be there with him.

LORRAINE AND JAMES PARRY

Lorraine Parry is a witness who has had several close-encounter experiences, as well as experiences of the wider paranormal related in a previous chapter.

Displacement in Time/Space

In 1982 Lorraine Parry, then in her late teens, had a paranormal experience that is suggestive of UFO contact. It occurred in Wembley, a suburb of Greater London. She was going up Lancelot Road to the High Road to buy spinach. Just a year or so prior to the experience Lorraine had become vegetarian. As she described the experience:
'As a result of neglecting my vegetable intake, I had anaemia at the time, and I was very, very low. I was on my way up Lancelot Road to go and get some spinach from the vegetable stall. So I was carrying a bag in my hand and I had shorts on. It was summer. And I was walking up the road and just before I was getting to the hill that takes you to the top on to the High Road I felt ... well ... where has everything gone? I stopped and I thought I had seen an aeroplane. And then the next thing I was aware of [was a] feeling that I was standing in water. I was definitely removed somehow and into

some ... other state ... some other experience. I was kind of looking around with my eyes closed but I could see.

'I could feel the same feeling under my feet. I knew I was standing on the pavement but at the same time I was [somewhere else]. It was a very tactile experience.

'I have often thought that, maybe because it was a busy road, somebody would have come up to me because maybe I was there for a little while. I don't really know the duration of this. I was aware that I was in a lake and I think I was at the deepest part. It was more or less in the centre and the water was up to my thighs. It wasn't cold, it wasn't warm. I just knew it was wet. Around me it was desert-like but it wasn't like a desert that I am aware of here.

'The sky was kind of pink, a pinkish kind of colour. I remember thinking at the time it was very pretty. And the sand was kind of yellows and browns but a bit brighter, most definitely yellow and brown, not just sand colours.

'And I was looking around and not once did I think, "What am I doing here?" I was just busy being there and experiencing it. And I felt like I was being watched. I looked around to see if there was anything actually watching me. I could see nothing.

'And [then] there was a craft going through the air. It was like an oblong shape. I think it must have been some kind of metal, it was silvery in colour and it had some windows. I found it quite humorous; I had the distinct feeling it was like a bus. It was just like a bus, it was just like a form of transport to take whatever from one place to another.'

The object made no sound though Lorraine was apparently aware of sounds around her, particularly the movement of wind. She continued:

'That's how it was used, like a shuttle, I suppose. And I looked up and it was quite a way in the distance and I could see that it had windows. I couldn't see into them. But I wanted to. I wanted to see what was going on and I thought, "I want to see what is in that." And then [it] was [as if] I was right up at the windows – but I hadn't moved. I could still feel the water and my feet were still touching ground. And I was up close to the windows. There were creatures in there; first of all there was only one, very small like a child peeping out of a bus window.

'It looked like it was jumping up and down with excitement. The creatures had large eyes, small nose, not a pointed chin but a chin with very small lips. I couldn't see ears but I was aware there might have been little holes there. It didn't have any clothes on; [I could see] it had quite a thin neck and squarish-looking shoulders and body. I could only see to its chest. And it was kind of waving around its arms. [It had] thin arms and thin fingers; I don't know if their hands were like ours, with five fingers on. I'm not really sure, I don't think I took that detail in.'

This is a description of an 'alien' often known as a 'grey', made famous by the front cover of Whitley Strieber's book Communion, *but at the time Lorraine had no knowledge of this, and the experience pre-dates Strieber's book by several years. Lorraine has since seen that picture and agrees that it resembles the entities she saw.*

'Then another creature came. It looked distinctly male, this one. And I thought "It is its child and this is an adult." Then a female came as well; the male adult called the female.'

I asked Lorraine what gave her the impression of gender:

'The eyes. The eyes were slightly different, not

extremely different but you could tell. There was a slight difference, a slight softness I suppose.'

The eyes always seem to be a focal point of these encounters; many witnesses remark on that. Eyes are, of course, called the 'windows of the soul' and they are the only surface feature on the face that is actually alive; the upper skin layers are dead.

Lorraine has a feeling of 'knowledge' and 'contact' with these types of creatures. Apparently long before the Communion *cover or having this sighting she talked to James about the eyes of these beings. She would tell James:*

'But they don't have black eyes, they are a deep, deep purply blue and it shifts. I saw them very close up and it was as if [there was] a shifting beautiful quality of movement within the eye, a really beautiful alive quality. The eye can be touched, it's very resilient. It looks soft, and is to the touch, but it's extremely resilient.'

Returning to the encounter, Lorraine continued her description of the creatures:

'And the little one was a boy. I hadn't assumed what the child was yet, but when I saw the other two I knew [the young one] was a boy because you could tell which is a male and which is a female and this was a boy.

'They were all excited, and pointing, and I thought, "They are pointing at me." But [they were] pointing at me in the distance. I didn't know if they knew I could see them up close. I really wasn't sure.'

I asked Lorraine what she thought the nature of the experience was, particularly the movement from 'normal' space to 'alien' space:

'I don't know. Maybe it was a kind of astral projection. It felt [similar] because I have astral projected. It kind of felt like that. But I was there, maybe not in [the] physical but when you astral project you still feel you are actual physical material, you are still aware of your shape. But I don't know, I haven't been able to explain it all.'

As James put it:

'She had gone somewhere else. [What] we don't know was how long was she there? Was she there for the duration of the experience? Or was she there for a moment out of time? Still in duration as I call it. Five seconds in the dentist's chair is not the same as five seconds sitting in glorious sunshine: [it's a] very different space of time.'

James had talked to Lorraine about her experience many times over the years. He pointed out that the thing that had fascinated him most was her description that the aliens looked surprised – perhaps even shocked – to see Lorraine. We discussed this and speculated that if Lorraine was in some way moved to another location perhaps she was the 'intruder' – suddenly seen by the occupants of a passing vehicle within their own normal habitat.

Was she herself a strange-looking 'alien' in someone's lake, somewhere, sometime?

James speculates that perhaps aliens brought Lorraine into some sort of psychological 'link' and created an intimacy during the encounter. Lorraine said it was a very enjoyable experience. She loves being in water anyway, and considers that perhaps the nature of the experience was a way of relaxing her.

The entities, she thought, might have been alarmed at the sight of her but she herself did not feel frightened. She felt immobilised but not in a frightening way; she could not move but the feeling wasn't unpleasant. Indeed, she has humour in her recall; she found the young one funny because he was so obviously shocked to see her.

Suddenly, 'normal' perception returned. Lorraine

realised she was back in the street and thought 'I'd better start moving.' She was in exactly the same place she had started; she had apparently not moved at all. Nobody had noticed anything – she was not being unduly watched by other pedestrians. If she did 'move' then her disappearance and reappearance must have been instantaneous, even simultaneous. As James put it, 'She may have got out of the co-ordinates of linear time as we perceive it. I'm not surprised at that because first of all we do not know the nature of time or the quality of it.'

The Second Displacement

Approximately two weeks later Lorraine had a similar, and perhaps related, experience.

She was returning home and again she perceived a shift of location back to the same landscape. She was not, however, in the water this time. The colouring and general ambience suggested to Lorraine that she was in the 'same' place, though possibly at a different precise location. The sky was kind of a greenish, mid-green, not pink like the other time.

This time, however, Lorraine did not feel comfortable with the experience, though she has no specific reason for that feeling.

'[I was in] the same street [Lancelot Road], [but] on the other side. I stopped and looked around me because I felt like I [had] stepped into another time.'

Lorraine described the buildings she was seeing in that 'other' landscape:

'They looked like they were maybe glass or metal – I didn't actually go and touch, but they looked as though they were. They were reflecting a lot of light. [They were] a light, silvery colour. They had extremely sloping roofs, they were quite pointed.'

James thought the description reminded him of solar panelling. Lorraine continued:

'I didn't see anybody in them [but felt I was looking at a] mixture of dwellings; people living in there, but also [they] might be work [places]. It felt like a working feeling. They weren't just living there. And even though they looked separate I felt as [though] they would meet up inside; that was just a feeling, I couldn't see that.'

While looking at the strange buildings she also saw, again, a similar air vehicle. This had no windows, however, and was larger than the one she had seen in the previous experience. Again, this made no sound as it flew.

The Man in White

Lorraine and James went on to describe another experience, one that was highly suggestive of the claims of 'Men in Black', though this had the twist of being a 'Man in White'. Lorraine began:

'It was about April, May, or June. We were living in Cornwall. There were four of us altogether. I can't really remember why but we were all having a blazing kind of row that was upsetting for everybody. And as usual – I am a very emotional person – I probably got the most upset. I did get very emotional and it ended up with me not being able to be in that environment any more. And I just blazed outside the door, grabbed a jumper and just went.

'It's a very small village and I just went down the road and there is one bus shelter in the centre of the village and I went down there and sat at the bus shelter. I think it was just past midnight because as I came out of the house the church clock had just chimed midnight. I remember that because I came out and thought, "Ah, the sound of bells was lovely after all that noise." I was sitting on the bench and the sky was very clear and I was looking at the stars because they seemed very bright that night. And sort of opposite me there were a few cottages, quite tall but they call them cottages. But above these cottages I was watching the stars and I was watching this particular one because it was very bright and I thought, "Oh, I have never noticed how quickly stars go out." And I thought this was normal at the time. And it was suddenly going down. It seemed ever so slow, like, I just thought I had never noticed it before. And I disregarded that and I thought, that's interesting. And I think by this time I probably heard the clock about twice [it chimed every quarter of an hour so that would suggest a half hour had passed.]

'And then I heard in the distance – it was very unusual really [because] tourists had only just started to come down and there weren't that many people around – I heard this screeching of a car in the distance.

'And I thought, "Surely it won't come down to the village making all that noise at this time of the night." I heard it come zooming down the hill and when it actually got to where I could see it it was a white car, big, American, and I thought this was unusual. I had never seen a car like that in [that] little village and I knew it wasn't a local's car because I would have seen it. And it came down and it was making a lot of noise.

'And it came down and slowed down once it got to the bottom of the hill, and went at a kind of normal speed, it could be about thirty miles an hour. And it went around the back of me – like I said the road goes right around the green. It went around the green and had to come right around and in front of me. It pulled up in front of me. And I stayed sitting there.

'It was all white inside, the upholstery was white and the steering wheel was white. Everything in there was white but the tyres weren't black. I don't know what they were but they weren't black. There wasn't a contrast of dark tyres. So I don't know what they were but I remember the hubcaps were incredibly shiny like they were new and buffed and they were very, very polished. And I thought, "Wow, this is a new car." It looked really new.

'And there was a young man sitting in there. And he had a white, like, a polo-neck sweater. His trousers were white, shoes were white, everything inside was white. He had a baseball cap on that was white. [He was] bronze-skinned and very tanned. His hair was blond and strangely shiny, like a doll's hair. Like nylon. The only thing that was dark were his shades, his sunglasses. They were dark, sort of squarish, not men's sunglasses.

'He didn't look at me. I just saw him in profile and he looked like a very good-looking man. There was nothing unusual. It wasn't an unusual face, from the profile it was a very nice-looking face. No moustache or beard or anything like that. And I knew, I sensed, that I could go in the car if I wanted to. I was so emotionally upset that I just wished that I could just get out of [that situation I had been in in the house]. I didn't want to experience any more of that; it had been a very distressing situation. And this car was here and I knew that I could open the door and get in and go. Goodness knows where I would have gone. But I nearly did. I actually nearly decided to do it. I thought, "Yes, I am going to do it. I am going to go."

'But then I decided. I didn't speak, but I just basically [thought], "No thank you, you can go." He didn't go straight away.

'There wasn't any sound at this point. There was no ticking over of engine, no exhaust, I couldn't smell any exhaust fumes. I'm very sensitive to exhaust fumes; I would have noticed. I would have been coughing and spluttering by this time if it had been that close to me. It was very silent; there was all that noise of it coming down the road, all this great screeching and speed and now it was strangely silent. And obviously nothing had stirred in the village. A few birds maybe but no people. And [the car] just went. It pulled off and started to make sound then when it pulled away. Up to then it had been very still. And it pulled off and I just watched it go to the bottom of the hill and then wasn't aware of it again.

'And as soon as it had gone I had a sudden feeling like a fear. I suddenly was very frightened and I didn't know why. And at that point I became aware of the clock and I'm sure that it was either quarter to two or two o'clock. And the start of the experience was roughly about half twelve, quarter to one and for a moment I thought, "What? an hour or so? That can't be right." But it wasn't wrong when I got back to the bungalow, so there was that lapse of time. It may have taken an hour to make up my mind ... I don't know what happened. But instead of just getting up and walking back to the bungalow I actually ran. It's a bit uncharacteristic of me to run. I don't feel comfortable running at all, it's not something that I find comfortable to do, but I ran. I wondered why I was running but I knew I was running because I was frightened and it was very confusing because I didn't know what I was frightened about. And I was running up towards where the bungalow is, up this little hill.

'And [then] there was a very loud sound of a helicopter. I looked up and it was just beside me. It was black and I don't remember any lights. I don't remember actual flashing lights like landing lights or that kind of thing. It was going roughly my speed, and in my direction. It wasn't going fast and it was very loud. And I suddenly thought, "Oh why aren't [the villagers] opening their windows?" That really scared me; I thought, "There's something going on here." I started to run faster and it went faster. [The helicopter] had, like, a searchlight. I looked up and it was going across the road. [The light] didn't funnel out like a torch; it was straighter and brighter but it wasn't like a laser. It still looked like a defused kind of light like a searchlight but it didn't actually come into a big circle once it hit the road. It was still quite small. And I thought, "That's for me. I've got to stay out of that light's way." So I stuck really close to the hedge and the wall that went along where I was going. Fortunately it went all the way round. And I knew as long as I stayed close it couldn't get to me. I can't explain why I knew [that]. I got to the bungalow and [the helicopter] was still there. It was actually still above me when I was banging on the door. I didn't take a key. I was banging and James came to the door and I said, "A helicopter is chasing me and I'd just like to get in." And he was looking around, and he said, "There is nothing here." And I said, "There is, it's just gone, it's gone." But James said "But it can't have gone that quickly. I'd see it, I'd hear it in the distance." But it had been there.

'[James] ran out straight away [but didn't see it]. I even asked villagers the next day if they had heard the helicopter, but they hadn't.'

The other people in the house did not hear the helicopter either, but they had remained inside and the house had been double-glazed, which could have accounted for that.

When reviewing the notes with James and Lorraine, James pointed out the strangeness of Lorraine being able to comment on the colour of the car driver's shoes from her seat at the bus stop. Lorraine was quite certain she did see the colour, but was uncertain how. Speculation would include that she stood up; that she did in fact get in the car but no longer remembers that; or that she had the same sort of 'double perspective' vision she described during her first entity sighting in Wembley.

Her story is clearly reminiscent of the 'Men in Black' accounts of earlier years; yet it is interesting that the imagery was not followed through with the 'Man in White' being angelic. He seems still to have been potentially sinister. This suggests little dependence on mental 'image bank'. 'Bad' men in white are a rare image even in science fiction; my only clear knowledge of one is the *Twilight Zone* episode entitled 'Welcome to Winfield', in which Death gives up the black cloak, scythe and chessboard and dresses all in white and drives a white 'supercar' in pursuit of his victims. But even he turns out to be a compassionate and caring Death.

The Group in the Room

Lorraine related a story from earlier in her life, which also contained accounts of entities similar to those she had seen in Wembley:

'I had never read anything or seen any footage or any books or anything about [UFOs]. It wasn't an interest. And I was sitting on my own in a room in the house and I closed my eyes and I felt very tired. And [I was] in a [different] room. There were other people in the house who would have noticed if I had gone if they had come into the room [I was originally in], which they didn't. I was on my own in there for about forty minutes, I suppose. It probably wasn't the duration of the vision but that's how long I was in there until somebody came in.

'[I had] a white gown on, right from my neck and covering right down to my feet. I don't know if there were sleeves or not, I'm not sure. If there were any they were all white. And around me in, like, a semi-circle there were ten people. I think it was ten. They had these gowns on as well. All I could see was their heads really, and occasionally I'd see a hand. And there were different people sitting and listening and some were taking notes, and recording. One of the people was a child. Female, it wasn't a male.

'[The] tape recorder was a huge thing, it was like a big one with reels going round. I think it had a largish microphone on a stand.

'I think I was seeing the whole situation, and I could see me, as if I was looking at a picture. I could see everything. There was no fear at all. Their fingers were long and they looked bony, whether it had bones or not I don't know, but they looked bony.'

Lorraine described that the creatures were floating in mid-air, and their arms were somehow floating also. Lorraine had the impression that their garments were not, however, defying gravity but were just hanging on the creatures' bodies. James pointed out that that would mean that the creatures could manipulate their own weightlessness but not that of other materials; he speculates that this could indicate that their weightlessness is a natural part of their environment. James points out the similarity to the descriptions given by Whitley Streiber, though this experience also predates the book.

Lorraine continued:

'Their eyes were big, almond shapes and the heads were . . . call it [the] classic shape now, but I didn't know that [then]. I was fascinated by the eyes. I always want to say [they were] black or blue but I'm not sure. I see them as dark but I also see them as light. That's what makes me think they have changed. Because I see them as dark and shiny and then I see them as sort of spongy, like they changed. It was very odd.'

The final case in this section is quite different. Whereas Janice, Bryan and Rohan seem to be struggling with an understanding of their experiences Sten Lingren, a Swedish contactee, is very certain that he understands what is happening. His contacts are 'classical'; and from the Adamski, Menger, Daniel Fry 'school of experiences'.

STEN

Sten started by referring to the triangular UFOs reported in Europe over the last few years. They had been seen mainly in Belgium, though there had been reports in France and England. There were now many reports from Sweden, from an area north of Gothenburg. 'It is a modern version of the old Adamski-shaped craft; three balls [underneath].' These types of UFOs are a central part of Sten's story.

Phase One

Sten saw his first UFO in 1957, near his parents' country house:

'Something came down from the sky, staying at about a hundred and fifty metres high. [It] was a sphere about ten metres in diameter [coloured] green-yellow. The other [people] said [that it was] a meteor but I [knew that it wasn't] because my father was an amateur astronomer. A meteor could not stop in the air and stay [motionless].

'It was hovering there for five minutes. I felt [that I was] being watched. Then it went up with tremendous acceleration. I didn't know what it was but I understood [that it was] something which was controlled.

'One year later, in the same place and at dusk – about six or seven o'clock – [I and a friend] were playing badminton. [Just] when I was [about] to smash the ball I saw a mother ship. I didn't know [then] that it was a mother ship, but I saw a cigar-shaped metallic object without windows, without any wings, without sound, coming slowly over the area, perhaps one kilometre from us. Probably it was twice or three times [the size of] an ordinary aeroplane in length.

'It was a metallic, reflecting object. But I didn't know what it was. I thought, "What a strange thing without wings." I had heard about zeppelins, but it was not such a thing.'

Sten later confirmed that his badminton partner, and others, had also seen the object.

'They saw it but they rejected it as if [it was] of no importance. But I stayed and looked.'

Sten told me that his friends had dismissed the sighting as being of a meteor.

'About one half-year later my father was informed by a friend, an amateur astronomer, about "things" happening in the United States called flying saucers. He had got copies of pictures; I wanted to see them. When I saw these pictures and heard the stories I connected [them] with my own observations. [I] then started to read books because I was ignited with interest about this subject.

'Moving on to about 1963: I and my girlfriend were going into the town to meet some friends. We were going to take a train. We were leaving this house [the house in which Sten still lives and where we conducted this interview] and when we [got] outside about five or ten metres I got the [compulsion] to look up. When I looked up there was, [at a height of] about one kilometre, something metallic so I ran in and got the binoculars. [I] came out and had quite a good look at this object. [It was a] spacecraft with three spheres under it, three balls. I got my parents out and we [all] used the binoculars, looking at it for about ten minutes. Suddenly the craft tilted, the balls went into the craft, they disappeared, and then it accelerated with an extremely "forced" movement.' [Sten used his hands to demonstrate rapid acceleration upwards.]

'Then I remembered the time. We should [have] missed the train [which had left] ten minutes [ago]. But then I got a strange impression – a kind of telepathic direction: "Go down to the station, the train will be there." So we did that. We went down [to the station] and the train was standing, waiting, at the station. When we [got there] the driver came out, we [boarded] the train, and came into the city.'

Sten clearly believed that the train had been held up for him; later conversation was to indicate that he believed this was alien intervention, guiding and assisting him.

Sten went back to his description of the sighting:

'The type of craft was the same as one [photographed] by Daniel Fry's wife.' [Daniel Fry is a celebrated contactee from America, who first reported sightings in the 1950s.] [By] the later part of 1963 I had begun wondering why I had had the opportunity, from 1957 to 1963, to have about six [to] eight observations of craft, different types of spacecraft: one mother ship and some other kinds of discs [and] things going in strange patterns over the area. I began wondering, "Who am I, who am I to have had this opportunity?" "That's strange," I thought, "to see one spacecraft – that's great luck – but to see six or seven, that was strange," I thought.'

Sten's next story had a suggestion of more direct contact.

'I was standing [in Stockholm, waiting] to go [by] tram [to see] a friend. It was in the daytime, in the late summer. I was waiting for the tram to come, and I was looking around [at various] people. [There were] about ten people standing in a little area around [me]. Suddenly, when my eyes were sweeping over the area, [I saw] a girl [and] something happened. From her eyes two very powerful rays were emitted. [Like a] laser beam. Take a laser beam which is one centimetre in diameter from each eye. It was so powerful; these [rays] coming out. She radiated [them] from her eyes and at the same moment she transmitted this [telepathic kind of] contact, [informing me of] who she was. She was an extraterrestrial being with a mission to contact me to open up the contact. And she told [me] some other things. And this took place in about one second; all this information was coming in. I was not afraid but my thoughts were operating like a propeller after that. Tremendous [speed of thought].

'I didn't know [what to do] because at the same moment the tram was coming in; the tram which I was going to take. I went on the tram; I didn't know [what else] to do. And she also went on the tram. There were a lot of people. We were standing in the same part of the tram, at the end of the tram there is a little platform [where we were].

'I didn't know [what to do]. At that time I was very shy [with] girls; I wouldn't normally [approach] a girl and talk with her. And in this case this was not a normal girl. So I was not afraid but I was shy.

'[When the tram reached the destination] I [got] off like a robot. She also [got] off. I [was looking] at her. She turned around to me, smiled, turned [back] and left in the same direction as the tram [had] come. I was confused [by] this thing but I was very inspired also. It was a tough experience, but a good one, very good. I felt very good, but excited.'

Sten moved on to another observation the following year:

'One year later, in 1964, I was walking near the plant, the gas installations [which had been pointed out to me earlier during my tour of the area – JS]. It was during the night. Suddenly I could see a little cigar-shaped object, about one hundred metres in length, which was visible partly over the clouds and partly under the clouds. [The sky] was not wholly clouded, it was partially clouded [at that time]. This craft had windows of some type, big windows. Suddenly something strange happened. Inside my head, a clear voice was heard. It was a male voice, [apparently] age about thirty years old, talking to me in perfect Swedish, saying: "Sten Lingren, we are going to contact you in the future." And then the ship disappeared and nothing [else] happened; only this little transmission.'

[Of the voice] 'It was metallic and [it] also [had] a little reverberation in it. I was later told – [of] this communication – how they did it. It was not telepathic, it was electronic communication, [and] they did it from the ship by directing an electronic beam, modulating the hearing nerve in the ear.'

Sten went on to close his account of this first 'phase' of his encounters by telling me of a different type of contact:

'Later on, I was contacted in some way by a woman. I will use the name Bea. This women was later to inform me about "things" and later [gave me] more and more [information]. I understood that this person was in connection with some group of cosmic visitors who were here. Later on I understood more about it; who she really was. She was human, like you, like me. A normal person in Stockholm, [or at least] looking like a normal person. She contacted me in some way but some parts [of my story] are kept out of information [that I am giving you].'

Sten went on to tell me that he felt he could only impart about ten per cent of the information that he had discovered; that it was not the right time yet to impart more.

We discussed Bea for a time, as I was unclear as to her 'origins'. I asked if he thought she was an extraterrestrial sent here to do a certain mission, or whether she was a human with alien contact:

'It's absolutely impossible for me to acknowledge or deny. Maybe all of you are also space beings, I don't know. But I know that she was very kind and that many, many things she told us have been correct. Bea was the main contact. I think if I put the question to her, "Are you from outer space?", she would not answer the question. I think she was, or is, a space person. She could bend her fingers but backwards, a physical thing which I can tell you normal people cannot do. I think she is a space woman, not only [some] one working with the space people but I think she is real [extraterrestrial] because I have seen things that you [haven't]. I've seen things. She could also call from the spacecraft with communication equipment connecting to the telephone line. They could call with a normal telephone receiver from the spacecraft like we use mobile telephones now.'

Phase Two

Sten made a clear distinction between what had happened up to then, and what he was to begin telling me about in 'phase two' – my choice of words, incidentally:

'In 1965 [a] friend of ours [named Daniel] received his

first contact in a [place] called Nävsjön; it's a lake one hundred and fifty kilometres from Stockholm. He was alone in a nature reserve very far from civilisation. A big craft came down; [it was] about two hundred metres in diameter. It landed and a ramp went out and out came a "person".

'[Actually it was] hovering over the lake, [over the part called the] swamp. You can walk [there] but you [might] go down in the mud.

'This person was [walking] but he was not putting his feet down in the mud. He was [walking] like a robot. He wasn't a robot but he was [moving] like that over the [swamp]. He came to Daniel, [to within] two metres [of] him. [The person] had a helmet on; the [face] shield went down with an electrical noise. [Daniel] could hear a little motor as it went down, and he could see two human eyes looking at him. This person was about two hundred and ten centimetres high, a very big [person], like a bodybuilder. He had a belt on with lamps flashing, or blinking.

'No communication was happening, only some gestures with the hands. [Then the person] withdrew into the ship and it took off; Daniel was shaken by this.

'Some weeks after[wards] they started to communicate [again]. [The aliens] contacted [Daniel] again. [For] a couple of contacts they talked English, they talked Swedish later.

'[During] the first contact [the person wore a] helmet. [During] the second contact [there were] two men in helmets; one took off his helmet and talked by mouth. [Communication was] not good at that moment but later on – some months after – they had normal communications. A couple of contacts happened in the time from about July 1965 [through to] October. Daniel [had been] selected as a contactee and most of his contacts took place in this area.

'Now we go on into interesting things. You know Bea was one of the contacts in Stockholm now; we are finding that there are people who have connection with a group from outer space.'

Sten brought Christer (who was another contactee) into the discussion. He had been at the interview throughout.

'Christer and I were told [about] the space people, for [whom] we use the word CBH – meaning Cosmic Brotherhood. It's the same group that [contacted] [George] Adamski, [Howard] Menger and [Daniel] Fry. They have persons stationed in Sweden, outer-space people working here. [Not only Sweden but] I just talk about Sweden.

'From one of these contacts we received [information] that [the CBH] would do a test over Sweden. [On] 29 October 1965, at the exact time of seven o'clock in the evening, they would perform a test. And at seven o'clock [on that] evening there were about thirty mother ships and about three hundred spacecraft – and smaller things also – coming in from south Sweden [and] going north. It [caused] a lot of reports in the papers; every Swedish paper had these things on the headlines.'

Sten had many press cuttings which he showed me, and the several people at the interview translated the text for me, reading through the newspapers that I was indicating.

I asked whether we were discussing daylight discs or night lights. At that time of the year, Sten confirmed, it would be dark at seven o'clock in the evening. However, he was certain that the sightings were of objects, not just lights:

'Big objects with windows,' he described. 'The mother ships were the biggest ones [at] about one kilometre in length. But most of them were not so big; they were about one hundred, two hundred and three hundred metres [in] length. [There were] also small Adamski-shaped crafts. They went over all Swedish cities.

'Olov Lagercrantz, the chief editor of [one of the main] newspapers, *Dagens Nyheter*, was in Stockholm and he was shown one of the cigar-shaped craft which came down over where he was. [He wrote] big, excited information about seeing this fantastic cigar-shaped object. He first thought it was a big aeroplane, then he thought it was a zeppelin, then he understood it was a tremendous object.'

Christer Janson introduced himself for my tape recorder, and he and Sten together took up the narrative. For ease of reading I am not specifying which of the two said any individual passages, it was very clear that they were checking and confirming with each other throughout the discussions and that they had no points of disagreement.

'I have known Sten for about thirty years and we have worked together in many cases connected to the UFOs and observations of the sky, also working with the whole phenomenon of the UFO and "new age" and such things. Together we have had many experiences. [Regarding the] one which you have just heard about, it was a big event. It was a psychological test taking place from the south part of Sweden up to the north part. It took about one hour, this overflight.

'About three weeks later, Sten and I were invited to [be with] Daniel [the person involved in the "lake" contacts – JS] about fifteen Swedish miles south of Stockholm. [It was] to be a special occasion, on a Saturday evening. We had a kind of psychic preparation, a mental preparation, during the hours we were with Daniel and his family at that time: we had some rules to follow, to take away watches and metal objects on our bodies and [it was demanded of us that] we be [in] a –

call it – higher state of mentality and not in a lower, or vulgar, [state] of mentality. [We had to have] good behaviour.

'Before we approached the landing area we [received] a scanning procedure. You sensed [as if] someone had put an electrical grid or helmet over your head and it was going down in the brain; it scanned the brain in some ways. [There] was no dangerous feeling, no hostile feeling. It was very comfortable, very nice to experience, nothing hostile or dangerous. It didn't [do] any harm or hurt. It was something we checked with each other later on after this evening's [events]; and we confirmed that we both had the experience.'

Moving on to the time of the event:

'We were sitting in [Daniel's] car, driving to Lake Nävsjön, the lake where we were going to have this [event]. At a special time we were told not to speak to each other but [to] be completely silent and try to "listen inwardly".

'Daniel signalled with the car's headlights two kilometres from the lake. Beside the lake [ten metres] was the landing point. We were asked to get out of the car. There was Sten and I standing [together]. The other group [consisted of] Daniel, his wife and a fifth man – a friend. They were walking towards a shining object, the shining point, like five-by-ten halogen lamps in a sports stadium, dimmed, and an Adamski-type craft was visible, about fifteen metres diameter, six metres high and about fifty to sixty metres away from the parked car. A "being" had come out of this lighted area, and was shining a yellow light, something like a sodium lamp.

'Daniel took a flashlight from his car when the being came out and he made three short blinks; the being took something from his belt and made three blinks with a laser-like light.

'At the same time there were two other spacecraft overhead; three hundred metres up and six hundred metres up.

'[One of the men – the fifth man] had an envelope in his hand when he went out [to the spacecraft]; and he came back with no envelope.'

I asked about this man and the envelope; no one seemed keen to discuss this part of the event in detail. Sten told me that he had had a few meetings with the fifth man, but they did not work with him regularly:

'After a while, five minutes or so, we were asked to go [back to] the car; still being directed inwardly, still being silent, good behaviour and so on, no metallic [objects]. And we were driven by Daniel maybe five kilometres away. Then we were asked again to leave the car; we got out of the car and were standing at the border of a field many hundreds of metres in diameter. We looked up at the sky and something very strange happened.

'It was like our senses were magnified or like the stars were coming maybe ten times closer to us, a zooming effect of some kind. [It was] like we took a part of the universe inside us in a completely different manner than we ordinarily experience things. But we experienced it with our eyes; it was a physical magnification.

'Later, Sten and I confirmed that we both had experienced the same thing at the same moment. Never afterwards or before have I experienced something like this. [For] all [of] this evening, and [for] maybe some days afterwards, we were – like – in another consciousness, a higher level consciousness.'

Sten spoke about the early days when he and Christer had started working together:

'We had started, in Sweden, a UFO group. Christer was with us in the beginning. We started it up sometime in the 1960s. We made contact with all observers of

UFOs from the newspapers, we contacted them and served them by [providing information on] books [they might want to read] and [we arranged that] they could borrow slides. We did it in a non-commercial way; serving them. We called [this little UFO group in Stockholm] the Inter-Galactical Federation. We were about twenty persons. We had a lot of communication with letters around the world; about three hundred letter contacts we had. It took a lot of time to do that. One of the observers was Heinz Böhme who had had close encounters [at fifty metres], seen G.A.-type ships, scanning discs, seen a mothership and had a car stop [engine stop] with craft close to him in Åtvidaberg, Sweden.

'In Sweden we were doing [UFO-related] work – Bertil Kuhlemann, me, and others. I remember we were working with a scientific project; small remote-control stations containing an electrically driven camera with wide-angle optics. [There was a] triggering mechanism for magnetic disturbance in the atmosphere which caused the dome to open and the camera to start. The project was going to place these stations all around the meteorological stations in Sweden. [The meteorological station staff] were to change the batteries and film. This was a costly project. It was a big project and it took us about one month to do all the writings to the scientific [bodies] and [to do] the grant applications.

'We were [working on this] at the Royal Academy of Engineering Science on the night of 17 August 1968 at nine o'clock in the evening. You understand that at this time I had been trained for communication, I had met Bea, I had learned about the space people. I had been training for communication. Suddenly at this [exact] time I received a message: "Get in contact as soon as possible with Heinz Böhme." So we telephoned Düsseldorf to find Heinz Böhme but we didn't manage to do that because [he] had no telephone. So we sent an express letter that evening just to open the communication with him, [as instructed] by the CBH. That same night Heinz Böhme woke up in the night, about two o'clock. He felt that he had to get up and he went to the back of his house. Hovering over the ground was a little craft about five metres in diameter. From the top of the craft they radiated a message to him, a transmission, you can use the word telepathic if you like, but it is not normal telepathy. It's electronic transmission. They told him: "Get in contact with the people in Stockholm as soon as possible for a mission you will do before the end of 1968." So he was very excited. He couldn't sleep that night and he sent a letter the next day. Our letters crossed [with] each other.

'So when we received his letter we were [wondering] what [would] happen; we didn't know. In the coming months there were plans to do a television [series] in Sweden, of twelve programmes called *The Hour*. [And now] they were going to make the last, the twelfth, programme. In the television team there was a new man [called] Ulf. They were trying to create the last programme but they had no idea what it would contain. [Ulf] managed to create an idea, [to do a programme on the] "new age". [The television company agreed to this.] So they [started to] research; they were looking for material. [Ulf] had heard that someone in Stockholm had pictures and films [of] UFOs, and he [obtained] my telephone number. When he called me – at that time I lived in Larsberg – the lights in my home began to pulse. Every time when he called it [happened].

'When he called the first time I remembered Heinz Böhme. So I told him about things happening in Germany, and also incidents with us. [The television company] was interested.

'Bjarne [a colleague] and I were up there talking about, and showing, films. When we did that, strange things happened inside the television company.

'There was a group of about eight persons, the editing team for the programme; and they wanted to see the films. We went into an area where they "cut" the films. They were putting films together, sixteen-millimetre [film] at that time. They put the film into the "showing equipment", pressed the button and "bang", the lamp exploded. They changed the lamp, put in another one, pushed the button and it [also] exploded. Now they did not have a new lamp. There are about thirty small [cutting] rooms and they were all occupied. So they had to wait for the next room to be ready. We went into this half an hour later, put the film in, pushed the button, and the transformer burned [out]. So we had to wait.

'Now it happened that one of the people in the team had to leave for a domestic flight to another part of Sweden; and [his attitude] was very negative [about] UFOs. [After] he disappeared they put the film into a new room and it went OK.

'So now he was [out of the way] and they said, "Let's take this Heinz Böhme and make UFOs the main theme." [Up to] that time we didn't know it would be the main theme. And it was [planned] that Heinz Böhme was to be taken from Düsseldorf to Sweden [by] aeroplane, and I was also to be in the programme.

'I told Bea about what happened and she told me [CBH] were going to make a big test over Sweden, [a] psychological test. I was instructed to tell some people about what would happen.

'The programme was recorded at four o'clock in the afternoon and broadcast at eight o'clock in the evening. Some of the television people were told that before, or during, the programme there was to be a "space operation" [UFO sightings] over Sweden; the CBH [were going to] make a big psychological test of the reaction of the people [to] seeing the films and pictures on the television. They had a kind of triggering signal, a triggering pulse, and in some way they were going to use the television broadcasting transmitters around Sweden. At a specified moment they [would] measure how the people reacted.

'And one of the spacecraft [came down] down over the television building during the recording session. During the recording [session] I was in communication with the craft [from] the studio. They had a communication line with me during the programme. You could call it telepathic.

'They had complete access to every movement in the studio. There were three cameras; call them one, two and three. They knew exactly when [for example] camera three [was] going to switch on. They had one hundred per cent control of everything.

'The evening papers [were] telling about spacecraft over Stockholm, over the city. People [saw] the spacecraft operating over Stockholm and also around Sweden [in] about twenty places, and where the craft came down close to the transmitter of the television tower. The project was one hundred per cent good for CBH.

'When I talked with Bea I asked her [to] arrange that Ulf Hultberg and Mona Sjöström, who was his girlfriend, also working as a producer at the television company, should see a spacecraft. "Take down a spacecraft so they will have a look." And [Bea] said she would probably [arrange] it.

'In the spring of 1969 the chief editor of the other biggest Swedish Newspaper, *Svenska Dagbladet*, [was] Allan Hernelius. His wife, Jeanette von Heidenstam, was a famous Swedish television announcer presenting the programme. [One evening] they were in a mansion one hundred kilometres south of Stockholm, and Ulf and Mona were there. Ulf Hultberg was the main channel of this twelfth broadcasting programme, *The Hour*, and he was the one who caused everything to run one hundred per cent. Remember I [had] asked Bea to fix an observation for them. When they were at this mansion one of the spacecraft came down. They were inside the house but they felt they had to go out for a walk.

'It was a clear evening in the spring, without snow, a crystal clear sky, it was dark outside. They were looking at the stars and saw these millions of little dots and felt they were part of the universe. Suddenly a bright glow appeared: it was a craft which looked like a bus in size. They felt very affected in their hearts and souls, they felt very excited. They went back to the mansion and talked about what had happened and when they were there talking the craft came back and flew outside the windows. [Mona] was very happy to see these things; she was impressed by these things in her heart and it caused her to be inspired. She said it was fantastic and that she [would] never forget [the] experience.

'The CBH can find a person anywhere on the planet or in the universe. They told me that every person has a specified frequency.'

Other Swedish contactees and researchers have told me the same thing, including the suggestion that using something similar to dowsing people can be 'tracked' by aliens. It is not so far removed from the American view that people are tracked by having devices inserted into their noses and ears – just a less technologically dependent version of the same theory.

Christer and Sten talked randomly for a time about sightings they had shared. They sensed, I think, that I was having some trouble taking in all that I was being told and they were at pains to point out that many sightings were shared, that there were multiple witnesses – including the two of them – to several incidents. They regarded it as important that I should know they could confirm what each other was saying.

For example:

'We were [together] in a place outside Stockholm when a George Adamski-type craft came within one hundred metres over us. It radiated a force field which was so intense that I had to drive the car to the side and stop. Every cell in the body was receiving vibration. A tremendous force.'

Sten took up some different points, first referring directly to me:

'Bea told [me] something which could be of interest to you. In Scandinavia there [were] about twelve to sixteen space people working here: in Denmark, Sweden, Norway and Finland. There were other countries also but they talked about Scandinavia. The main communication and transports they had were to England. So I have drawn my own conclusion that the operation they did was in some way connected with England because they had some kind of centre in England for Scandinavia. So Scandinavian channels were directed towards England. These space people, they talked a lot of languages. [This would have been] between 1965 and up to 1980 [when] Bea was stationed in Sweden.

'I was "disconnected" from her then. She left Sweden in 1980 and I was to do my own mission and I have [since] been in connection with them by communication only. So I cannot reach them except by telepathy but they [can] reach me.

'I will tell you what's going on now because you are going to see things happening in this world of which you are one of the first people outside Sweden to know.

303

When you [leave] this house today you will be confused but you will see what's happening just now. Hopefully confused on a higher level.

'Something you need to know: Bea confirmed that Adamski, Howard Menger and Daniel Fry, every one of them was a true contact of the same group [CBH]. They were true contacts. But a lot of people have caused them to be seen like frauds.'

Sten took up the narrative:

'In 1981 I was going to give a lecture in a place in Stockholm and my car [was] in the garage under my workplace. I came out with the car into the street and there was a spacecraft over the area. I followed it up to Ropsten and then the craft went out to Lidingö and I followed it just up to this place where it was [hovering]. I [got] out of the car, aligned my attention on the object and then I received a message that during [that night's meeting] there would be an important contact.

'I gave a lecture talking about UFOs. When there was a break one person, who had come to watch me, had a talk with me. That was a very important person in the television company, Jeanette von Heidenstam. [She] told me about the observation in the mansion south of Stockholm and about [the] things which happened when Ulf and Mona saw the craft which was ordered by Bea to come down.

'When they fixed the transmission for me it was two hours before the lecture. They knew exactly how important this meeting was to be with this Jeanette von Heidenstam at the lecture. This caused – later on – contacts to be established with the news media, with the television company. They helped me in different ways to fix contacts. They arranged everything. I don't need to do so much, they fix it. They fixed up Heinz Böhme to be on the television from Düsseldorf up to Stockholm.

And they knew that the [lecture that night] was important and they knew that before it happened.

'They are checking now. They know that you are here and there is a plan in which you are involved in some way. But I don't know it yet. But we will see.'

Sten moved on to an operation he conceived in 1984, one which Bertil Kuhlemann commented was something of a 'successor' to Project Hessdalen:

'I asked my [CBH] contacts to try if they could do a special operation in Sweden. We talked about it, we fixed it together. There were two people in Sweden who knew about it before it happened: Bertil [Kuhlemann] and another person from Dalarna [in Sweden]. My plan was to ask CBH to fix an observation station over a specified place in Sweden. In the middle of 1984 I told Bertil that I was going to order an overflight operation over an area. On 28 December I was up in Dalarna and gave a lecture for about thirty people. During that lecture I [received a] transmission from them [the CBH] that they would start the operation soon. About one week after that they started one of the biggest operations that they have done in Sweden; about two hundred and fifty operations in a period of two weeks over a specified area. There were big mother ships [and] different sorts of craft reported. That was the week that shocked Dalarna. [It was] the biggest UFO outbreak we ever have seen in Sweden; [in] the geographical area [around] Dalarna. Every newspaper had this in the headlines every day for fourteen days.' We were all reading the press cuttings of the outbreak. Bertil Kuhlemann translated a question one of the newspapers had asked: "Has the phenomenon moved from Hessdalen into Dalarna?" Bertil commented: "I thought it was a very good idea to have the Hessdalen phenomena move over to Sweden because of the inconvenience of the area where the Hessdalen phenomenon was occurring. So I simply confirmed to Sten that I knew he had told me half a year before it started happening and then on 28 December [Sten] told the group of people up there [in Dalarna] that they would be seeing things. I also told Sten that I thought it would be very much more convenient to have them in Dalarna.'

Sten went on to discuss other contacts:

'[In] 1970 Bjarne Håkansson, myself and a girl, Ritva, and her daughter were going by car from Stockholm to Nyköping where we were going to meet a person. When we [were] about sixty kilometres south of Stockholm, Bea contacted me by communication channel and told me that they would come down with a carrier or a mother ship and I was to inform the people in the car before that happened so they would have a proof of communication. So I told the people in the car that a craft would come down and a couple of minutes later they [sent] down this very big ship, about one kilometre in length. It came down over E4 [the main road in the area – JS]; it was in the morning so [there] was no heavy traffic; no [other] cars. From the ship Bea told me that there were three people aboard the spacecraft who [had a] connection with our group in Sweden. Three people; the rest of the crew – about seven or eight hundred persons – had nothing to do with us. But three people on board – one was Bea – and two other people had something [to do with us]. They did that for proof for the people in the car because Bjarne, who was the target of this operation, was to have a proof of my contact with CBH; it was a proof for him.

'By that time he had had his own experiences, but he had no communication [at that time], only [a sighting of the] craft coming down. Then they told me by communication channel that they [could not] stay in the area because of radar and other things. They didn't want to be observed. So they told me to tell [the others] in the car that they [would] raise the craft in a specified angle and then take off like that. [Sten used his hands to show a steep upward glide.] Just for communication proof; and they did that. They tilted and . . . [flew upwards].

'I am trained for [these communications]. The normal person cannot take the communication channel one hundred per cent. It's very difficult to have communication established and have it running. You have to know visualisation and concentration. I have been given a lot of exercises just to train concentration.

'We go on to 1982. I [was] on my way in to Stockholm City when a little cigar-shaped craft came down. It was about one hundred metres [in length]. [With] this craft I [could] see the force field, it was in the daytime. The play of the force field is so beautiful. At this time there was heavy traffic so I couldn't get into the right lane. You know we have right-hand traffic in Sweden. There was heavy traffic so I wanted to slow down but there were so many cars I had to look when I was driving. [It was] at this moment I received instruction for the URD project. The next step, you see, was contact with the Research Department of Defence of Sweden to get their material out of the files to put it into the computer. [CBH] fixed that.

'I have been told the following: from the spacecraft they have a kind of ray they use. They can select a geographical area [and] put out the transmitting rays. Some of the people will react. In the ship there is an automatic response indicator which takes the receiving signal back and they do a kind of test. They put out something and they receive something. And the receiving is checked after some time and then they select people who are responsive to a kind of consciousness level. These are the people they are looking for. And they have some people [under] observation for ten years, for twenty years or so.

'If everything is OK the contact will come. And they have a lot of different patterns they use. Technical, social and spiritual awareness have to be in balance, they say, just to handle civilisation in a good way.

'[Of the] esoteric knowledge of the brothers: they say that one of the most important steps we haven't understood in this world yet is the "common denominator principle".'

Sten demonstrated by diagrams how different types of connections can be made by people and indicated that people must try to find their common areas and build on them, rather than concentrating on their differences. As the author of a book on corporate change planning, and a trainer for industry in that subject, I recognised this as one of the principles of getting people to accept change, and build a dialogue leading to understanding. Presumably Sten's CBH contacts are well versed in getting people to accept change – as indeed they would need to be!

'Bea told me [in 1967 or 1968] that they were operating on a thirty-year plan. That means that the plan is ending – at the latest – about 1999 [even] if I [am] one year [in error] and if the plan only just started then. That means that the plan is running in [its] final [phase].

'They have contacted a lot of governments. [These governments] are fully aware [of] the existence of CBH and other groups also. There are about ten different civilisations doing projects on this planet now. That does not include perhaps hundreds of civilisations visiting this planet, and leaving; they are not involved in the planet project. Most of them [look like humans] but not all. I do not know of [all these civilisations] in detail; I know only that six, seven or eight are co-operating.

'CBH is one of them; CBH represents about six hundred solar systems which have a lot of different civilisations, but it's one group in my [figures].

'I know that they travel in a couple of hours in the galaxy [and] in a couple of days outside the galaxy. [Their] travel is very fast; time is not a problem, it's the start and the stop which is a problem – and navigation. The travel is no problem. But they have navigation problems and security problems or safety problems. I don't know, I am not given [this] information. We are so stupid in comparison with them that we cannot understand [other than] a small fraction.

'It will be shock for people when they know who they are. They told us that we have common ancestors. We who are living on this planet now have been colonised a lot of times from different sources. They have placed people here and these people who [were] sent here have forgotten the knowledge and the civilisation they have. And there have been wars and civilisations have come and gone, a lot of times.'

I asked Sten what his 'mission' was – in the broadest terms:

'When you get in contact you get a responsibility inside you and it causes you to act. First you understand yourself and your connection with them. Then you understand the Earth people and the problem the Earth has. When you can see both the Earth situation and their society then you think the people here are completely mad. And then you feel compassion, I think, for the Earth people and there starts a process inside just to evolve in some way the consciousness which causes you to try to help in some way. What I try to do is to try to [communicate] my own experience to people in Sweden, [tell them] just what I know exists. I know that [CBH] exists and I know how the Earth is and I know that if I can focus the people to understand [CBH] we can lift mankind up in some way.'

I commented that UFO activity was very high in Sweden at that time, with many 'triangular UFOs' being reported north of Gothenburg.

'What is going on just now in Sweden is probably the opening up of a kind of big operation for the whole planet. The CBH will manifest themselves in Sweden and Scandinavia. What I don't know is if they will do the same [thing] at the same time in other countries. But what will happen here is that they will break through.

'You know in Norway you have Hessdalen. This was a psychological test in some way, I don't know exactly. I know that when they picked up people for Dalarna they selected the forces which were stationed in Hessdalen and moved them to Dalarna. You know there are [CBH] people assigned to [certain] countries, assigned to specific projects.

'This plan is not Scandinavian, it's a global plan and it has segments with different parts of the world. If we are opening up for a finalisation of the plan right now there should be [similar] things [happening] in different countries.'

Sten then turned the tables and challenged me, asking whether I was able to believe the things he was saying to me. I stated, as always, that I keep as open a mind as possible but that I was a researcher – not a believer – and in the end I needed some sort of proof. I do not restrict my thinking or my research to presently accepted sciences, but I know that in the end we have to find an appropriate science. It was interesting that Sten's conviction was so strong that he found my lack of belief difficult to comprehend. He said: 'Is this so complex for you that you can't grasp that they have physical beings stationed on this planet in different countries, that they have a network? You haven't taken this and accepted it as reality yet. It isn't quite clear for you that it is so because you have no experience of [CBH]. What proof would you require?'

I suggested that I would certainly welcome the landing of an Adamski-like saucer then and there. It was certainly not the only proof I would accept, but since Sten had arranged something like that for others perhaps he could arrange something for me; I indicated a spot in a park outside Sten's window. Sten pointed out that there had been plenty of sightings. I made the point that he had had personal contact; could I not have the same? I suggested I was quite happy to stay awake that night and wait for a landing if he could arrange one. [Bertil, with some humour, pointed out that since I was staying at his home at that time that would mean having a landing in his garden, and he wasn't so sure he liked that idea!]

Sten concluded by suggesting that I would have my wish, but it would be some time in the future, not yet. I shall look forward to it.

I have covered my beliefs about the UFO experience in early chapters and choose not to comment further on these four cases here. As much as possible in a book written by one person and therefore expressing his views, I want to leave these cases open for the readers to consider for themselves.

Over to you . . .

20 Gaia Intervention

T he *popularity* of the image that aliens are coming to Earth for a variety of possible purposes has its origins in our 'science-fiction' culture, even if that image also happens to be true. Other possible interpretations are being missed in this 'rush to the stars'. With no more scientifically solid evidence to support a Gaia intervention than an alien intervention, I have included the following cases in this chapter as there is at least some indication that 'Mother Earth' could be using the UFO phenomenon as a guiding or teaching tool of her own. Many contactees, and abductees, have felt a kinship to the Earth; if the alien experience is not the same as the 'eco-friendly' experience it might be linked in some way.

The alternative view would suggest that those who believe their experiences are simply themselves creating a reason why they should hear what they expect to hear, and be told to do what they want to do. Whatever the truth, these experiences are beneficial for the percipients, and presumably for the ecology if a heightened ecological awareness occurs as a result.

I am not trying to 'push' this Gaia alternative, but merely to give it a hearing amidst the clamour of ETH-theories. I start with the experiences of Bertil Kuhlemann, a colleague who has been involved in UFO study for many years of his life and is a prominent UFO researcher in Sweden. The context into which he fits his beliefs is much wider, and much more profound.

BERTIL

'It was in the middle of the fifties, 1955 I think, and I think it was a couple of days before Midsummer Day. I had for a year or so been discussing "life" issues with a young man living just opposite my flat. He was chauffeur to a Swedish millionaire. His employer would spend nine months of the year in Bolivia where he ran a wood company and come back to Sweden for three months over the summer.

'This young man started to provide me with articles from weekly papers, mainly about reincarnation cases based upon spiritualist mediums and their conversations with the souls of dead people. I needed to have a thorough discussion with him and it was set up to begin at eight o'clock in the evening. Our discussion went on for hours and suddenly at five o'clock in the morning we got in what we later called a situation where we were in "a swing with God". [I cannot find a better term for it.] After the experience, it might have lasted a quarter of an hour or something like that, I went across the road back to my flat and entered the garden. We lived in a cottage with a garden at that time and there were beds of beautiful roses. I knelt down and I got in touch with one of the roses: I was actually part of its system of juices running through the stem up to the rosebuds and it was such a magnificent feeling. I was really enlightened. I had a couple of hours' sleep and in the morning my wife and I went off to a summer resort. We were staying there for a fortnight and I tried to share the experience with other people. There were a lot of people around; academics, reasonable people, lots of common sense, and so forth. Most of them respected that I had had an experience but none could understand what I was trying to share.'

I knew something of the depth of feeling that Bertil was trying to express. I can still recall a morning when I was young, nine years old or so, and I woke up under stream of brilliant light pouring in through my bedroom window. I could hear the sounds of birds noisier and yet more harmonious than ever before and I could smell the grass and flowers so clearly. I attached no mystical significance to the feelings, then or now, but I was passionately moved inside by it. I knew then that I would remember that day forever, and I remember it today as clearly as then. As I lay there in bed I remember thinking, 'This will always be my special day.' When I see streaming sunlight as strong as I did that morning I instantly return to that feeling with great clarity, and it always makes me feel tranquil and optimistic.

I spoke to a lady in Scotland about a similar experience, which she described as being like a spiritual revelation. She was waiting for the results of a biopsy following an examination of a lump on her breast. She hadn't heard from the doctor, although she had by then expected to. In fact the hospital had given the results to the doctor but he had not contacted her thinking that the hospital would have directly informed her. The result was, incidentally, clear. One morning, while waiting for the results, she was in bed and had more or less decided that 'My days were numbered.' She held an orange in her hand, and then had this extraordinary spiritual feeling. She felt completely at ease with the world, thinking, 'I have the gold of the world in my hands.' A complete feeling of tranquillity came over her. Her perspective totally shifted; it no longer mattered what happened to her, or however bad the results of her test might be. That all

*became insignificant because of this feeling that the world
was wonderful, perfect. She told me: 'I can face anything
now because of the feeling from holding this simple object,
grown from the earth. It just took a second or so to pass
through my mind but it was like a revelation, it summed
up our place in the universe. It was a signal of life's
strength and continuity. I felt nourished and strengthened
by the whole experience. I have never felt anxious about
life ever since, except minor little things day to day, of
course. But the totality of existence is now not a concern
to me.'*

Bertil continued his account of his experiences:

'About thirty years afterwards, in the middle of the
1980s, I started becoming more and more conscious of
the inner living nature of plants and trees and so forth.
Animals seem to be animated beings, of course, like human beings, but I came to realise that plants also are
animated in a way. I started trying to get in touch with
trees and plants and I succeeded. Now whenever I like
I am able to be in touch with plants and listen to them
and really get messages.'

I asked what kind of messages Bertil received:

'Well, it normally starts by me orienting my awareness towards the plant in question, with gentleness, and
then just feeling into the plant for whatever kind of feelings the plant may have. Is it contented? Is it feeling that
there is too little water available for it? Should I water
the plant? Is there too much sunshine so it becomes hot
and cannot thrive as it would like? Mostly, though,
plants are contented. You could ask yourself, is that
Bertil projecting himself, his feelings, his thoughts, his
expectations on to the plant? The gentle approach requires me neutralising myself in that sense. I need to
openly listen otherwise it would not be possible for the
plant to speak to me. I was participating in a course in

Holland a couple of years ago; the course was about [increasing awareness] about ecological issues. It was a three-day course. In the middle of the course we were asked to disperse in the garden around the house. We were twenty-three people and what we were asked to do was to choose a silent place, sit down, contemplate and try to get in touch with Mother Earth. [We were to say]: "Hello Mother Earth, how are you?" Then [we were to] see what happened. Of the twenty-three, one was the leader of the course, so he was not doing it because he had [done] it several times before. Out of the twenty-two participants, twenty-one had similar experiences [but] the twenty-second had another kind of experience. The same experience [that] we [twenty-one] all had was a warm, loving response; "Hello, I'm fine. How are you?"

'It was [in the form of] words appearing in my mind; not going through the ears. Of course we were all astonished; we were all expecting [Mother Earth] to [tell us of] her miseries and all the bad treatment we give to her, and so forth. But she [said], at least to me, "But you humans could perhaps take it a little easier and think about things you are doing." That was all.'

I asked Bertil why he did not think that he was hearing words from his own mind, perhaps his own wishful thinking, or even his own guilt:

'I couldn't know that using any kind of logic. But I knew it [in my] heart; it was not me. You see, the twenty-second one did experience what we all had expected to experience; Mother Earth moaning and unhappy. I think that [in his] case he was hearing words from his own mind.

'During the last few years I have been lecturing a lot. One of the main issues in my lecturing is that the base for our conscience is our heart. There is a point in our heart where we know what's right [and] what's wrong.

That's the point in our system where we can discrimi-
nate between what are our own things and what [comes
from outside of us]. And that's the point where we can
know that the extraterrestrial hypothesis is not a hypothesis but the truth.'

*Bertil has always been very clear that he believes the
UFO experience involves the visitation of extraterrestrials:*

'The teaching "game" of ufology is about giving individuals very clear experiences which are extremely
difficult to share in a defined way. So when you share it
is in a vague way, but you are coming out of your experience. You are transmitting to the other [person] your
energies caused by remembering and re-living your experience. And by doing so you give the other party the
possibility of sharing and recognising, [in their] heart,
the truth.'

*I suggested that people respond to what they believe,
not necessarily what is true. On that basis Bertil's idea
would still hold good, even if there were no 'real' UFO
phenomenon:*

'True. But [there is] another side. We start with the
beliefs people have. For example if five people are on
the same spot at the same time, in company, and two of
the people are experiencing UFO [events], even [those]
two might report very different experiences, while the
other three may report they had no experience at all.
They didn't even see a UFO. And by beginning at the
beliefs we have we tend to narrow our sights, tend to put
on coloured glasses and blindfolds. The phenomenon
does not necessarily only belong to the physical matter,
it could, if it has intelligence, which is highly probable,
choose to express itself in the form of wavelengths [and]
frequencies which are available for observation only to
certain people. [And] I'm talking about any kind of
paranormal experience, not just UFOs.

'We were talking about the possibility of getting a kind of a relationship with plants and, of course, animals. To me it's very much a question of allowing, to begin with, for the plant to have its own individual consciousness distinct from the collective consciousness.'

Bertil compared this feeling with one he believed vital for the relationship between researchers and UFO witnesses:

'The relationship of a UFO researcher or field investigator to a UFO observer or abductee needs to be sympathetic and compassionate. It must allow for the individual to express him- or herself in their own natural way of being; their own peculiarities, eccentricities and so forth. That is important also in order to make it possible for you to be listening on all levels to that person. You will not be fully open to the other person or be able to share everything which might come out if you have a narrowed type of listening. That person would sense that unconsciously and would be reluctant to share it with you. So you would miss part of the picture.'

What Bertil was saying was very much a model of witness-driven investigation. Although I originally created that technique from work done by Ken Phillips, Bertil had been part of my early influence in coming to the conclusion that witnesses needed a more self-fulfilling role than the 'investigator-driven' techniques of the 'old school' allowed.

MARIANNE

When I had been in Sweden in 1988 I had spent time with a woman I called Marianne, whose story was in my earlier book *Perspectives*. On a recent visit, in 1993, I was able to meet her again and see what further changes there had been in her life.

To quickly summarise her story as recounted in *Perspectives*: she had been a 'repeater' witness of several night lights and one daylight disc. Her sightings had not been particularly exotic; it had been the effect on her of her sightings which I had thought so important.

She had been around twelve years old at the peak of her sightings, during the 1974 local outbreak; they had lasted around two years.

Marianne had a total of around twelve observations in the period. The closest, and most significant, was connected to artwork. She had been sitting at her desk drawing; she found she had drawn a flying saucer, and that it was a better image than she had ever created before. At this point she felt compelled to go to the window and there she saw a silvery disc moving across the fields behind the house where she lived then. It was just above treetop height and moving slowly, and appeared to be about one and half centimetres at arm's length. As the disc started to descend, Marianne went downstairs to see it through the living-room windows. She wondered whether or not to go out, but felt she should not. She did not see a landing, nor did she see the disc again. Her belief was that this sighting was destined for *her*, that it and other sightings were designed to give her life a more spiritual dimension.

When I interviewed Marianne in 1988 she told me that she believed that the object might represent a force designed to search out those who were yet to become 'aware' of Earth, and help them to do so in a beneficial way. Certainly this had been the result for Marianne; she spent many years passionately concerned for ecology and the planet.

In the years since there had been changes:

'It seemed like the ecology interest was weakening as time went by. Not that I was not interested; it was more like I realised that to really change people's behaviour you had to change their way of thinking. So I think it was around 1986 or 1987 when I read a book called *The Awakening Earth* by Peter Russell. But there I read about the skin-encapsulated ego; that you derive your identity from the outside world. I had always felt that there was something more than just the physical body. I think it was a process that I developed in other directions, so I went further and further away from the ecology orientation. It was still part of a goal to transform the world.

'The strange thing is that we hadn't really found any direction for the work until this autumn, 1992. [Marianne refers to "we"; there is another person involved in the work she is undertaking. That person has confided various paranormal experiences to me but does not wish to be identified in the book.] In Sweden a lot of people are not into going to church. They don't want to go to church because they don't feel attracted to it. There was a research showing that fifty-seven to sixty per cent of the population are privately spiritual and believe in something higher but they don't want to go to church.

'I think the message they [the church] have, that we are sinners and we have to behave so well to be loved by God, doesn't appeal to people today.

'So they feel maybe that there is something more to this existence but it's not what the church is saying. We had read a lot of books including channelled books. And it's really inspiring material because you see that you are part of a whole. They are kind of practical books you can work with.

'I think these books brought us to the point this autumn where we said that we have to create a kind of a new church. Not a "real" church but something that can give people power and knowledge.

'We haven't really started to do that much yet because we have a lot of research to do. This church would include lectures, seminars, meditations, singing, dancing, and also research into all kinds of phenomena.

'What I feel is that I am here both to heal myself and to transform myself and to help other people do that. But I don't know the form yet. Of course our books are also part of it. [Marianne is part of a small publishing group dealing with esoteric subject matter.] What I feel is that when you are ready to understand something and be transformed, then a book, or a person, or a lecture or something comes along. I'm also beginning to understand that I create everything I experience.

'I am trying to [re-create myself] but sometimes I don't have the best self-discipline. I know I should re-create my thoughts but maybe one or two years ago it took a much longer time. Now it is much quicker.'

I asked whether Marianne had had other encounters. She had not, but reminded me that she had felt the original ones were to 'awaken' her, and that now she was awake and did not need them.

'I think I'm awakening more and more. It's like you take a big step to work into all kinds of different philosophies and things like that. You read about different things, then you come back and see what [the meaning is for you]. You see that you are here in the physical world, you are here to learn things and you are really a part of the whole. So I think I've awakened a lot in, let's say, one year.'

I asked a theoretical question, to which I realised Marianne could only guess an answer: if she distracted herself in some way. and became less spiritual, did she think she might have another UFO encounter that would bring her back on course?

'I don't know. Maybe I would have something else happen. I believe in reincarnation so I think before I decided to be born here I decided to wake up to a certain degree here and that could have happened in different ways. Maybe I created them [the flying saucers] or they were here and I saw them. Because I wonder if [others] would have seen them if I wasn't there. I think it was visible to me but I don't think it was visible to others.

'It's difficult to really remember all the different steps I have taken. I mean it's been a gradual awakening all the time.

'My ultimate goal is to ascend in this life to be so spiritually developed or whatever you want to call it that I can decide what I want to do with my physical body. That I can keep it young forever, I can live for five thousand years or that I can dissolve it and take it with me and be somewhere else.

'I think that a lot of people haven't started to wake up yet but I guess they have to. There will probably be big changes.'

Mankind has always personified the forces of nature. When we tried to understand wind and rain and thunder we believed them to be manifestations of the activities of Norse gods. Now we know differently, but the wind and the thunder still continue. We understood the mechanism, that is all. I suspect some part of the alien mythology is personification of energies we have yet to understand. Technological man creates aliens because he needs a technological personification. When we understand these energies it will not make them go away, we may even be able to work in harmony with them. Whether or not our current Gaia or ecological beliefs come from an intelligence in the Earth, from ourselves, or from random natural forces misinterpreted probably makes little difference in the long run. It is still in our interests to heed the message.

21 Human Intervention

This chapter looks at cases which suggest at least some self-development of the sighting on the part of the witness. The cases are unique, as are all cases, yet they are similar enough to other cases in this book to make my 'classifications' quite unrealistic. The witnesses will have their own interpretations of course. The cases here reflect those who are open to the source of their experiences. They know they have experienced something, they recognise that the alien interpretation is strongly 'pushed' by a host of people I have called myth-makers, but they are resisting labelling their encounters. They know they are real, but they search for answers to their nature.

One case that shows the diversity of experience that people undergo was told to me by Peter Holding. There are those that would argue that his 'main' experience is nothing to do with UFOs. I take a different view: that what we label 'UFO' has artificial boundaries. There are too many similarities – cause and effect – between Peter's case and other contactee stories for them to be ignored.

PETER HOLDING

When Peter Holding was around fourteen years old, in 1973, he had two experiences which he connects, occurring as they did within a short space of time. He cannot now recall which experience came first but his family confirm various aspects of both experiences. The first sighting described took place on a dark winter's night between around nine and eleven o'clock in the evening. The family arrived at their home in Barnet, just north of London, in their car. As they were parking they saw a bright light in the sky. Peter's father, who was driving, stopped the car at its normal parking place and the family got out. Peter's father lined up the light with the side of the garage to see if the light was moving. It was definitely still for the fifteen to twenty minutes of their observation. Peter described the light as very bright and not pulsating, not too high and not like a star. A guess, admittedly based on very little information, suggested to the family that the object was some two or three hundred feet high. When I asked Peter's father to hold a two-pence piece at arm's length he confirmed that the light was much bigger than that.

After fifteen or twenty minutes of hovering, the object moved slowly off towards the south, in the direction of London. As it left their vision it picked up speed and moved off very quickly. There was no sound throughout the whole event.

Local newspapers and so on offered no solutions. For all of Peter's family this event stuck vividly in their minds.

The second incident Peter related to me took place around the same time.

At around two or three o'clock in the morning Peter was in bed, sleeping. He woke up, got out of bed and pulled the curtains open. This followed a feeling that he was compelled to do it; that he *knew* something was there. Peter was certain that he did not see any light coming through the curtains; just had a 'feeling'. Peter pulled back the curtains and faced the window.

Outside was a very round, very bright light with swirling colours in it. The centre was like a ball turning on an axis. Peter described the inner core as turning as if independently. He looked at it for around three to five seconds, he believes.

Peter described the window as seeming to have 'gone'. It was not like looking through a window; the light swamped everything and totally filled Peter's field of vision.

Then the whole image seemed to 'implode' (to use Peter's word). It became tiny and then disappeared. Suddenly Peter was just looking through the window which was, as always, closed; only the curtains were pulled open.

Peter went back to bed. He did not go downstairs or see any members of his family. He, and his father, recall that he then slept for 26 hours. It was fairly normal for Peter to stay in his bedroom, and indeed sleep a lot, so the family did not find this uncommon and did not interrupt him.

Since that time Peter's artistic talents have flared up, and there is considerable emphasis in his art on the swirling coloured patterns that were part of his experience.

When I spoke to Peter he had a vague idea that his sister, Jane, had had something similar happen to her. I was later able to confirm with Jane that she had indeed had nightmares at that time and described it as 'something like a black hole she felt she had to go into'. Jane thought that her experience was before Peter's and that the nightmares stopped after Peter had his experience. She confirmed that she has had no experience since. Like Peter, Jane spent all day and night asleep which her mother thought, in her case, was strange.

During the experience Jane described a feeling in her legs, hands and feet that they were not part of her body, that she had herself become 'out of proportion'.

Jane did not feel that the experience had had any lasting effect. She had never been artistic and has not since become so. By the same token she has not suffered any adverse effects from the events she merely described as nightmares.

Peter's Artistry

Prior to the experiences Peter was not artistic and described his rudimentary attempts at art as 'painting a few pictures of birds'. However, Peter was certain that the event was a 'turning point' in his life. His interest in all things paranormal started at that time and his first attempt at art, photography, took place around the age of about seventeen. He took creative photographs, some of which have been published, and himself pointed out that many of his images centred on crosses. Even architectural pictures show window positions on buildings taken a 'cross' form. To some extent Peter said his experience was 'religious' and he recognised that his photography was a deliberate expression, albeit a subconscious one, of his feelings.

More recently Peter has taken up painting and has sold many works. Many of his paintings are centred on the swirling circular patterns of colour that are based on his experience. One painting shows a face or portrait-like image inside the swirling lights. Peter had the feeling that this face or image was there when he saw the original patterns outside his bedroom window.

Peter is self-taught in both painting and photography, and feels that his art is without doubt a method of expressing his experiences.

The next witness is around sixty years old. Elsie Oakensen is probably the most prominent UFO abductee in

England, and a wonderful and charming woman with whom I have had the great privilege to have worked. More than any, her attitude enforces my belief that the *effect* of close-encounter experiences is more important than the cause. Elsie seems to me to have realised that the toys are toys. Now she is consciously playing with her own self-development.

ELSIE

Elsie Oakensen had a close encounter in Northamptonshire, in the English Midlands, on 22 November 1978. Not only was it an event that was to change her life completely, it may well be a case that will help rewrite UFO research for the better.

Elsie was driving along the A5 at Weedon when she saw a smooth, grey, dumb-bell-shaped object literally straddling the road. She could see a bright red light to the left-hand side of the road and a bright green light to the right-hand side. She estimated the object to be some 100 feet above her head and 50 feet across.

Already there was an element of mystery to the encounter. Elsie is an articulate and down-to-earth person, not given to mischief or fantasy. For many years she was the head of a teachers' centre in Daventry. Furthermore, the after-effects of her encounter suggest *something* definitely happened, though admittedly cause cannot yet be linked to effect with any certainty. What was the mystery then?

Simple: Elsie's sighting took place at around 5.30 p.m. – the height of the rush hour. The A5 in that area at that time would have been very busy, yet no one else reported the object. Indeed Elsie herself points out that when she encountered the object she felt compelled to stop but could not do so because of the potential danger caused by the traffic.

Some will dismiss Elsie's claim on this basis alone, yet there must be room to believe that UFOs – whatever they are – are a phenomenon that requires a certain state of mind for their perception. Perhaps Elsie was in that state of mind at that time. Elsie also believes that perhaps the object was there for *her*. This is difficult to prove, but that is no reason to dismiss the possibility, however much it conflicts with the structure of a world we only think we understand. Marianne, whose story is outlined in the previous chapter, told me much the same thing in Sweden, and like Elsie she has changed her life as a result – whatever the real or perceived cause.

For the moment let us follow Elsie's encounter further.

She passed under the object, travelled further up the road and turned right off the main road towards the small village where her home is. Car stops and electro-magnetic effects are commonly reported in UFO encounters; Elsie was to report this as the next manifestation. The electrics of the car 'played up', to use her words, as she passed underneath some trees; shortly afterwards, on a small country road near her home, Elsie found herself cloaked in darkness. 'When I came out from under the trees I suddenly found myself in darkness, absolute pitch-black darkness. As I sat in the car I could not see the road, buildings, trees or anything else.'

She sat in the car watching a metre-wide circle of bright white light shining on the road to the left of the car. For some time she then watched a variety of light effects around the car, and at one point Elsie saw the lights shining on the wall of a nearby cottage. 'As I sat there thinking about it I was absolutely fascinated by the whole thing. *I think that the lights were there not for any particular purpose other than to take my mind off what really happened* [my emphasis].'

Another element of the abduction pattern so often reported is that of 'missing time'. Elsie was to discover what she believed was a short period of time missing from her journey. Indeed, she lost part of the journey itself and found herself in normal daylight about 30 yards further down the road from where she had originally seen the object. She was driving normally, though she speculates that for a time the car may have been remotely controlled. But the fifteen-minute journey had actually taken about half an hour: fifteen minutes of time had been lost.

Later that evening, at about 7 p.m., Elsie felt a tightening sensation around her head; it reminded her of that similar feeling earlier in the day.

Elsie has an interpretation of these events which she herself is sensible enough to recognise as speculative only. Elsie believes that she was somehow selected by the UFO at lunchtime, that she was scanned by it during the encounter and then released later in the evening, when the sensation briefly returned.

Elsie believed that she might have been given some sort of message which may not come to the fore for many years. She also believed that during the encounter she was examined, but she stresses that she believes the examination was 'spiritual' rather than medical. The possibility that the 'message', still to come to the fore, is the development of her spiritual abilities is irresistible.

Such development was to follow. And Elsie believes that her developed abilities are connected to her UFO encounter.

In late 1989/early 1990, Elsie encountered several healers and mediums who told her that she had the power to heal. They told her she could develop this power, and that she could enter mediumship through healing. As she told me in 1990 during one of our many meetings and discussions: 'I am beginning to be able to do this with the help of a very good friend who is working with me and giving me additional power. Together we are working to heal the sick. I think that is a gift that I have and I would be silly not to develop it if I can help people.'

In October 1991 Elsie went into some detail for me about the period of almost two years of her development.

Towards the end of 1989 two friends were struck with tragedy when the husband discovered he had cancer of the colon. He'd been given about three months to live. When Elsie said hello or goodbye after their visits together she used to hold his hands and kiss him. Sometimes, afterwards, she would find that on the way home she was suffering pains and headaches lasting for up to an hour and a half. A friend suggested to her that she [Elsie] was a healer, that she was giving healing and actually taking on his pain. She got used to it.

Later, in February 1990, Elsie was introduced to a medium and trance healer. She had a reading with him, the first spiritual reading that she had had. The healer confirmed to Elsie that her pains were the result of her becoming a healer, and he said to her: 'You have the gift and it would be a pity not to use this. The choice is yours.'

A friend helped Elsie to set up a clinic. They assumed that word of mouth would send people to them for healing; if they helped people, word would spread.

In fact the first 'client' Elsie helped was her own daughter-in-law, who had hurt her back. She was in considerable pain and due to go abroad for a holiday in just a few days. During the treatment Elsie's daughter-in-law sat on a stool, Elsie's friend stood in front and guided Elsie. 'Stand behind and take your hands over her head, not touching, just outside where there was an aura,' she explained. Elsie was not familiar with auras (and hasn't seen one yet, she points out) but she followed the directions to 'test' the area to act by using her hands over the body. 'Over her right shoulder my right hand went cold and further down her back my right hand went cold.' Elsie's daughter-in-law pointed out that the pain was not there, but Elsie followed her hands, as she had been instructed. Elsie started on the right shoulder and her daughter-in-law reported that her hands had got hotter than she had ever felt them before. This went on for about a quarter of an hour.

Then Elsie concentrated on another part of her back and did the same for about half an hour. And then she asked, 'How do you feel now?' Elsie's daughter-in-law felt immediately more mobile and freer of pain.

Elsie met her daughter-in-law at the shops the next day; she was walking normally and carrying a large bag of groceries. Elsie wanted to help her more, but was told: 'There is no need at all, yesterday afternoon I realised that all the pain had gone out of my back and it's perfect.'

Elsie's success continued within the family. Her granddaughter, who suffered severe hearing defects, had had ten operations on her ears. Her granddaughter had been forced to wear two hearing aids, and the house was set up for a deaf child with devices to enhance hearing. Elsie gave her contact [touching] healing as well as absent healing in the form of 'directed' prayer. After a while the girl's hearing became quite good, though it later deteriorated and she had to have another operation. After further absent healing the child was cured;

the hearing aids were gone. 'She runs about, dashing around and screaming and plays like a normal child now,' Elsie said.

Healers are thought by some to be channelling from 'the other side', and as such they have 'guides' in 'the other world'. Elsie was given a message through the trance healer to tell her to stop contact healing: a message from his spirit guide. She was advised to do absent healing only.

Elsie explained: 'You have to ask for your channel to be open because I don't do the healing, it's done by spirit guides and I am the channel through which they work. I have a guide named Mukelib. He says he is a North American Indian. I got that [information] through [automatic] writing.'

Elsie has a special time of the evening for her absent healing. 'Even if we are out – I don't stop going out with [my husband] just because of it. Yes, if we are out I find a quiet spot and open up my channel and list these people's names and do the usual thing. And then I carry on as normal. My hands are hot all the time that this is happening and then when they cool down I close myself down.'

Elsie believes that the energy used comes from the spirits. She has become what she described as 'spiritually aware' and from my work in this subject over the past twenty years I would agree; I am also well aware of the changes that have developed in her in the years I have known her.

Of the connection between the events with the UFO and her 'spiritual development' Elsie can only guess. She feels they are connected, but clearly cannot prove it. She believes that she was given her abilities during the fifteen minutes of missing time but adds: 'I honestly don't know what happened in those fifteen minutes and unfortunately, or I don't know if it's fortunately, I didn't have any more hypnosis.' (Elsie had one session of regressive hypnosis but has ruled out further sessions, recognising that she is now 'contaminated' with knowledge that might come through – wrongly – as her own experience. It is an example of her common sense that she has considered these problems.)

Elsie has more recently ventured into dowsing, another of the paranormal areas generally supported by all but the most sceptical.

I did an experiment with her while we were being interviewed for a radio show. Elsie dowses with a small pendulum that moves differently, depending on the answers to her questions. She claimed that by holding a pendulum over an object, and asking the right question, she would get the right answer. In my wallet I had a recent eye-prescription from my opticians on pink paper. I kept the wallet closed, never letting her see the paper. I told her only that there was a sheet of paper in the back of the wallet and asked her to find its colour. I did not tell her it was a prescription, which might have made her think of yellow or pink, the traditional colours for such items. The pendulum swung to and fro to every question – 'Is it green?', 'Is it blue?' – indicating 'no'. To the question 'Is it pink?' it immediately swung in a circle, which she had earlier stated would be the way it would 'say' 'yes'. I tried to bluff her that it was not pink, but she was adamant, and of course correct. I suspect that at least one of the interviewers believed we had set the whole thing up, I can't prove we didn't, but the fact is we did not – indeed I had not intended to talk to Elsie about the dowsing at that time.

Very recently Elsie sent me a letter about new dowsing experiments she had done – this time on leys (commonly known as ley lines) near her abduction site.

In late 1992 Elsie and a friend had dowsed in the village of Farthingstone and located a ley in her friend's garden, and under her house.

Elsie linked her own abduction site – the area where she had sat in darkness and seen the strange lights moving – to a ley she had found on a map. She dowsed there and found the site was indeed on a ley. The same ley, Elsie discovered, connected to the point where her car electrics had 'played up'. This seems to have been of both surprise and interest to Elsie; however I had gone through this expansion of the encounter into the wider paranormal before.

One case in particular was very similar to this latest development of Elsie's. When I had been on one of my visits to Sweden in October 1988, I had worked with 'new age' researchers who had helped a witness to examine his own abduction case. (In my book *Perspectives* I refer to this witness by the pseudonym 'Anders'.) It was one of my first 'witness-led' cases – Elsie is one of the first English witness-led cases – meaning that the investigators follow the path the witness demands, rather than that demanded by the investigators. One of the routes Anders wanted the investigation to go down was the dowsing of his abduction site. The dowser in that case discovered that Anders's abduction had taken place at the convergence of several energy lines and near several runic stones. The special, ancient sites are – in many countries – recognised as significant in paranormal research.

Elsie is one of many people I have worked with from across the world who show that UFO encounters may be more extraordinary – and more benign – than often supposed. Her story makes connections between so many paranormal areas: the UFO itself (which I think is part of the paranormal 'spectrum'), but also dowsing, healing, automatic writing, the spirit world, ley lines and so on.

I believe that this enforces my belief that UFOs are not the invasion of alien astronauts that the Americans, in particular, tend to believe they are; the idea of 'conventional' aliens having a mission to link people up to native American Indian spirit guides seems absurd even in this exotic context. The search for the answers must take a different path than the one UFO research is presently taking.

I find it more reasonable to consider that paranormal experiences, whatever they are, become interpreted according to the witness's background and culture. Whatever the varying interpretations, the *experiences* are essentially the same for Western technological man and rural African village dweller. Elsie's claims remind me more, in fact, of the world of Aboriginal shamans than they do of America's 'greys'.

22 Conclusion

I have forced you, the reader, to flounder around in the UFO phenomenon while you have read this book, rather than take you on the guided tour some authors feel able to offer. I make no apologies for this; I have no idea what the ideal guided tour should cover. In truth, I haven't felt that the other guided tours have answered any of the legitimate questions about the UFO phenomenon.

The UFO phenomenon is still almost entirely a mystery, and my book reflects that truth as I see it. I could have tied up the loose ends only falsely, if I could have done so at all.

This book is nonetheless open and truthful. I have presented the images of the UFO phenomenon that need to be appreciated by readers; and I hope that I have opened the way to understanding some legitimate alternatives to the all-too-prominent belief in extraterrestrials that is actually holding UFO research back.

And I think this book shows that even the term 'research' is a rather grand title for the search we are conducting. Before we can begin research – at least on one level – we must find out what it is we are to research. I think the clues are here in this book; you must help me to find the direction that we must go in from here.

This book is also 'open' in that I have tried not to interfere with the opinions of the witnesses whose stories are included while at the same time giving my own views outside those accounts. It is a difficult path to walk, I hope I mostly succeeded.

However, it is only fair to round off my own book with a summary of my opinions while in doing so realising that I can only be partly right at best. If I told you I had answers I would be fooling myself as well as you.

I believe that there are two unconnected UFO phenomena brought together falsely. The first, the distant sightings, are probably mundane, Earth-based phenomena for the most part, but may include some unknown natural forces such as earth energies or atmospheric phenomena. Scientific investigation in these areas will, I suspect, uncover some new understandings of natural mechanisms at work in the world around us. I do not believe that there is sufficient evidence to conclude that distant sightings are of alien spaceships, though I admit that I would be displaying an unreasonable bias if I suggested that was impossible. For the time being let's call it highly improbable.

The second UFO phenomenon is the close encounters on which this book is focused. This could be divided into four front-runner possibilities (with complicated sub-sets): (a) alien intervention; (b) intelligent but terrestrial, Gaia-like, energies; (c) natural, non-intelligent energies we have yet to understand; and (d) human consciousness.

I have little regard for the idea of 'conventional' alien intervention by 'invasion'; let's call it 'highly improbable'. Gaia-Earth and perhaps more subtle forms of alien intervention I think are possibilities, but I still rate them very low down the scale.

I favour a combination of (c) and (d) (and reserve the right to change my mind next week!): the conclusion that there are natural earth energies of a kind that we have not yet understood, and that people are experiencing encounters with those forces. People seek to understand those encounters and interpret them according to their predispositions and the normal, natural limitations of human thinking processes. I think that, perhaps separately and perhaps as a by-product of these encounters, people are driven to develop themselves. This self-development can take a variety of forms and an even greater variety of expressions – often in forms of art. Some expressions are less pleasant: fear and anxiety, such as that felt by 'Mark'. I do not believe that such negative feelings arise directly from the experiences, however.

Whatever UFOs are, and whether they are put there by some other force or constructed largely by ourselves, they are a toy we choose to play with. Like the model trains we place in front of children, they amuse and occupy the conscious awareness while deeper, developing processes are happening in other areas of the mind.

The voices people hear, or the channelled writing they receive and often attribute to aliens, I believe to be expressions of their own higher consciousness. Many people live without realising that their subconscious is collecting a variety of data and impressions that guide them through their lives and feed the conscious mind as and when necessary. The occasional contact with the information in that 'pool' can be surprising and even frightening at first. The development which the fascination of the paranormal brings about increases those contacts with those areas of ourselves.

Playing with the psychic toys of the paranormal allows a person to connect the conscious and subconscious minds, to access the information pools in the higher conscious areas. Such 'playing' allows for the unity of mind, body and spirit; thus witnesses develop into more 'complete' people as a result of their experiences, and can access their creativity and express themselves in a variety of ways we label 'artistic'.

UFOs are not a discrete set of events in their own right, but are a part of a broad range of events across the 'paranormal' spectrum. To understand UFOs it is necessary to understand those other experiences of the witnesses. That some people are 'prone' to certain energies – that their minds can perceive what others' cannot – is important.

The presentations in this book show how these other paranormal areas are involved in people's overall 'cases', as well as showing the development and expressions of each individual witness.

I have left the conclusions witnesses have arrived at without too much comment; I think it is the fair way to present the stories. It is obvious, though, that I would not always agree with the witnesses' own *interpretations* of what has happened to them. That really doesn't matter; I have presented the case in the witnesses' own words for you, as reader, and I hope I have made clear that I am not in any way refuting or denying the basis of the witnesses' claims or experiences. Interpretation is only one stage, and a subjective one at that, in the study of this extraordinary mystery.

As to solving the UFO mystery of close encounters, perhaps there is no 'solution' simply because there is no question. Perhaps the phenomenon is there, like wind and rain and sunshine, to be used as appropriate. If so, then a positive attitude and an open and receptive mind will let us all use it to make us all better people, to build better relationships and ultimately to let us all build a better world.

And that may be why the toy is there to be played with.

Index

Anyone wishing to report close-encounter or other paranormal experiences can contact the author at the following address:

The Leys
2c Leyton Road
Harpenden
Herts
AL5 2TL
England.

Details of BUFORA – The British UFO Research Association – can be obtained through the same address.

BUFORA also operates a 24-hour UFOCALL telephone line giving details of current research from around the world, latest national and regional events, and other information. Calls are at special rates. The number is 0891 121886. A similar service is also operated by The House of Jupiter: the number is 0839 114485. Special rates also apply.